BRITISH AND IRISH WOMEN DRAMATISTS SINCE 1958

GENDER IN WRITING

Series Editor: Kate Flint
Mansfield College, Oxford

Difference in language, in subject matter, in form. This series seeks to explore what is distinctive about women's and men's writing, and to examine the theories of sexuality which attempt to explain these differences. Writings of all periods and genres will be looked at from a variety of radical perspectives: some explicitly feminist, others examining masculinity, homosexuality and gender politics as they are constructed through the writing and reading of texts. The series will draw on recent developments in literary theory in order to examine all aspects of gender in writing.

Published Titles:

British and Irish Women Dramatists since 1958
Trevor R. Griffiths and Margaret Llewellyn-Jones (eds)

Writing for Women: The Example of Woman as Reader in Elizabethan Romance
Caroline Lucas

Gender in Irish Writing
Toni O'Brien Johnson and David Cairns (eds)

Writing Differences: Readings from the Seminar of Hélène Cixous
Susan Sellers (ed.)

BRITISH AND IRISH WOMEN DRAMATISTS SINCE 1958

A Critical Handbook

Edited by
TREVOR R. GRIFFITHS AND
MARGARET LLEWELLYN-JONES

OPEN UNIVERSITY PRESS
BUCKINGHAM · PHILADELPHIA

Open University Press
Celtic Court
22 Ballmoor
Buckingham
MK18 1XW

and
1900 Frost Road, Suite 101
Bristol, PA 19007, USA

First Published 1993

A catalogue record of this book is available from the British Library

Library of Congress Cataloging-in-Publication Data

British and Irish women dramatists since 1958 : a critical handbook /
    edited by Trevor R. Griffiths and Margaret Llewellyn-Jones.
        p.   cm. — (Gender in writing)
    Includes bibliographical references and index.
    ISBN 0-335-09603-4. — ISBN 0-335-09602-6 (pbk.)
        1. English drama—20th century—History and criticism.
    2. Feminism and literature—Great Britain—History—20th century.
    3. Women and literature—Great Britain—History—20th century.
    4. Feminism and literature—Ireland—History—20th century.
    5. Women and literature—Ireland—History—20th century. 6. English
    drama—Irish authors—History and criticism. 7. English drama—
    Women authors—History and criticism. I. Griffiths, Trevor R.
    II. Llewellyn-Jones, Margaret, 1938- III. Series.
    PR739.F45B75   1993
    822'.914099287—dc20   92-29695
                                                                   CIP

Typeset by Inforum, Rowlands Castle, Hants
Printed in Great Britain by St Edmundsbury Press,
Bury St Edmunds, Suffolk

Contents

Contributors

Susan Croft was formerly Director of the New Playwrights' Trust and lecturer in Creative Arts at Nottingham Polytechnic. She was joint organizer of the first Second Wave Young Women Playwrights Festival. She is now working freelance, completing *Also Wrote Plays: A Women Playwrights Source Book* for Methuen.

April de Angelis is a playwright. She was writer in residence for Paines Plough Theatre Company 1990–91. Her latest play *Hush* was performed at the Royal Court Theatre in 1992.

Rose Collis worked as an untrained performer and writer in theatre and music from 1979–86. She then became an equally untrained, but more successful, journalist and researcher. Her work has appeared in many publications, including *The Independent, City Limits* and *Time Out*.

Trevor R. Griffiths is Director of Media and Interdisciplinary Studies at the University of North London, where he teaches Drama and Theatre Studies. He was chair of Foco Novo Theatre Company until 1988. His previous books on drama are *Stagecraft, The Longman Guide to Shakespeare Quotations* (with T.A. Joscelyne), and the *Bloomsbury Theatre Guide* (with Carole Woddis).

Margaret Llewellyn-Jones has recently rejoined the staff of the University of North London where she teaches Drama and Theatre Studies. During the writing of this book she was a lecturer at Nene College, Northampton. She is currently preparing an edition of *The Contemporary Theatre Review* on women's performance language and strategies.

Anna McMullan is a lecturer in the Film and Drama Department of the University of Reading. She has research interests in performance theory, women's theatre, post-war Irish theatre, and the later drama of Samuel Beckett.

Lib Taylor is a lecturer in the Film and Drama Department of the University of Reading. Her research interests include performance process and analysis, contemporary women's theatre and oriental theatre and its relationship to current avant garde practice.

Susan C. Triesman is Director of Drama at Strathclyde University, Glasgow, where she runs the Drama Centre, a city centre theatre. A pioneer of Theatre Studies and Performing Arts courses in the UK, she is a theatre director, actress, playwright and critic.

Introduction

Trevor R. Griffiths and Margaret Llewellyn-Jones

Writing in 1988, the theatre critic Carole Woddis remarked that 'Women and the way they work in the theatre tend to be invisible'.[1] This study of British and Irish women dramatists since 1958 is an attempt to record, celebrate and interrogate the nature of the achievement of women theatre writers and to begin to redress the balance, because the standard works on British theatre pay scant attention to women's writing.

It has been argued that studies devoted exclusively to women writers inevitably place their subject as the less privileged term in a binary opposition: there are (male) writers and 'women writers', authors and 'authoresses'.[2] While we recognize the theoretical force of such arguments, the fact remains that our ground has been defined for us negatively, by the vast majority of those who have studied the British and Irish drama of the last thirty years, in the absence of women from their chapter headings, their indexes and their studies. For example, John Russell Taylor's *Anger and After: A Guide to the New British Drama* (1962, revised edition 1969), covers nineteen male dramatists in its chapter headings but only three women writers and Joan Littlewood. There are no women dramatists in Taylor's *The Second Wave* (1971) or Oleg Kerensky's *The New British Drama* (1977). Littlewood is the only woman in Katharine J. Worth's *Revolutions in Modern English Drama* (1973) and Ronald Hayman's *British Theatre since 1955* (1979), where she shares a chapter with five male directors.[3]

The 1980s saw little improvement: John Russell Brown's *A Short Guide to Modern British Drama* (1982) offers brief discussions of twenty-five plays by twenty-five writers, of whom two are women; his index refers to over

forty dramatists active during this period in the British Isles, of whom four
are women (curiously he manages to include Jonathan, but not Pam,
Gems). This pattern is unsurprisingly continued in compilations of reviews
such as John Elsom's *Post-war British Theatre Criticism* (1981), which reprints
critical reactions to seventeen plays first staged between 1956 and 1978, of
which only *Oh, What a Lovely War* and *A Severed Head* might be regarded as
having female 'authors'. Similarly, Gareth and Barbara Lloyd-Evans's *Plays
in Review 1956–1980* (1985), reprints comments on plays by forty-one
writers, of whom two are women. David Ian Rabey's *British and Irish
Political Drama in the Twentieth Century* (1986) mentions twenty-eight writers, of whom two are female, including Margaretta D'Arcy who appears as
an appendage to John Arden. The two most recent substantial studies,
Richard Allen Cave's *New British Drama in Performance on the London Stage:
1970 to 1985* (1987) and Colin Chambers' and Mike Prior's *Playwrights'
Progress: Patterns of Postwar British Drama* (1987) do little to alter this pattern:
Cave mentions eight male dramatists in his chapter headings; Chambers
and Prior mention six men and two women (with D'Arcy again an adjunct
of Arden).[4]

Of course, these simple numerical analyses do not reveal the full picture,
particularly with Chambers and Prior who also offer chapters on 'The
Gender Gap' and other socio-political themes to remind us of the danger of
judging purely on the presence of names; nevertheless the books mentioned
appear frequently on reading lists as the standard reference points for a
consideration of postwar drama, thus playing an important part in canon
formation. Nor do we argue that questions of gender representation hinge
on an essentialist equation of a writer's gender with a particular socio-
political perspective, simply that the established critical consensus has
played down the significant contributions of women writers, which form
the subject matter of this book.[5]

Moreover, the two women who do appear in many of the studies
illustrate significant points about women's theatrical creativity and critical
responses to it. Neither Joan Littlewood nor Margaretta D'Arcy fits neatly
into standard categories of authorship, which stress the uniqueness of individual vision in a way that has traditionally proved problematic for collaborative activities such as theatre and cinema. The anomalous presence of
Littlewood in chapter headings indicates the difficulties of categorizing her
achievements: Littlewood's contribution to the theatre is enormous and
well attested, but her precise contribution to the shape of individual plays is
unclear.[6] Similarly D'Arcy earns grudging recognition as co-worker with
John Arden, but tends to be cast as the villainess of the piece, as Arden
himself has noted.[7] Her Irishness also leads to a double marginalization in a
British theatre unwilling or unable to tackle Irish subjects.

In creating this book we have been aware of the kinds of marginalization
exemplified in the treatment of D'Arcy and Littlewood, because women's

theatrical work often takes place in 'fringe' venues outside the mainstream (male) theatrical tradition. For this reason we have attempted to discover, record, and analyse works that have either been inadequately treated or that seem in danger of slipping into neglect. Despite the quality and increasing volume of women's theatrical writing over the last thirty years, its absence from the standard accounts may lead to it being gradually forgotten.[8]

The reasons for the relative lack of attention paid to women's theatre writing, both in terms of number of productions staged and critical reactions to them are complex. Our general reading of such issues and of the plays themselves is indebted to a number of theoretical studies that raise general points both about the socio-economic context in which the plays were staged[9] and about the ways in which we 'read' works of art. The important pioneering studies of women's theatrical achievements by writers such as Helen Keyssar, Sue-Ellen Case, Lesley Ferris, Michelene Wandor and Karen Malpede,[10] which cover substantial ranges of issues and suggest possible theoretical approaches, now need to be supplemented by more detailed and specific analyses such as ours which concentrate on geographically and historically limited periods.

Useful potential links between ideology and form have been traced in Catherine Belsey's definitions of both the classic realist text, which operates in the declarative mode 'imparting knowledge to a reader whose position is thereby stabilized' and the interrogative text, which 'disrupts the unity of the reader'.[11] According to Belsey, the former type of text is one which in closure reinstates the dominant ideology; the latter is questioning, often metatheatrical and unclosed, without a hierarchy of discourse, and in its interplay exposes the split nature of the subject and thus may be ideologically subversive. The affinity of the latter definition to Brecht's dramatic distancing techniques indicates a potential means of describing aspects of the theatrical practice of women dramatists and their shifting relationship to the naturalistic theatre. Some women writers in the 1950s were clearly in tune with the social realist concerns of 'kitchen sink' drama, when merely to reflect domestic situations as such seemed relatively radical. During the following decades, although other experiments flourished, the reworking of naturalist techniques in the declarative mode remained a prominent feature even in the plays of some of the most performed women writers whose work reached major venues. Indeed this approach, less radical in terms of form and ideology may well go some way towards explaining their popularity as opposed to that of more overtly experimental feminist plays, which often remain in fringe houses because few theatres are likely to take Box Office risks in supporting plays with radical form and content.

Changes in the economic context have been particularly significant in terms of the growth and then waning of Government and other funding. Increases in the cost of running theatre venues and companies have been a profound factor in the scheduling not only of fringe/alternative theatre but also of the major 'national' companies as well as commercial theatre. Even in those plays by women that have been performed, dramatic strategies such as doubling, which may have partly originated in sexual politics, now have an extra ironic bite, because they have become economically desirable. Similarly commercial reasons may have led to the exploitation of certain themes to voyeuristic or ideologically conservative effect in mainstream theatre productions and particularly in television or film versions of potentially subversive women's drama. Material factors have been crucial in affecting the degree to which drama written by women, especially if it is more radical, has been able to flourish and reach an audience. Although very small companies, such as the all female Hogwash Theatre Company operating from the Sheffield area, ingeniously manage to get under way, originally through the one-year Government-sponsored Enterprise Allowance Scheme,[12] these groups tend to exist in a hand-to-mouth way, living on a very basic economy once the funding lapses, rarely managing to pay Equity rates, but reaching a varied, and often local, audience.

The nature of the audience for gender-conscious plays written by women is itself also a matter of debate. A widespread popular myth suggests that this audience – as for political theatre – is a stereotyped and limited one. Certainly the dynamics of venues and audience are crucially linked with the criticism that the most successful plays in terms of West End performance or major company productions are often those of writers like Louise Page, who might be considered as bourgeois feminist.

Our 1958 starting point was determined by the production of A Taste of Honey, which seemed to offer a new way forward for women's theatre, with a division into decades reflecting the growing impact of the women's movement after 1968 and of the Thatcher Government in the UK after 1979. The growth of women's theatrical activity in the 1980s is reflected in separate sections dealing with 'mainstream' successes and with the fringe scene. Women writers in Ireland, Scotland and Wales, black writers and lesbian theatre are dealt with separately because of the specific issues that relate to each constituency.

As a means of indicating some of the shades of difference across the spectrum of approaches to form and ideology in women's theatre writing, an appropriation of terms from literary criticism and film theory respectively may prove useful. Elaine Showalter uses the terms 'feminine', 'feminist' and 'female' to describe phases of women's writing that apply respectively to imitation of dominant literary modes and values, outward protest against these and a phase of more inward turning self-discovery.[13] Without using these terms in a misleading evolutionary way, it is possible to combine them with the terminology of Patricia Erens, in a way that indicates more about dramatic form and creative methodology, and which links to Belsey's ideas about the relation between form and ideology. Erens uses the term 'reflectionist' to cover an artist's appraisal of her own feelings and relationship with society; the term 'revolutionary' for the direct challenge in form and content to established norms, particularly with a concern for the group and the term 'ritualistic' is given to a stage of equality and possibly androgyny when the act of creation itself, and the means of expressing sensations and feelings, are paramount.[14] We may amalgamate and extend the terms, using feminine/reflectionist to describe the largely declarative text, which shows the situation of women, exploring their feelings without overt challenge to dominant ideology or conventional dramatic forms, such as Mary O'Malley's *Once a Catholic*. In *Once a Catholic* the discourse of religion and sexuality circulate in juxtaposition throughout the play, in a comedic way that softens the transgression of the critique of patriarchy. But even in such a declarative play the subversive use of domestic objects, the presence of taboo items like sanitary towels and, especially in performance, the interplay of verbal and visual discourses allows a staging of subversion.

Feminist/revolutionary could be taken to describe largely interrogative texts that are subversive in their questioning of both ideology and declarative dramatic forms, using techniques of a Brechtian nature to reveal the notion of gender as a construct, such as Caryl Churchill's *Cloud Nine*. Female/ritualistic could be extended to cover the most experimental often group devised pieces 'which extend the boundaries of the medium',[15] particularly those in which the emphasis on visual language and non-verbal means of signification is developed in a celebratory way, perhaps more on the lines of Performance Art or the Artaudian theatre practices applauded by Julia Kristeva. Although writers such as Dale Spender have made a simplistic case that language is 'man-made', the debate on the possibility of a female language – l'Écriture Feminine – is expressed in the more complex writings of French feminists, such as Julia Kristeva, Helene Cixous and Luce Irigary.[16] These ideas – though not identical – are rooted in psychoanalytic and linguistic theories, including those of Jacques Lacan, which suggest that language is acquired at the expense of a 'split' in the human subject, between the conscious, speaking self, which enters the symbolic order of language and the repressed, unconscious self.[17] According to Kristeva the patriarchal structures of language and society, the symbolic order, can be subverted by 'semiotic' forces, which she associates with the bodily centred drives of the pleasure-seeking unconscious. Her ideas are in sympathy with Artaudian notions of polyphonic, total theatre, present in such carnivalesque drama, which she suggests embodies these pre-speech semiotic forces, since it 'destroys the monologic of representational discourse and sets the scene for a kaleidoscopic and pluralist way of writing.'[18] This description could be applied to the female/ritualistic approach to creating non-linear, group-devised performance, which though sometimes finally scripted, may reflect the attempt to challenge and subvert not only mimetic dramatic framework and techniques, but patriarchal discourse itself through a battery of visual and multivocal aural experiences. These may be either predominantly non-verbal or may reinvest or transform the process of signification in a fluid way that predates language and its fixing of the psyche within the social and language contract.

As the restrictive order of language is identified with the laws of patriarchal society, feminists have begun to explore many performance strategies, especially a new concept of writing-the-body, through which women may discover their own mode of expression, which has means of access to the unconscious. French dramatists such as Cixous, Marguerite Duras and Nathalie Sarraulte have drawn upon some of these ideas and in Britain traces of these semiotic incursions within more traditional dramatic form may be found in some of the work of writers early in the period, such as Ann Jellicoe, who could not have been aware of these theories.[19]

However, many women currently writing for theatre are well aware of this theoretical debate about the nature of langauge and its ideological implications; for example Caryl Churchill based her play *Softcops* on Michel Foucault's *Discipline and Punish*.[20] New writers with academic as well as theatrical credentials, such as Lisa Goldman and Sarah Tuck, whose *On the Bridge*, a deconstructive exploration of Ibsen's women, was performed at the Oval House in January 1990, claim to use 'a carnival of visual verbal transformation' as a deliberate means of challenging traditional forms and ideology.[21] The possibility of women's theatre language is also the subject of theoretical debate and practical experiment in the Magdalena Project, a Cardiff-based international organization that encourages research and exploration by writers, performers and academics through a range of opportunities including practical workshops and festivals.[22]

A number of strategies are significant in women's theatre practice. Feminist/revolutionary dramatic form interrogates ideological and naturalistic dramatic practice in ways that reveal the split in the subject, especially in the context of gender construction, and in particular through metatheatrical devices that may subvert stereotypes. The spectacle within a spectacle of Stas, the physiotherapist, dressing herself for her role of call girl in Gems' *Dusa, Fish, Stas & Vi* is an instance of this technique. Another, common to many plays written by women as a means of pointing out the way in which identity is socially constructed is 'doubling', in the sense both of one performer playing several roles and of one role being played by several performers, often irrespective of gender – to highlight the notion that gender is a construct. An extreme illustration of this technique is the fragmented personality of Verity in Olwen Wymark's *Find Me*, where the role is played by five performers. Churchill's *Cloud Nine* doubles characters of different age, race and gender across time barriers. This fragmentation of subjects may be extended to a breaching of chronological form, including even the reappearance of characters known to be dead, or the mixing of characters from a range of historical periods or indeed from fiction and history, as in Churchill's *Top Girls*, a use of time akin to Kristeva's theory on 'women's time'. Another strategy is the use of repetition of words, events or physical image patterns, a notion related to Freud's notion of 'the uncanny', as a vehicle for the return of the repressed. Such repetitions occur in Wymark's *Best Friends*, and uncanny manifestations like the Creature in Liz Lochhead's *Blood and Ice* who haunts Mary Shelley, embody further aspects of repression and inner conflict.[23] Further changes in traditional dramatic practice have been claimed as instances of semiotic incursions of the symbolic order, when elements of the feminine/unconscious breach patriarchal logic. Some of these strategies are also associated with the female/ritualistic model, particularly notions of repetition. Whereas, however, unlike the interrogative mode, which tends to open up the gap in the signification process in Brechtian style, this mode, particularly in fringe venues where it is possible to use space more adventurously, tends to blur the distinction between audience and performer, in a carnivalesque suffusion of sensuous impressions, often intended to reclaim and celebrate the female body in a non-stereotypical way. This welter of experience is also semiotically charged, in Kristeva's sense, akin to the experience of the pre-speech child – before gender differentiation, a condition that Artaud recognized in Balinese Theatre practice as 'a state prior to language'.[24] Here, too, there may be greater use of the strategic silence, polyphonic discourse and non-verbal sounds, which sometimes also occur in other modes. This kind of semiotic disruption of symbolic order syntax through a range of sounds that can be associated with bodily drives is seen by Kristeva as a 'mark of the working of the drives, appropriation/rejection, orality/ anality, love/hate, life/death.'[25] Though not all French feminist theorists would agree with Kristeva's use of binary oppositions, their views would support the notion that such linguistic disruption in women's drama is also ideologically subversive. Clearly, no piece would ever conform exactly to the three models that the above terms loosely describe, and indeed might bear the elements of more than one mode. Some drama, such as some of Olwen Wymark's work, might be read as bridging the gap between feminist/revolutionary and female/ritualistic modes in its relationship to the qualities of a potential dramatic 'Écriture Feminine'. Furthermore, some plays written by women may conform both ideologically and formally to the established patriarchal norm, for example Agatha Christie's 1950s Poirot-style plays, notwithstanding Miss Marple's appropriation of such apparently male skills to solve mysteries in other plays. This is not, however, the place to dispute the biological specificity of dramatists – the concern is with the work produced by women in a particular historical moment, and most especially those which in different ways stage gender difference.

8

Just as the three models vary in form and strategies, so there is a difference in balance in the treatment of issues which, like the return of the repressed, recur across the geographical and chronological spectrum, which may indicate changes in the social perceptions of women's role as well as developments in feminist perspectives. Among such themes are the exploration of family values, mother–child relationships – particularly with daughters, absent fathers, sexual relationships, friendships between women, images of women, recuperation or demythologizing of famous women, the celebration and restoration of women marginalized in history, women and institutions, lesbian and black women and others in oppressed and minority group contexts. Curiously, it seems that in Scotland and Wales – though not particularly in Ireland – there is a tendency to explore issues through a naturalistic form that merges with the poetic – often in a historicized or quasi-mythical context. More complex issues, such as the gender constitution of the gaze of the audience,[26] the relationship between different shades of feminism in the theatre, the problems associated with the multiple voices of group creativity such as the attribution of authorship to devised pieces, and what one contributor to this book calls 'the tyranny of structurelessness' have yet to be fully addressed. It may seem that, since the heady burgeoning of women's drama post-1968, the consequent gradual evolution from an emphasis on political content to a stronger concern with the theatrical could, like other factors such as the current movement back from collectivism, be more than an economically pragmatic move. Not only shrinking funds, but also gender attitudes as revealed in Clause 28, the moral panic about AIDS and the Thatcher Government's evocation of Victorian family values, indicate a move away from public feminism, which is affecting the nature of women's drama as presently performed, particularly in major venues. This shift also seems to be affecting the work of the most widely known women writers. Their emphasis seems to be shifting from a concern with an inner world of issues relating to women, to the wider outward sphere of broader philosophical and political interests, and to theatrical experiment *per se*. Whether this tendency, as well as the persistent elements of naturalism, will gradually affect the increasingly struggling fringe, alternative and community venues, creative writing courses and performance groups that remain as the front line for women dramatists remains to be seen.

1

Early stages: Women dramatists 1958–68

Lib Taylor

In a sense, always, women are the bearers of society: of its continuing
life, of its settlements, of its practical inheritance.
(Raymond Williams[1])

In 1952, *The Mouse Trap* opened in London and has continued to play in
packed houses ever since. It is now, with over 16,000 performances, the
world's longest running play. In 1956, the year that *Look Back in Anger* took
the theatrical community by storm, a new play, *The Chalk Garden* proved
to be the most commercially successful play in London. Both *The Mouse
Trap* and *The Chalk Garden* were written by women, Agatha Christie and
Enid Bagnold, two accomplished writers who, although they had succeeded in penetrating the theatrical establishment, were in a small minority
for both the 1950s and 1960s, which follow the familiar historical pattern of
being characterized by the absence of women playwrights. Noted as a time
of challenge to the prevailing theatrical establishment, the particular conjunction of historical events of the 1950s, and the subsequent social and
political climate, gave voice to a generation of rebellious, disaffected young
men, but did not operate as the same catalyst for the generation of women.
What is frequently termed a progressive period in theatre history is, ironically, noted as regressive for women. For a woman to become a successful
playwright, she had not only to negotiate the prejudices of theatrical institutions but also to overcome a set of social and political structures that
deterred her entry or voice in this public arena.

In the post-war decade it became increasingly evident that the promised
restructuring of Britain would not materialize. With the newly-elected
Conservative Government of 1950, radical opportunities faded as traditional values were gradually re-entrenched. Disillusionment was expressed as a
predominantly male frustration, hence the novels, plays and films of the

time coalesce male crisis and social dislocation in the 'angry young man', the anti-hero of literature written by a group of largely left-wing writers who focused on rebellious and alienated youth culture. Reference to women in such texts largely operated on a metaphorical level, often as a reinforcement of male entrapment, but ignoring women's issues. No space was left for women to express their own discourse.

What was a crisis for the male became a significant setback for the female in her bid for self-determination, returning her to a pre-war position from which she had just begun to escape. The economic independence won during the war, when women were in demand on the labour market, was reversed so that by 1947 only 18 per cent of married women were in employment.[2] The contradictions of the female role became evident, for while hegemonic forces urged mothers to seek fulfilment within the home and family, the material demands of an affluent society placed pressures on married women to find paid employment. A wife, popularly defined as comforter, carer and nurturer of children and husband, was discouraged from working outside the home, yet the growing economic boom opposed these ideals and encouraged more and more women onto the employment market towards the end of the 1950s.[3] However, ideological forces ensured that working, married females did not become a serious threat to male supremacy in the labour force. Consequently, although by 1967 as many as 29.7 per cent of married women were working, they remained at lower – hence uninfluential – market levels.[4] Within the theatrical institutions, the male establishment maintained a stranglehold on managerial and artistic positions of power, whilst women occupied peripheral low status and poorly paid jobs. Commercial theatre was dominated by a form of naturalism, which placed the male perspective centre stage, whilst the few experimental theatre spaces focused on a form closely allied to social realism that, essentially concerned with the male dilemma, sometimes revealed deeply rooted misogynist attitudes.[5] As alternative and fringe spaces were rare, female playwrights wanting performances were forced to negotiate an entrenched and antagonistic mainstream structure.

In a Foreword to French's edition of *The Chalk Garden*, Bagnold pays tribute to her American producer Irene Mayer Selznick, who spent two years trying to get the play accepted for performance: 'She flew, she cabled, she battled'.[6] She obtained a London production only after the play had proved itself in the USA – and this struggle was for a writer already established as a novelist, with some previous acclaim as a playwright. In 1970, twelve years after the play's 23-month London run, Bagnold reflected that it had never been '. . . asked for by Chichester or the National Theatre: though the National Theatre's Literary Manager, Kenneth Tynan, once wrote of it: ". . . It may well be the finest artificial comedy to have flowed from an English (as opposed to an Irish) pen since the death of Congreve." '[7]

However, as pockets of women questioned their role in both family and society, with no organized Women's Movement, no formulated political objectives and no public platform, it was difficult for the rumblings of discontent to find expression. To a degree, the theatre provided a forum for critical analysis, as a small handful of female dramatists began to present a world that did not correspond to received notions of family life. Only by dissecting their personal function in society could women begin to take account of their ideologically and socially constructed position in society; a necessary analysis before embarking on the process of change. The 1950s and 1960s became a time when, with the possible exception of Christie, those few women writers who had access to the theatre, reflected these concerns by finding ways of subverting the ideology of the family, predominantly by focusing on the role of the mother.

1958 can be identified as a crossroads for women dramatists, for while two of Christie's and one of Bagnold's successes were running in the West End, a group of women began to filter into the more radical spaces where they could experiment with finding their own voice. The first public performances of works by Ann Jellicoe, Doris Lessing and Shelagh Delaney in 1958 marked the beginning of a search for a theatrical form appropriate for the representation of women.

The West End – collusion or subversion

The woman playwright synonymous with popular stage success was Christie, whose name spelt prosperity for theatre managements and whose works continue to be revived, particularly by amateurs. Her acceptance in the West End can be attributed to both dramaturgical and political factors: pleasures of problem-solving and the reassurance of restored order. The ideology presented through Christie's plays conforms to the dominant British value system, recalling an unproblematic, halcyon pre-war era. She addresses the middle classes, showing working class characters as either untrustworthy or comic. Gender is represented stereotypically – women's roles rarely extend further than virgin or whore, mother or blue-stocking. An ideologically defined, if implicit, sense of moral justice is never dislodged but always executed, even if this fails to correspond to legal justice. Murder victims are revealed as dispensable – either weak, unpleasant, invalided or somehow deserving their fate – their presence disturbing the 'natural' order. The criminals therefore become the agents of justice, even if they are disposed of in the process.

Both *The Verdict* and *The Unexpected Guest*, opening in London in 1958, concerned the murder of invalids who made their spouses' lives untenable. The former's plot involves an improbable refusal of the victim's husband to disclose the name of his wife's murderer, as a result of some misplaced

sensibilities. Consequently, his wife's cousin Lisa, whom he loves unre-
quitedly, is tried for the crime instead and becomes the real victim. A
highly educated woman, she has chosen domesticity instead of academia in
order to care for the wife of the man she loves. She denies her own future
in favour of his and even after prison – in a sense her punishment for her
transgression against the marriage vow – she continues this sacrifice despite
her apparent awareness of male oppression. The second play starts after a
murder, with the apparently guilty party, the wife, confessing. The plot
unravels the past of the degenerate, bitter victim, whose crimes surpass
those of the apparent murderer, and whose own mother will not even
defend him. Justice has been done but the crime must be solved legally.
The father of a child previously killed in an accident caused by the victim,
appears, becoming the agent of moral justice – but a mentally unbalanced
scapegoat is accused and conveniently pays the final penalty. The audience
remains uncertain who the murderer was.

Although both victims meet a 'just' and merciful death, the restoration of
the moral codes sanctifying both life and marriage is central. Redemption
comes through the suffering of women whose only crime is their sexuality,
whilst men remain irreproachable. The legal restoration involves im-
probabilities of plot, such as scapegoat murderers – an over-privileged
'loose' woman or a retarded boy, neither of whom occupy secure positions
in the Symbolic Order,[8] and who can be despatched without compunc-
tion. The women collude by rejecting the possibility of challenging their
oppressors, preferring the *status quo*.

Structurally, *Go Back For Murder* (1960) is one of the most interesting
Christie plays; it engages in metatheatrical devices, shifting the play from
drawing-room naturalism. The second Act is in flashback, as the past inter-
cuts with the present. A solicitor takes on a stage manager-type role,
controlling the action and enabling a re-enactment of memories. Each
character offers a differing viewpoint on the narrative, and finally a replay-
ing of one scene reveals the unreliability of recall, unveiling the 'true'
murderess.

Christie is certainly here raising questions about linearity, and in representing multiplicity she foreshadows the preoccupation of feminist writers,
but ultimately her play moves towards a closure. Like many Christie detec-
tives, the solicitor functions uncritically as male author, sustaining the narrative structure and 'speaking for' characters, especially females, thereby
denying plurality in favour of singularity and resolution. This deconstructive process reinforces rather than dislodges stereotypes, as the perceived
villainess now coincides with the 'true' murderess, and the mother is restored to her ideologically defined position. Moral justice prevails: the *status
quo* remains undisturbed. Christie's 1962 programme of three one-Act
plays, *An Afternoon at the Seaside, The Rats* and *The Patient*, present an
interesting conceit, but do not carry the weight of her full-length plays,

which generally show her skill in hermeneutic coding – pleasurably misleading audiences and maintaining suspense.

Where Christie's plays reveal an underlying collusion with patriarchy,
there is an insistent questioning voice within the works of Enid Bagnold.
While negotiating the same rigidly structured institutions as Christie, she
works to challenge prevailing ideologies. Although not offering a blueprint
for a Christie-style success, Bagnold's reputation as a serious writer was
endorsed by the casting of established heavy-weight theatrical stars. Her
rather artificial, epigrammatic style is not popular today, but her attempt to
examine family structures is in tune with modern feminist writers. Bagnold's plays could be termed early feminine/reflectionist in that her conscious concern is to expose the situation of women; she also indicates
possibilities for dislodging entrenched beliefs. Her plays are traditional in
form and the society she presents is essentially middle class but it is one
where social conventions are flouted and disorder is courted. Bagnold's
families are fractured and incomplete; the mother is presented as a figure
who does not conform to the caring stereotype. Her women are strong,
centre stage and not desirous of male protection. Bagnold's plays might not
be radical but neither do they accept social systems without question.

The Chalk Garden (1956) provides a good example of the operation of
Bagnold's critique. The play's title refers not only to the real garden of the
house, which has to be carefully nurtured to remain fertile, but also the
young girl, Laurel, who is vaguely unbalanced and in need of attention.
The 'family' of The Chalk Garden are anything but conventional. The
mother function is shared between surrogate carers: the grandmother, a
slightly fey manservant and a governess/companion, Miss Madrigal. This
incompatible group is completed by a disabled butler, Pinkbell, a patriarchal figure who never appears but continues to exercise authority over
house and garden. Ever since anyone can remember, the house has been
governed by standards and rules set in place by Pinkbell, whose control, like
that of any patriarchal system, is pervasive and invisible. Exposed as ob-
solete, ineffective but impossible to dislodge, Pinkbell's regime is challenged by Miss Madrigal as the crux of the play. Despite her introduction of
new ways of working and organizational systems, resolution is only con-
ceivable in terms of Pinkbell's death. At the point of closure, Grandmother
and Madrigal tend the garden together, using the latter's alternative knowledge, while rejecting Pinkbell's empty tradition. In The Chalk Garden the
maternal order is the natural order.

Bagnold's next play, The Last Joke, which survived for less than a month
in the West End in 1960,[9] continued to explore the mother's role, focusing
on the redemptive qualities of woman. The plot concerns Prince Ferdinand
Cavanti's desire to restore to its rightful position the stolen portrait of his
mother. Like Pinkbell, the Prince has suffered a stroke and wishes to
renounce the world but is blackmailed into remaining alive by his brother

Hugo. Despite a slightly morbid tone, the play maintains an ironic humour in its central exploration of the Oedipus complex. The portrait has been stolen by Portal, a rich, shady character, who keeps this image of the mother-figure above his bed, hidden from the gaze of all other men. In this picture he recognizes his idealized woman, whom he wishes to possess completely, and upon whom he models his own daughter, Rose. Redemption can only come through Rose, who conspires to reunite the mother and sons by returning the portrait to Ferdinand and agreeing to marry Hugo – thus underscoring the Oedipal pattern, for Hugo is marrying his mother's image. The play is antiquated in its artificial and 'poetic' use of language, but remains an intriguing piece of work in its exploration of the notion of split female identity. Rose's biological mother has sacrificed all maternal claims in favour of being Portal's anonymous servant. The objectified, idealized woman and the desexualized carer cannot be reconciled within the maternal.

This sense of fragmentation is explored further in Bagnold's *The Chinese Prime Minister*, staged in London in 1965 after a New York production in 1964. An elderly actress, referred to as 'She' in the written text, decides just before her seventieth birthday to abandon not only her career but also her roles of mother and wife. She wants to reclaim the 'ME in me that I have never lost.'[10] In declaring 'I want the whole of myself – and not half again',[11] she not only acknowledges that self-determination and the shackles of marriage and motherhood are incompatible, but recognizes the plurality of female identity. The title refers to the attitude towards age in the ancient East, 'when age was near paradise and not a prison'.[12] Hence She is only able to take steps towards independence when released from her responsibilities by her advancing years. Bagnold here presents a very positive view of old age in which maturity brings realization of power.

Her final play, *Call Me Jacky* (1968), however, presents a less affirmative yet still potent image of age with an old woman slowly deteriorating within a delapidated house. *Call Me Jacky*, a ranging and unfocused text, is concerned with a complex struggle between an old and new order. The central character, Mrs Basil, is an elderly woman who refuses to give up her old house to modern development. She is opposed by her grandson, Niggie, and his quarrelsome friends, whose lifestyle stresses the immorality of ownership. The house survives but only in a derelict state. In this humourless, desolate play any pretence of conventional family life or sustaining relationship between the sexes has been abandoned: Niggie's marriage is an arrid affair and his friends are involved in sterile homosexual and lesbian relationships. This notion is crystallized in the absence of the mother, without whom the house crumbles. Any optimism is ultimately restored through the arrival of Elizabeth, an unconventional maternal figure, who inherits the house and sets up home with her alternative family group of culturally and racially diverse children, unconstrained by the presence of a father figure. As in *The Chalk Garden,* the Law of the Father has been supplanted.[13] Mrs Basil, possibly like Bagnold, opposes revolutionary action, but in her call at the end of the play 'to raise the bricks again'[14] she is asking for a total restructuring of society and, more importantly, a repositioning of the mother figure.

Literary 'ladies'

That Christie and Bagnold both achieved success as novelists before writing for the stage, might have eased their passage into the theatre. Whether the same is true of succeeding female novelists is open to debate but as the influence of the New Wave filtered into the mainstream, scripts reflecting these changes were sought, providing the opportunity for more novelists to experiment with playwriting. Two such were Doris Lessing and Iris Murdoch, whose brief incursions into drama and consequent influence on the development of women's theatre cannot be dismissed, despite their largely literary reputations.

While Lessing had a struggle to achieve only a single Sunday evening performance at the Royal Court for her first play *Each His Own Wilderness* in 1958, her second was performed in the West End in 1962. Focusing on women, these plays question notions of freedom and responsibility. Where the earlier play addresses the dichotomy of the public and private carer embodied in the mother-figure, the latter's female protagonist is a single mother, seeking her freedom unhampered by social conventions.

Each His Own Wilderness refers to the traditional female concern with campaigns for peace, prefiguring many Greenham issues. It portrays the conflicting desires of Myra Bolton, who wishes to relinquish her maternal responsibilities in favour of public service, and of her son Tony. Their opposing views are crystallized in their political positions: Myra's fiery socialist idealism prompting action, conflicts with Tony's disillusionment and lethargy, signifying disaffected youth's alienation from the political sphere. Tony both desires and despises his mother, castigating her for refusing the role of a 'proper' woman. This Oedipal relationship is underscored by Myra taking as a lover her close friend Milly's son, whilst there is a reciprocal sexual encounter between Tony and Milly. However, Lessing presents a refreshingly liberated perspective on motherhood. Both Milly and Myra are unfettered from the burden of their role, and the final optimism of their play lies with Myra's life-affirming exit into the world, rather than her son's timid retreat.

In *Play With a Tiger* Lessing presents a 'rootless, declassed people who live in bed-sitting rooms or small flats',[15] alienated by their cultural diversity and marginalized by a resistance to conventions of family life. The central characters; Anna, an Australian, and Dave, American, exist in a state of limbo, balanced between decisions. Anna has just rejected a marriage proposal while Dave is considering matrimony. Beginning naturalistically in Anna's room, the walls fade away on Dave's appearance, and the room becomes part of a broader landscape. This shift enables the characters to engage on a different level, exploring the inner realm of the mind as well as the nature of their relationship. Employing these deconstructive strategies, they make a bid to recover their identities through a process resembling psychoanalysis, evoking their pasts, desires and dreams.

In 1972 Lessing wrote a postscript that this should not be interpreted as a 'woman's play'[16] for, although taking account of gender issues, it does not privilege the woman's point of view. However, the focus is on female territory and Anna's transgressions exceed Dave's, as she is an economically independent single parent who refuses to conform to gender role or social conventions. Poised between two role models, Mary, her repressed 'old maid' landlady, a widow like herself, and Helen, the oppressed wife of her friend Harry, Anna rejects both, leaving open the question of whether she can find a satisfactory alternative. This unresolved ending draws attention to women's uncertain direction. Where *Each His Own Wilderness* conforms to the naturalist tradition, in writing *Play With a Tiger*, Lessing set herself 'an artistic problem which resulted from [her] decision that naturalism, or if you like, realism, is the greatest enemy of the theatre'.[17] Recognizing its formal limitations, she implicitly acknowledges naturalism's inadequacy in representing the female perspective, thereby anticipating the central project of many future feminist playwrights.

Iris Murdoch's invitation into the West End indicates the comparative ease with which already established novelists achieved theatrical recognition, particularly as she initially reshaped existing novels rather than create new fictions for the stage. Confronted with the problem of finding an appropriate theatrical voice, she turned towards experienced male counterparts, enlisting the help of J.B. Priestley and James Saunders in adapting her material. Saunders's statement that her '. . . dialogue didn't have the right dramatic quality. Perhaps one might say that Iris is a better novelist than I am, and I am a better playwright than she is.'[18] raises questions of authority, and hence, in Murdoch's first two plays, as a female writer's ideas have been modified by the male pen, a man 'speaks for' the woman.

The Severed Head and *The Italian Girl* are similarly short, fast moving, comic novels, with male first person narrators. It has been suggested that *The Italian Girl*, more successful as a play than as a novel, prompted Murdoch to separate her novelistic from her dramatic writing,[19] as she afterwards wrote *The Servants and the Snow* (1970) and *The Three Arrows* (1962), neither of which originated in novels. Most recently, with *The Black Prince* (1989), she has returned to adaptation.

The Severed Head (1963) presents an incestuous web of sexual relationships in a corrupt, middle-class society. This superficial and avaricious group of people, revealed as morally contemptible egocentrics devoid of any sense of affection or guilt, exist in a sterile world reflected by the private interior settings and introspective form of the play. It is the narrative structure that becomes of central interest as Martin Lynch-Gibbon, the novel's narrator and apparently pivotal character of the play, systematically becomes decentered from the text. What begins as Martin's story, gradually becomes fractured and multilayered as the perspectives of other characters take on equal status to his own and his secure authorial control is undermined. Each new perspective offers the spectator differing narrative possibilities until linearity is totally dislodged and narrativity discredited. Ultimately it becomes apparent that several alternative narratives have been played out during the course of the play, to which the spectator has not been exposed. A dark, mythic thread running throughout is embodied in Honor Klein, an enigmatic anthropologist. It is to this powerful mother-figure, whose capacity for violence and knowledge remain mystical, that Martin is ultimately drawn, seeking reunification with the maternal.

The Italian Girl (1967) bears many resemblances to The Severed Head in its focus on sexual intrigue and disturbed social conventions. Though not as tightly structured or comic, this play is concerned with a less brittle if equally odious set of people. Edmund, the male protagonist, has returned to the family home after his mother's death, yet remains elusive and non-committal. Like Lynch-Gibbon, he is neither aware of surrounding relationships nor able to control his own existence. The play's tone recalls the relationship between Gothicism and subversion.[20] The setting of overgrown trees and a blackened brick house, offsets a macabre tomb in the centre of the stage space. Members of the household are revealed as in thrall to a somewhat fey, hostile couple, whose presence disrupts the family, exposing its fragmentation and incompatibility. Malignant bearers of disorder, restoration depends on their destruction.

Murdoch's plays do not fit neatly into any category of women's theatre, for, unlike Lessing or even Bagnold, her concern is not to reveal women's situation or challenge a form of social organization that specifically oppresses the female. However, for Murdoch, woman connotes strength; in both these plays the Oedipal pattern is evoked in resolution. As Klein represents the maternal in the earlier play, so Maggie, the Italian girl of the other's title, represents a succession of mother substitute figures in the life of Edmund, to whom he is ultimately reunited.

In the workshop

As the history of women's theatre makes evident, when women dramatists have flourished, it is on the fringes rather than within mainstream theatre. The political expediency of occupying a marginal position is not something

that can be considered here, but both the English Stage Company at The
Royal Court and Theatre Workshop at Stratford East were companies operating in ideological opposition to the mainstream and, as such, have a significance, though a somewhat contradictory one, in the development of
women's theatre. The work of Joan Littlewood at Stratford East has already
been well-documented but no account of post-war women playwrights
would be complete without consideration of her practice on two counts.
First, she developed a working method that, in some ways, provided a model
for feminist groups; second, although there are no theatrical texts ascribed to
her, her contribution to a body of written material must be acknowledged. 'I
do not believe in the supremacy of the director, designer, actor or even the
writer',[21] wrote Littlewood, and with Theatre Workshop she set about
constructing an ensemble company who worked collaboratively. Wishing to
overthrow a rehearsal process inherited from the fortnightly repertory system, Littlewood introduced working procedures aimed to empower all
members of the company. Hierarchical structures that privileged author or
'star' were dismantled in favour of group decision-making and equality of
pay. Improvisation was at the heart of her methods and she encouraged each
performer to participate in the processes of research. Training and the reshar-
pening of performance skills were to become integral to this working method, thereby enhancing some of the most exciting theatrical pieces of the
1950s and 1960s. Although Littlewood was essentially a director, the imple-
mentation of her working practices indicates she was responsible for partially
shaping new texts on which she worked. Certainly, both Shelagh Delaney
and Brendan Behan have acknowledged their debt to her and it is clear that
Littlewood's distinctive influence is present in their work.

In choosing to work in an East London community, one of Littlewood's
central intentions was to break the stranglehold of the middle classes on
theatre and to place representations of the working class on the stage. In
Shelagh Delaney's script *A Taste of Honey* (1958) she saw the opportunity to
do just that – the play reveals the squalid existence of a mother and daughter living in a seedy Salford flat. The central focus of the text is not on the
plot, but on the female characters, unconventional relationships and dialogue. Action is largely confined to one room and the episodic structure
slides from scene to scene with little regard for temporal shifts. Littlewood's
hallmarks are evident as the dialogue takes on the quality of a comic double
act and music becomes a central feature of the play. The play attempts to
explode myths surrounding the notion of motherhood. Both Jo and Helen
resist functioning as traditional homemakers, and although they express
some vague understanding of what is expected of a 'proper' mother, neither
can conform to this ideal. The relationship between the two is seen as
unsentimental and abrasive: Helen avoids any responsibility for her daughter and Jo refuses to accept her obligations to her unborn child. Delaney
is questioning two deeply rooted conceptions; that motherhood auto-

matically denotes fulfilment for a woman and that it remains the exclusive province of the female. She represents the maternal state as burdensome and undesirable for the women, whilst Geof, the male, demonstrates the greatest sense of care and takes on the surrogate mother role.

Delaney's play is often cited as an early example of a feminist text, and could be called feminine/reflectionist in its conscious focus upon women characters and the female condition. The question, however, remains as to whether gender stereotyping is challenged, for although Jo and Helen resist their assigned roles, they cannot escape them. Jo accepts her pregnancy unquestioningly and they both demonstrate an interdependency that suggests their biological relationship takes primacy. Thus motherhood is defined as 'natural' for women and, although it fails to satisfy, neither Helen nor Jo are given alternative aspirations. Geof, too, resists his prescribed gender role, but is only allowed to 'stand in' for Helen, and is finally evicted from the house as an inappropriate mother substitute. By placing her central characters within a socially marginalized group, black, sexually ambivalent and shady, Delaney constructs her women as 'other'. They exist on the periphery of society, despite Helen's attempts to penetrate the social order. Where *A Taste of Honey* offers a breakthrough for women dramatists is in the representation of Jo, who is constructed as a subject and not as an object of male desire. The Oedipal pattern is confounded because, despite her pregnancy (or perhaps because of it) Jo is perceived as sexually 'neutral', while in Geof she finds a partner whose sexual ambivalence renders him ineffective. He cannot find redemption through Jo.

A Taste of Honey was an enormous critical and commercial success, moving from Stratford East to the West End and thence to New York. Delaney's only other published play, *The Lion in Love* (1960), initially produced at the Belgrade Theatre Coventry, before moving to the Royal Court, met with nowhere near the same acclaim. Stuart Hall identifies both the strength and weaknesses of the play: 'Naturalism in its purest form is certainly to be seen in *The Lion in Love* . . . it came as close as any play of substance in the period of reproducing the naturalism of everyday life'.[22] In presenting a slice of working-class life in its minutiae, Delaney paints a very sharp picture of a shabby market community in the back streets and bomb sites of a northern city. She focuses upon dreams, thwarted ambitions and disappointments, revealing life as a set of inadequate illusions. However, although the play's structure extends familiar notions of naturalism, with unresolved, diffuse scenes that intercut apparently haphazardly, the presentation of such closely observed external detail allows no space for a selective examination of the rather ill-defined social context. Consequently the play lacks the political dimensions and critical framework of *A Taste of Honey*. The play's preface, 'Nothing can be more fatal to peace than the ill-assorted marriages into which rash love may lead',[23] crystallizes its central theme, focused on the unsatisfactory marriage of Kit and Frank. Women characterized as positive, powerful and assured provide the community's strength. Kit, the unconventional mother-figure, is seen as courageous and defiant, whilst Nora, Frank's mistress, not only has a far more realistic grip on life than he does, but has achieved financial independence. Peg, Kit's daughter, embodies any optimism in the play as the only character whose aspirations have credibility. Delaney's conscious intentionality is revealed in the strange fairy story Peg relates, where the Queen, the tale's protagonist, chooses to throw herself into the sea, thereby becoming a rock, rather than be reunited with her husband. Clearly conveyed here is the strength Delaney observes in women, expressed in resistance to what she sees as the female capitulation in conventional happy endings. The woman is thus placed centre stage. To an extent, John Russell Taylor's comments on Delaney proved prophetic:

> Her future career remains a big question-mark in the English theatrical scene; it is quite possible that she will never again live up to the achievement of her first play.[24]

Despite her occasional television and screenplays, most notably perhaps *Dance with a Stranger* (1985), Delaney has written no more theatre texts. There are indications that, without Littlewood's support, her work lacks crucial dramatic qualities. Essentially, the collaborative working method enabled Delaney to develop her own voice within a framework of theatre strategies developed by Theatre Workshop to meet their own set of political, cultural and theatrical objectives.

These strategies are most clearly evident in *Oh, What a Lovely War*, which emerged out of collective rehearsal processes and, characteristically, is not attributed to Littlewood alone, but rather to the entire company. *Oh, What a Lovely War* (1963) presents images of the First World War, framed by a pierrot show, juxtaposing stark realism and sentimental romanticism. Rather than present a single, cohesive structured narrative, with identifiable central characters, the protagonist becomes an oppressed and abused class. Littlewood raids the British theatrical tradition to develop a form embodying song, dance, acrobatics and slide projection, which attempts to dislodge entrenched suppositions and shift perceptions. Brecht's influence is evident as the comfortable and familiar music hall acts and pierrot turns are intercut by satire and documentary material in order to develop a critical perspective on those in power.

Formal changes

The theatre most clearly identified with new dramatic writing since 1956 has been the Royal Court. However, despite its claim as a place where 'risks can be taken' and 'where new writers can be continually tried out,'[25] the number of women whose work has been produced there is alarmingly small. In the twelve years between 1956 and 1968, out of over two hundred productions, only fifteen were plays written by women, six of which were single Sunday performances. Yet, without the Royal Court, and its commitment to new work, there is no doubt that the evolution of women's theatre would have been diminished. Where early isolated opportunities provided groundwork for development and the search for a feminist theatre form, more recently, as later chapters of this book indicate, rather more new women writers have been supported through workshops and productions at the Royal Court or its Upstairs studio.[26]

Perhaps the most significant woman writer to overcome the prejudices of the Royal Court was Ann Jellicoe, who not only had material presented but became part of the directorial team:

> I didn't feel isolated as a woman in the earlier days at the Court. I was awfully blind – I'm one of the ones that's been re-educated. I felt I'd done something remarkable, being a woman who'd got through.[27]

Many feminist playwrights today look to Jellicoe's works as demonstrating early signals of an embryonic female/ritualistic form that challenges theatrical limits in order to express the female voice. Rather than emerging from a literary background, Jellicoe's experience was in theatre; she trained as an actress, ran her own theatre company and was keen to direct. Her evident understanding of the mechanisms of theatre enabled her to draw upon a range of dramatic strategies, rejecting the primacy of the logocentric text and embracing a multiplicity of physical, visual and aural theatre languages. Her printed texts therefore can only supply a partial approximation of the experience of many of her plays.

Written in response to an *Observer* play competition, *The Sport of My Mad Mother* (1958) is set 'down behind a back street' in 'a protected corner,'[28] in other words, in an alternative space, governed by a different set of laws. Into this space comes Steve, a musician, who sets in place a formal theatrical framework for the play, exemplified by a musical metaphor:

> I just want to reach people, I want to make them feel, and with music somehow . . . music communicates, it reaches into people and they can forget their brains, their intellects and the way they've been taught to intellectualize about everything, they can just let music happen, let it happen physically to them.[29]

He is followed onstage by Dean, who invites the audience to move away from the 'main road'[30] to explore the side streets in order to examine the group of young people inhabiting this space. The play engages with issues of leadership and violence, embodied in the figure of Greta, the mad mother of the title, who becomes a symbol of both slaughter and regeneration. Her power and threat lie in her potential for motherhood ('Birth! Birth! That's the thing! Oh, I shall have hundreds of children, millions of hundreds and hundreds of millions'[31]) coupled with her destructive facility, and with this she exercises control over Patty, Fak and Cone, who constitute the existing order. On to the stage wanders Dodo, a woman 'apparently about sixteen years old with a plain old face. She might even be an old woman.'[32] This physical ambivalence and her strange mixture of costume and props mark her as 'different'. Both Greta, an Australian, and Dean, American, are outsiders, and thus aligned with Dodo, but with the means to assert power. Dodo has no coherent language and therefore no means of representation, while Dean's articulacy makes him a candidate for leadership. He challenges Greta's position of authority, wishing to replace her primitive, violent and maternal rule with his sense of rational, moral responsibility. Finally the play becomes a struggle between these two ideologies, with Greta ultimately triumphant.

The use of language becomes fractured and fragmented as there are no fully coherent exchanges between characters, and the verbal text is not the principal bearer of meaning. Any notion of rationality is arbitrary as sounds and phrases intercut with more conventionally structured dialogue. As repetition and free association offer alternative ways of using words, not confining them to the production of any logical meaning, the strongly rhythmic language becomes ritualized. The spectator is offered a range of possibilities through the interplay of verbal, movement, costume, sound and gestural signifiers, underpinned by a percussive musical accompaniment, which governs levels of emotional tension. This complex text in many ways anticipates feminist theatre forms in its emphasis upon a multiplicity of theatrical discourses operating dynamically. That *The Sport of My Mad Mother* defines motherhood problematically as both destructive and prolific, suggests that for Jellicoe women connote strength; a notion she develops in her next theatre project. Commissioned by the Girl Guide Association to write a play for a cast of over four hundred guides and a few professional performers for their fiftieth anniversary celebrations, Jellicoe created a short pageant called *The Rising Generation* (1960). The central figure, Mother, is 'an enormous woman half-masked with padded headdress and shoes'[33] who seeks control of the world for women, wishing to expunge all trace of men. Men are sold, auctioned and physically destroyed; history is rewritten to erase their contribution. Regiments of women are organized to indoctrinate the populace with the new ideology:

Men are thick.
Men are tall.
Men are strong.
Men will tear you, beat you, eat you.
When you're older, you will know.[34]

Ultimately, mother's megalomania destroys the world as she sets off the bomb to prevent male reassertion. The surviving generation of men and women leave the poisoned Earth in a spaceship to find a planet where they can establish a new mode of living. The reading of women's politics remains contradictory here, as although demonstrating the dangers of abused power, the critical focus becomes unclear, especially as Mother's signification of strength has a patriarchal quality. However, structurally the play is exciting and innovative, epic in scope and logistically ambitious. Although the Girl Guide Association rejected it, Jellicoe found a form that enabled her to write for a large body of people, embracing amateurs and professionals. More recently she has gained a reputation as writer and director of community plays, including *The Reckoning* (1978), *The Tide* (1980) and *The Western Women* (1984), all with roots in *The Rising Generation*.

Jellicoe's commercially most successful play, *The Knack* (1961), achieved both critical and popular acclaim in London and New York. Although adopting similar formal strategies to her earlier texts, in this play they serve to underpin a strong narrative, hence this finely tuned process makes for a very powerful piece of theatre. Ritualized movement and fragmented language patterns reinforce sexual and social power struggles. The disrupted domestic setting provides an interesting inversion of the traditional female space, with the significant absence of the mother figure. In the process of being transformed for the male, the room is scattered with objects, chest expanders and step ladders, that signify masculinity, with a bed as the dominant feature, sharpening the sense of sexual tension. Focusing on male sexuality, the play's central conflict lies in three men: Tolen, a libidinous, macho type, who sees every woman as an opportunity for exercising his sexual prowess; Colin, a sexually inept innocent, who admires and envies Tolen's facility with women; and Tom, a person for whom sexuality is not an overt statement of himself. Into their shared house comes Nancy, an ingenuous young woman who triggers the ensuing struggle for supremacy between Tolen and Colin. Nancy's own sense of power is not realized until the end of the play, when she erroneously claims she has been raped, thereby confounding Colin and Tolen, both variously intrigued and fearful of the assertion. Although this charge temporarily dislodges Tolen's confidence and repositions Colin, it in no way effects change for Nancy; her claim finally reinstating male control. The use of rape therefore functions to reveal the processes of manipulation and power relationships but the issue of rape is in no way addressed. Serving to raise doubts around masculinity, it does so by defining the woman as a victim colluding in her own exploitation.

Neither of Jellicoe's last two plays within this period were as successful as *The Knack*. *Shelley; or, The Idealist* (1965) is an account of the poet's life. Representing a surprising departure for Jellicoe both in terms of a return to naturalistic form and an unchallenging representation of women, the play shows Mary Shelley as merely an extension of the male ego, defined only in relation to her husband, without reference to her independent life as a writer. In *The Giveaway* (1969), on the other hand, Jellicoe continues her pursuit of new theatre forms rather than the development of insights into problems of female representation. Following the absurdist tradition, this rather slight comedy is concerned with rampant consumerism in a materialistic society. Despite an intriguing use of language, the play fails to engage the imagination in anywhere like the same degree as *The Sport of My Mad Mother* or *The Knack*.

Jellicoe's writing provides a beacon for contemporary women dramatists and her early plays stand out as paradigms in breaking the stranglehold of patriarchal form. Nevertheless, there are contradictions, for while she triggers the imagination in a way that relates to female experience, many of her women characters remain imprisoned by male values and systems of representation. While she places gender issues on the theatrical agenda they are not framed politically and she is unable to release the woman as a subject.

Into battle

As sexual politics developed, questions of gender and equal opportunity began to be raised as public issues, although the theatre did not immediately reflect these. Indeed, by the end of the 1960s there were fewer women playwrights having work produced than at the end of the 1950s. Vivienne Welburn had three plays published during this time, but not all received professional productions. Her work focuses upon the identity crisis experienced by the young in their struggle for self-assertion. She rejects naturalism and the domestic space in favour of a more ritualized form enacted in bleak, barren landscapes. Welburn explores entrapping patterns of behaviour and social conditioning, using a mode of language that recalls the fractured quality of Jellicoe's work, with powerful rhythmic structures intercut by an abrasive realism.

An awareness of sexual politics struggling for expression is evident in her work, especially her short, first play *The Drag* (1965). An act of rape takes place at the beginning of the piece, becoming the context for the succeeding events. Burdened by a sense of irrational guilt, the victim cannot escape her initial 'crime' and she becomes imprisoned by a society from which she feels alienated. At one level, her experience is defined as universal; the act of rape becoming a metaphor for the experience of all women. Welburn recognizes the oppression in which women exist and draws attention to the interactive process of the personal and the political, foreshadowing the principal preoccupation of the early feminist movement. Her second and third plays, *Johnny So Long* (1965) and *Clearway* (1967), examine the nature of freedom, exemplified by groups of youths struggling for supremacy and control of their own lives. Both are set on waste, common ground, the former near a fairground, the latter near a motorway. Prompted by the

arrival of an uninvited outsider, characters are forced to explore their
unfulfilled aspirations and fears, exposing the deeply rooted conflicts and
tensions present within their aimless existences. Fair and motorway become
symbols of freedom and escape as the young people are forced to make
decisions about their own futures. In both plays, the metatheatrical device
of a narrator acts as bridge between spectator and audience. In the former
he is a clown in the Shakespearian tradition, in the second a 'recluse' owner
of a cafe where the young meet. The women in both these plays largely
function as objects of male desire and not as problematic subjects in their
own right. In *The Drag*, however, there is a clearly articulated insistence on
placing the woman as the central interest of the play. Constructed as victim,
the Girl remains as equally confined at the end of the narrative as she was at
the beginning, but in this text the issues of women's oppression are defined
by a conscious awareness of sexual politics. Both the evident subversive
intention and the interrogative form indicate that Welburn is providing an
early example of a feminist/revolutionary approach.

Within the changing theatrical contexts at the end of the 1960s, and a
developing embryonic Women's Liberation Movement, women playwrights began to make their struggles for independence the subject of their
work. Growing political awareness enabled them to confront gender issues
directly, instead of engaging in a process of negotiating the subplot. The
removal of the censorship laws allowed theatre venues that were more
appropriate for radical experimentation and women found more spaces in
which they could voice their own set of politically defined issues. This shift
is exemplified by Jane Arden's *Vagina Rex and the Gas Oven* (1969), a
multimedia text that was produced at Jim Haynes' London Arts Laboratory.
This play again recalls Jellicoe's work in its use of sound, music and ritual.
Rather than construct a single narrative, Arden presents a polemic in the
form of a montage of woman's experience, which identifies the issues of
sexual politics, defining the choice for women as 'Fight – submit – or go
mad.'[35] Using grotesque, shock tactics and forms derived from pop culture,
the play examines the process of male oppression and illustrates the ways in
which patriarchy maintains its grip; through manipulation, degradation and
domination of the woman.

Providing a challenge for women's theatre, *Vagina Rex* places the
woman unequivocally as subject of the play: it identifies the male indisputa-
bly as the opposition; it contends that only by acquiring a language and
history of their own will women find a form of expression. These are issues
that will act as the future agenda for female dramatists. The woman has
moved out from the confines of domesticity and the kitchen sink to confront the 'gas oven'. The play ends not optimistically, but prophetically,
'The rage is still impacted with us – I am frightened of the on-coming
explosion.'[36]

2

Claiming a space: 1969–78

Margaret Llewellyn-Jones

Contemporary reviews give some indication of the development of drama written by women during this period: Michael Billington, writing in 1972, laments the dearth of women writers of stature who are not 'myopically concerned with the problems of being a woman' (*The Guardian*, 4 February, 1972); by 1977 *Time Out* (394, October 21–27, 1977), was confident enough to devote its front cover to 'The Rise of Britain's Women Dramatists', in celebration of Pam Gems' *Queen Christina*, currently in performance by the RSC, Mary O'Malley's *Once a Catholic*, running in the West End and imminent new women's productions. At least six of the nine dramatists Ann McFerran interviewed still had works in print in 1991. However, only three women – Gems, O'Malley and Caryl Churchill – appeared in forty-eight photographs with brief accounts of 'Top Playwrights' in the *Sunday Times Magazine* (26 November, 1978).

Although the establishment orientation of the *Sunday Times* and the then 'alternative' stance of *Time Out* account for the differing extent of their response to innovative work, such references indicate the problems associated both with recording and with analysing the varied co-operative styles, dramatic forms, ideological positions and kinds of venue intrinsic to performance. Broadly, the work of women dramatists could be associated with the three categories indicated in the Introduction: feminine/reflectionist, feminist/revolutionary and female/ritualistic, although these approaches to form and content cannot be defined exclusively in terms of chronology, and may be mingled within the work of particular authors or groups. Prior to this period, women had on the whole worked as individuals. Michelene

Wandor has suggested there was a stronger emphasis on group-devised imagistic work from 1969–73, followed by a peak of subsidized collaborative activity from 1973–77, succeeded by a tendency towards individual writing as dwindling Arts funding reduced opportunities.[1] Major figures emerging from this period may have experimented creatively in individual reflection, unrecorded ritualistic fluid street happenings, collaboration in revolutionary agitprop or cabaret style, or commissioned writing of a script drawn from group devising or other sources. Throughout, there is a strong emphasis on non-verbal signification and writing-the-body in conjunction with other formal factors. Certain venues, like the Royal Court Upstairs and Soho Poly Theatre where the director/writer Verity Bargate worked, had policies that encouraged women dramatists, but the growth of the Women's Movement was intrinsic to the explosion of women's alternative theatre groups, also fostering the development of directors such as Susan Todd, Nancy Meckler, Midge Mackenzie and Clare Venables.[2] A brief account of three of the most influential groups, Red Ladder, The Women's Theatre Group and Monstrous Regiment, is indicative of their significance and the historical context.[3] Many groups began with an emphasis on the political rather than the theatrical, so the later tendency towards a stronger theatrical form at the expense of the political may to some extent mirror the current economically pragmatic move back from collectivism towards more directorial or writer controlled pieces.

Red Ladder, formed in 1968 following the AgitProp Street festival in Trafalgar Square, was a mixed gender, socialist theatre group with a high level of political commitment, an awareness of feminist issues and a collective approach to devising work, originally in short agitprop pieces. Then, from the period of the Working Women's Charter and the Equal Pay Act in 1970 came a full length piece *Strike While The Iron is Hot* or *A Woman's Work Is Never Done* in 1974. Influenced by Brecht's *The Mother* it centred on revealing the link between sexual and industrial politics.[4] In 1976 the group moved to Leeds, maintaining their record for new work by devising cabarets and plays for the Yorkshire working-class community. Currently, using what their Administrator calls a 'broader "socialist and feminist" label',[5] rather than defining themselves as a women's theatre company, their planning for 1989–92 aims to develop further their commitment to 'young people, to new work, to Equal Opportunities, to broadening audiences', particularly in the context of Youth Services and Youth Clubs.[6]

Two demonstrations indicate the symbiotic relationship between feminism and theatre in this period; one attacked the 'Miss World' contest in November 1970 and the other celebrated International Woman's Day in 1971, when the newly formed Women's Street Theatre Group paraded taboo objects such as giant sanitary towels and performed *Sugar and Spice*, devised with Bryony Lavery, which showed how women are trapped from childhood by their socially constructed image and the demand to 'keep

young and beautiful'. A founder member and participant was Buzz Good-
body, later the first woman director at the RSC, where she established The
Other Place at Stratford. Two other seminal events were the lunchtime
Women's Festival held at Ed Berman's Inter-Action's Almost Free Theatre
in London in 1973; and the Women's Theatre Festival held in the Haymarket Theatre, Leicester, in 1975. Writers such as Churchill, Gems, Wandor and Olwen Wymark participated in one or the other, or both. Born
from the first festival were the shortlived mixed Women's Company,
which intended to present feminist theatre with entertainment and without
'diatribe', and The Women's Theatre Group which, 'as a by-product of the
Women's Movement, has always functioned in a totally collective manner,
trying to avoid leadership and hierarchies'.[7] Touring to venues often associated with socialist theatre, the group generally also engaged in post-
performance discussion. Ten years later, the Group still maintained its
policies of didacticism and encouraging women's writing, through regular
rehearsed readings and workshops. Their approach 'The personal is political' is evident in the programme for Deborah Levy's Pax (1984) – where a
poem unites her personal creativity to history – or reference elsewhere to
the pending abolition of the GLC. During its first years, the Group devised
performances such as Fantasia (1974) an exploration of women's fantasies;
My Mother Says (1975) about contraception and Out On The Costa Del Trico
(1977) on a current industrial dispute. Since 1978 they have employed
freelance women directors and designers, and commissioned writers; the
first of whom were Eileen Fairweather and Melissa Murray with Hot Spot.
Alison MacKinnon of the Women's Theatre Group states that although
their creative method is still co-operative, the Group now rarely devise
work, but commission women writers, although few such scripts are
published.[8]

    Founded from the Leicester Festival by the actors Gillian Hanna and
Mary MacCusker, the Monstrous Regiment collective responded to the
poverty of female roles. Although the company included some men,
women took the major administrative and artistic decisions; such deliberate
assumption of group responsibility differing from the traditionally hierarchical patriarchal practice of mainstream theatre. An emphasis on scripts,
often from more experienced writers, and on touring the art/theatre circuit
evoked an audience slightly different from that of the Women's Theatre
Group. In 1976, their first plays – Scum by Claire Luckham and Chris
Bond, set in a laundry during the Paris Commune of 1870, and Vinegar
Tom, by Caryl Churchill, about seventeenth-century witchcraft –
illuminated the present perception of women through the perspective of
the past. Other early work employed music and strongly visual images,
including the development of group-written cabaret, such as Floorshow
(1977), or the very physical Yoga Class (1981). Despite restrictions imposed
by finances, the group still performs a variety of work.

Eileen Fairweather's article 'Getting Their Act Together' (*Cosmopolitan*, October, 1981) indicates the scope of groups like Beryl and the Perils or Cunning Stunts. Much of this imagistic, body-centred work, through anarchic, radical forms and polymorphously perverse spectacle, also celebrates female energy and ritual, thus reclaiming the female body from the stereotype, challenging male practices. Somewhat in this vein, are Jane Arden's *Vagina Rex and the Gas Oven* (1969), Maureen Duffy's *Rites* (1969) and Luckham's *Trafford Tanzi* (1978). Using a mixture of Brechtian and Artaudian techniques, reworked classical archetypes, with fragmented structures and a range of multimedia effects to reflect the destructive nature of gender conditioning, the former went some way towards creating a new female performance language. The second rewrites Greek myth through an exploration of Euripides' *The Bacchae,* in the confined space of a Ladies' lavatory, where a range of rituals reveal the pent-up destructive potential of social conditioning, and the notion of female space celebrated in later works such as Nell Dunn's *Steaming* (1981). *Trafford Tanzi* uses the image of the male wrestling ring as a metaphor for the same conditioning process. A combination of the violence of the contests and Brechtian comic songs partly draws in and partly distances the audience from the event, which is successful in entertainment terms, if ideologically somewhat questionable. Although the physicality of the piece, demanding real wrestling training, could be seen as celebrating the female protagonist's physical and moral strength in her triumph against the brutality of patriarchal conventions, the appearance and behaviour of her rival, Platinum Sue evokes traditional gender responses. Similarly, the final bout blurs metaphor and reality, producing competitive cheering and doubtfully voyeuristic pleasures, which thus override the didactic if comic discourse of the deconstructive songs that shape the piece.

Where much of the above work shares female/ritualistic qualities, the currently available printed work of the five writers from the *Time Out* article spans the spectrum from feminine/reflectionist in the case of O'Malley through Gems to the more feminist/revolutionary work of Wymark and Wandor. Not all these women necessarily subscribe to a specific feminist position, but a reading of their work is inevitably marked by the institutions of language and theatre which were, and remain, male-dominated. The tremendous variation of styles and form reflects the search for an appropriate audience, and there is a deliberate attempt to create new positive roles for women.

In 1977 Gems stated, 'I think that the phrase "feminist writer" is absolutely meaningless because it implies polemic, and polemic is about changing things in a direct political way', but she 'certainly had the intention of writing parts for women. The paucity of them gives me a sense of outrage' (*Time Out*, 394). Whether following this intention through reflectionist forms of drama merely reproduces women's situation without analysis, is open to debate. Nevertheless, as Mary Jacobus points out in her discussion of Luce Irigaray, woman's historical role – reproduction – can as mimesis be a means of knowing role-playing and thus a form of subversive exposure. 'To play with mimesis is thus for a woman, to try to recover the place of her exploitation by discourse, without allowing herself to be simply reduced to it.'[9] Even if women's appropriation of traditional language and theatre form in this mode could be claimed to have a quality of difference, during the period 1968–78 the most 'acceptable' face of the woman dramatist in commercial and reviewers' terms, was found in those plays that departed least from the classic realist form, were less radical in content, had a strong comic vein, or could be open to a more popularized and softened reading. The realist text, as defined by Catherine Belsey, combines mimesis with a hierarchy of discourse, which, especially in closure, reinstates the dominant values of a culture.[10] Hence the more traditionally structured O'Malley's *Once A Catholic* or Gems's *Piaf* escaped the wrath of nervous critics and gained wider audiences, whereas challenging subversive pieces in the mode of the interrogative text,[11] such as Olwen Wymark's *Find Me*, excited hostile debate and achieved fringe showing only.

The other four lesser-known writers featured in the *Time Out* article are symptomatic of then available options. Felicity Browne, having written fourteen plays in isolation before her success with *The Family Dance* produced by Tennants at the Criterion in 1977, comments 'What I hadn't realized until I had one put on is that you never see what you had written . . . No one has ever called me a feminist.' Gilly Fraser, a TV actress then writing for radio and TV as a protest against stereotypical roles, had *Do a Dance For Daddy* (1976) and *A Bit Of Rough* (1977) staged at the Soho Poly Theatre; in the 1990s she writes for TV's *EastEnders*. Cherry Potter, also a *Radio Times* TV Drama Award winner, who went to work with groups like Common Stock for *Audience* in 1979, is quoted thus, 'In the best of all possible worlds one wouldn't be thought of as a male writer or a female writer, but as a writer.' Finally, magazine journalist Tina Brown, recorded as winning a *Sunday Times Award* as the most promising playwright for *Under The Bamboo Tree* (1973), and with *Happy Yellow* at the Bush Theatre, denies in *The Guardian* (15 November, 1973), that her work has a 'Woman's Lib angle . . . the girl is exploiting the man as much as he is exploiting her.' Confident that 'discrimination works in our favour at the moment' (*Time Out*, 394), she was by, 27 July 1979, reported to have taken over editorial charge of *The Tatler*.

During this period, key themes that are significant for theorized readings' of all three modes of women's drama include: the definition of sexuality; the reclamation of the female body; the definition of oppression – particularly in terms of institutional frameworks; madness and neurosis as a means of subversion; redefinition of the family – often through other, usually female, networks; the tension between personal/private and political/public role – reflected in spatial terms; the demythologizing of certain images of famous women and aspects of history, as well as the celebration of the female.

As a prize-winner, O'Malley was then one of the most successful women dramatists. She won awards in 1977 from *Plays and Players* and from the *Evening Standard* as the most promising new playwright, one from the latter in 1978 for her BBC TV play *Oy Vay Maria*, and the first Susan Smith Blackburn Prize also for *Once A Catholic* in 1979, whilst the Thames Television Award for this play gave her a year as the Royal Court's resident writer. O'Malley's initial period of success, which began at the Soho Poly and the Open Space, was interrupted by a serious car crash, although *On the Shelf* was televised in 1984, and *Talk Of The Devil*, starring the pop singer/actor Ian Dury opened at the Palace Theatre Watford, in 1986. In a postscript to the *Time Out* article (October, 1977), O'Malley states 'I'm not an intellectual. I'm not a feminist . . . I'm not committed to any cause.' This comment suggests that her work falls within the feminine/reflective category: *Once a Catholic* (1977), a Royal Court transfer to Wyndhams and *Look Out . . . Here Comes Trouble*, an RSC Warehouse performance, reveal a degree of involvement with feminist themes, but a comparatively naturalistic form and setting temper radical tendencies. Particularly in *Once A Catholic*, as with Gems, the use of coarse, often body-centred language and a strong sense of comedy combine to give a wider audience feelings of pleasure and outrage, linking taboo-breaking with a voyeuristic insight into the ways of those thus seen as 'Other'. John Barber's *Daily Telegraph* review, reprinted on the cover of *Look Out . . . Here Comes Trouble*, states 'The abnormal are only people a fraction less able to cope than ourselves'. This patronizing comment indicates the safety effect that such distancing can lend to an audience enabled to laugh at painful situations without considering the underlying critique. In *Once A Catholic*, scenes quickly alternate between public spaces – school, chapel and homes – but there is no strictly private space where the girls are not harried by the power of patriarchal discourse, embodied in the nuns, who persistently repress any sexual or other energies felt by their resilient pupils. Even a retreat into the lavatory to read dubious Bible extracts fails. Punitive Father Mullarkey [*sic*] is more interested in food and raffle tickets than the heroine's actual social distress, whilst the crippled music teacher, a closet gay and rebel, offers her both a pagan locket and escape through music, which she rejects. Thus, despite breaking female taboos – officially issued passion-killer knickers are worn on the head, Tampax is flourished on stage, the girls swear and one finally adds a large wax penis to the crucifix – there is no real sense that the girls can escape their biologically determined fate. Outside the convent walls, sceptical predatory young males exploit the girls' sexuality, and it is an ambivalent triumph that while one becomes engaged, the innocent scapegoat heroine is barred from her spiritual vocation. Without moments of solidarity, the girls behave competitively, although they are all namesakes of the Virgin. The most telling, potentially deconstructive, moments are the parallel uses of ritualized questioning: those where the authority figures catechize the girls on religious matters, and those where knowing girls catechize the innocent on sex. Similarly, the biology lesson is intertwined with religious responses. Thus, through ritualized verbal and visual discourse, both sets of myths, the spiritual and the sexual, are comically debunked. However, as it was set in the 1950s, the satirical bite of the play's potential critique of gender roles would have been diffused by 1970s laughter. It purports to showing the girls as subversives, yet in closure reflects their ultimate fate as victims. Any radicalism is muted, whilst the potentially tragic elements are evaded through comedy that skirts class and economic issues like the heroine's poverty, by treating them as a joke. Similarly, in closure *Look Out Here Comes Trouble*, a naturalistic piece set in a mental institution, seems to reflect the ideological notion that there is no escape from the dominant hierarchy inside or outside. Cast for eight men and six women, the setting varies from the lounge to the psychiatrist's office to the female dormitory. The latter, although men sometimes intrude, is nevertheless a private female space where some crucial communication occurs. Through the behaviour of all patients, an implied critique of relationships is developed. Quasi-parental caring is symbolized by Dennis, a failed suicide, who gives others food symbolic of the lost love of his ex-wife. Lonely Olive ceaselessly eats chocolates and marmalade sandwiches. Janet, the anorexic, is gradually fed, metaphorically, by other woman patients and by a tentative relationship with George, who is obsessed by astrology. Sylvia, trapped in marriage by an over-solicitous (and possibly guilty) husband, enjoys flashy dressing and dancing, but perhaps realizing that she is equally trapped by the image she projects, destroys her clothes, dwindling into a bed-ridden state. Alternatively, Kieran, an exhibitionist, seems to suffer from an over-protective and self-martyring wife. The institutional discourse of the doctor, interviewing individual patients in scenes interspersed between group exchange, manifests less ability than the patients themselves in working towards cure. His ironic contribution about his profession runs 'And let us all work in the dark' (*Look Out*, p. 124). Although there is some subversive and quasi-comic body language, like Sylvia's struggling fit – a metaphor of resistance – institutional discourse is shown to 'frame' and 'label' the patients through the use of visual and verbal techniques as the nurses carry out a variety of restraining instructions. Again, there is little sense of the social and economic context which impinges on the institutional world. Sheila's housing difficulties are acknowledged, but it is the emotional needs of the patients – reflected in the inadequacies of traditional gender roles – that hold centre stage. Through remarks like 'People get these symptoms when they're anxious and unhappy about their lives' (*Look Out*, p. 99) the audience is guided towards liberally minded sympathy with individuals rather than radical political analysis.

Gems's plays range across a wide range of themes varying from the complexity of interpersonal relationships between private individuals to demythologizing historical and literary women. Traces of the three modes of writing – reflective, revolutionary and ritualistic – are evident in the evolution of her dramatic techniques. Past interviews and her own play introductions reveal that her success began at almost forty when, as a psychology graduate and mother of four children moving to London in the 1970s she first encountered the feminist movement, including those who 'saw theatre as a possible political weapon'.[12] Previously some radio and TV plays had been transmitted, but the Cockpit Theatre put on *Betty's Wonderful Christmas* in 1972/3. She wrote monologues for Ed Berman's Fun-Art Bus, for example, one about a girl drowning her baby in a lavatory, and following the Almost Free Theatre's lunchtime festival of women's plays, joined the less radical splinter group, the short-lived Women's Company for whom she wrote the mixed cast *Go West, Young Woman*, performed at the Roundhouse in 1974. Gems' ambivalent relationship with feminism is aptly encapsulated in Victoria Radin's *Observer* review of *Dusa, Fish, Stas and Vi*: 'But the play leaves a riddle somewhere between the feminist moan which it eschews and the female bravado which it so wholeheartedly embraces' (*Observer*, 14 December, 1977). *Dusa, Fish, Stas & Vi*, produced under the giveaway title of *Dead Fish* for the 1976 Edinburgh Festival, ran retitled in a Hampstead Theatre Club production transferring to the Mayfair Theatre on February 10th, 1977. This pioneering play, with an all female cast, was also created by women – designed by Tanya McCallin, costumed by Lindy Hemming and brilliantly directed by Nancy Meckler. Such relatively unusual circumstances may well have contributed strongly to its success and trail-blazing qualities. The four flat-sharing girls are the divorced Dusa, whose ex-husband is reported to have kidnapped their children; Fish, a patrician revolutionary who ultimately kills herself because her previous lover marries another; Stas who sells herself and shoplifts as a means of saving up for a marine biology course at the University of Hawaii; and Vi, an unemployed eccentric anorexic. Gems has recorded her surprise that, both then and since, some socialist and radical feminist critics have felt that the suicidal ending did not deal adequately with the tension posed for women between the personal and the political.[13] She eschews their view that the play is thus bourgeois and individualistic because the closure fails to deal with this wider context. Contemporary reviews also indicate that much of the play's power can be reappropriated by dominant ideology: 'The tragedy is hers: and I believe the dramatist is trying to say that she brings it upon herself by her refusal to be what used to be called unwomanly' (J.C. Trewin, *Birmingham Post*, 10 December, 1976); '. . . unabashed victims of their emotions' (J. Barber,

Daily Telegraph, 9 December, 1976); 'This is a play about personal not political anarchism . . . the bitter cost of such a bargain with oneself and with one's life . . . [it] condemns personal anarchy in a society where women go out in an obsessive search for some sort of loving security' (Nicholas de Jongh, *The Guardian*, 9 December, 1976). Such readings attribute blame to women, without a trace of the realization that society and theatre construct images and roles against which all women may struggle. Yet, within the performance – particularly the dressing and undressing of Stas as she switches between her roles, transforming herself from dowdy physiotherapist to glamorous 'hostess', the Aladdin's cave effect of the dressing-up tableau scene and Vi's appearance as a traffic warden – there are visual moments that, in Irigaray's sense, mimetically demonstrate this process of image construction in a way that is critique as much as reflection. The play also explores different ways in which women may use their bodies to redefine their sexuality – Dusa as individual yet mother, Stas as both male exploiter and scientist, Fish as a personal as well as political being, whilst Vi's starvation can be seen as a refusal to be bodily defined. Reviewers stating 'the frequent interruptions of inane radio interviews' are a 'mistake' (*Tatler*, 2 February, 1976) miss the point that these distressing sounds can be read as linguistic manifestations of the power of male institutions – significantly, Vi can only bear the TV without sound. According to Gems, the key is Fish's speech about Rosa Luxembourg, delivered directly to the audience in frame-breaking style: 'The nature of the social and political contribution of women is, at this moment wholly in question' (*Plays by Women 1*, p. 55). However, the struggle is too great for Fish, outside the anarchy, comedy and support of the female space, the flat. The others all manage some kind of recovery, but her birth/deathday note runs, 'My loves, what are we to do? We don't do as they want any more, and they hate it. What are we to do?' (*Plays by Women 1*, p. 70). Although the play ends on a questioning note as Stas reads these words aloud, the corpse is a vivid physical reminder of the difficulty of escaping the defining demands of patriarchal society. The play's setting is clearly indicated as 'not naturalistic' (*Plays by Women 1*, p. 48) and its imagistic moments, together with the anarchic quality of the comedy seem to depart from classic realism. Nevertheless, the characterization and time sequence remain relatively near traditional dramatic form, consequently the nature of presentation seems to be predominantly feminine/reflective.

The lack of ideological bite, in conjunction with Gems' typical comedy and coarseness – considered by some critics as misguided flippancy – could be seen as contributory to her other West End and RSC successes, as a more radical stance is less likely to be commercially viable. Other major plays less thematically dense than *Dusa, Fish, Stas and Vi*, go on to demythologize other constructions of the feminine. *Queen Christina*, probably the most radical, a fast-flowing open consideration of sexuality as construct,

nevertheless seems to end in a rather essentialist position typical of Gems'
paradoxical approach. A reassessment of the Queen of Sweden immor-
talized in the Garbo film, started in 1974, rejected by the Royal Court's
male directors, it became the first play by a woman to be performed in
Stratford's The Other Place, where Penny Cherns directed. Gems said of
Queen Christina, 'She was brought up to be like a prince and do everything a man can do. When it came time for her to marry she couldn't. She
had unlearned the business of womanhood. That was her tragedy' (*Sunday
Telegraph*, 19 June, 1977). Plain bisexual Christina is full of a disruptive
excess of energy, coarse language and manners, anger and even the intellectual ability to challenge Descartes and the Pope. Her polymorphous attitude to pleasure is in vivid contrast to her emaciated bred-out mother, who
keeps the head and member of the late King at hand in a box. Even so,
somewhat like Fish, Christina questions, 'I can't even secure my own
happiness. Am I, in my privilege, to derive contentment solely from the
nourishment of others?' (*Plays by Women 5*, p. 23). Potential subversion is
again sited in visual moments that embody the essence of gender construction, such as the masque or the wedding/abdication ceremony when
Christina emerges in riding gear from her ceremonial skirts. Provoked by
outrageous and unexpected events, the audience veer from sympathy to
admiration to hostility on viewing Christina's behaviour. The irony that
male-bonded Christina feels an interloper even among liberated and radical
French lesbians who welcome her, develops to a point when she realizes,
too late, that by identifying with male aggression and values she has lost the
chance to bear children. Having killed her duplicitous male lover, she sits
frozen, until a child gives her sweets – a food symbolic here of love yet loss.
She is a victim of a notion she expressed earlier, 'the privilege of action at
the cost of oneself' (*Plays by Women 5*, p. 43) thus, ultimately, reflecting
bourgeois individualism and maternal drives. This biological drive is found
in both the hairdresser and the radical woman in *Loving Women*, written as
The Project in 1976, revised and then directed by Gems' son Jonathan at the
Arts Theatre in February 1984. Less radical, somewhat satirical of the Left,
it is set more naturalistically. Though these 'rival' women establish a kind of
rapport – sharing the rather weak male, who will perhaps father the child
the radical now desires after devoting her past life to causes – a compromise
is typical of the price paid, Gems suggests elsewhere, for individual survival.[14] The demythologizing thrust of two other major plays is comprised
by an ambivalence implicit in performance potential; a possibility for softening implications of the verbal text through direction that can emphasize
selectively scenic and physical presentation towards a romantic rather than
deconstructive effect. Productions such as the Royal Theatre Northampton's *Piaf* (1987) and the RSC's *Camille* (1984/5) illustrate this point.
Piaf, the eponymous heroine of the play transferred between the RSC's
London and Stratford studios in 1979 and thence to the Picadilly in 1980,

shares many of Christina's energetic unrestrained qualities. The version printed by Amber Lane Press (1979) has a harsher, more Brechtian tone than the slightly muted revised version in the Penguin Plays series (1985), but the remaining circular episodic structure is open to an ambivalent production. Piaf's allegiance to her working class roots is emphasized, but not in an ideologically coherent way; greater importance is laid on her resilient sense of her own identity and sexuality. Disregard of taboos varies from pissing on stage, to setting up an orgy, to attacking medical staff who try to repair her after a car crash. Female support and camaraderie is important, yet Piaf's dependence on a series of male relationships is as crucial to her as the drink and drugs that affect her health. She is shown to nourish these younger men almost as substitutes for her farmed-out dead child, about whom she fantasizes when mourning her dead 'true love' Marcel. Despite the coarse language and comic tone of the text, which can keep the deconstructive approach to the myth of the 'Sparrow' dominant, there are points open to sentimentality, such as Piaf's song with her last young husband, Theo, and the closing moments, which repeat the opening concert. This softening possibility, the popularity of the myth and the music, with the strong nature of the original production starring Jane Lapotaire, may well account for the play's wide appeal.

Camille, transferred from Stratford to the West End in April 1984, sets out to demythologize romance, revealing it as a construct masking the exploitative nature of traditional notions of sexuality. Aspects of female solidarity are also celebrated, though again there is a focus on women's ability to survive through taking decisions against the odds – but at a cost. The cyclical text, which starts and ends just as the dead Marguerite's effects are being auctioned, and flows as if narrated by Armand to Gaston, could be open to performance in a somewhat Brechtian style. However, the RSC production demonstrated the difficulties inherent in Gems' tendency to mix the mimetic/reflectionist and interrogative/radical forms. The narrative framework opens up the possibility of demonstrating a dialectical relationship between the ideologies represented by Armand's romantic discourse and Madame Prudence's cash nexus attitudes. Labelled furniture for the auction of the dead Camille's possessions in the framing opening scene of the play is a vivid semiological indication of the condensation of sexuality and economics, which underlies all the emotional transactions. Marguerite's pragmatic insistence on one more assignation with the impotently drunk Russian Prince so that she can bring the returned Armand a dowry, finally loses the promise of reunion with him – he throws money in her face and leaves. Tension induced by the following interlude with the Russian accelerates her death through haemorrhage. Just as Stas could keep her integrity whilst using men to survive, Marguerite and the other demimondaines can distinguish between the constructed dream and the real. The men cannot, because it suits them to perpetuate the image of romance and the notion of moral, contracted marriage: Marguerite's 'Only a fool believes a lie' is counterpointed by coughing fits (Gems, *Three Plays*, p. 113). Although she sacrifices her love for Armand and her love for her son by relinquishing both, it is at the pragmatic price that her son will become respectable and educated, under the sponsorship of his natural father, who is also Armand's. The mismatch between the mythic construct of romance and the materialism of reality is encoded through various devices in the verbal and visual text: the white and red camellias indicative of menstruation; the carnivalesque circle games in which, under the ringmasterly direction of Prudence, partners are changed; and the offstage opera story and metatheatrical framing of the whole by Armand's narrative. The RSC production's main scenic background was made from mirror-like wall panels and the only open, unclaustrophobic scene was the secret garden where the lovers were happy. There is a strong anti-romantic and often comic discourse in the verbal text: references to abortion, masturbation, impotence and to Marguerite as 'A woman who has felt the private parts of every man in Paris' (*Three Plays*, p. 123); yet this production seemed to foreground the romantic discourse, through its use of visual symbols such as attractive pale costumes, banks of flowers and predominantly mellow piano music, which was not undercut enough by the hacking coughs or the coarseness of the bumping song. Women's tenacity and energy for survival sometimes surfaces in outbursts of violence and tension, which contrast with romping and poignant interludes in the play, hinting perhaps at the perverse pleasures of the female/ritualistic mode. Marguerite's solitary physical fading is ironically counterpointed with the gradual fattening of Clemence, who literally and metaphorically feeds off her suitor, the comic count. True to Gems' priorities, Marguerite breathes her son's name at the last – ironically, as an 'unfit' mother, she has bought him the myth of respectability. Her greatest sacrifice and loss is as a mother rather than a lover – death is the penalty for those women who defy the norms of status, materialism and sex. Piaf, Christina and Camille are figures who may have been demythologized within these plays, but at the expense of evoking another myth, the essentialist notion that motherhood is true fulfilment and its loss is inevitably tragic.

Gems's undoubted Box Office success, and pioneering qualities cannot be denied, but it is perhaps significant that her most recent work has been in translation/development, such as *The Danton Affair* (1986), whilst her more experimental pieces, such as *Aunt Mary*, an anarchic camp fantasy (RSC Warehouse, 1982), are rarely shown. However, Gems' re-working of *The Blue Angel*, with the eponymous role made famous on film by Marlene Dietrich, was scheduled for their 1991–2 programme by the RSC. Wandor criticizes Gems' depiction of women as 'powerfully and confidently sexually self-determining', demonstrating 'the bourgeois feminist dynamic of individual existential power over their lives' (*Carry on Understudies*, p. 166). As an extension of this view, it would seem that Gems's anxiety to avoid polemic and her concern to invest her plays with subversive energetic comedy, combined with her ambivalent attitude to feminism, is most strongly evident in her tendency to use dramatic forms, which mix near naturalism with elements of the interrogative text. Thus the deconstructive visual coding implicit in the verbal text is liable to be softened and underplayed through direction more appealing to a commercial audience, in reflecting the position of woman as victim rather than providing a critique which would imply the need for change. *Piaf* and *Dusa, Fish, Stas and Vi* are very popular in regional repertory, suggesting that the question of woman's status in society is still one that appeals to a less radical audience, providing that it is not played as an overt challenge.

The work of Wymark, also celebrated in the *Time Out* article, explores a similar range of themes, but is more radical in form and techniques, embodying many of the qualities associated with the notion of 'l'Écriture Feminine'. An American prematurely widowed with four children, she suggests she had used motherhood to postpone writing. Her plays have generally been performed in fringe venues and she was involved with 1975 Leicester Women's Theatre Festival. Productions of her plays have also won awards in America, many are still in print. Press coverage of *Find Me* (Orange Tree, Richmond, 1977), particularly a fierce dispute between Bernard Levin in the *Sunday Times* (30 October and 6 November, 1977) and Steve Grant of *Time Out*, shows audience response varied from emotional concern for the insolubility of a severely mentally disturbed girl's problems, to didactic condemnation of the inadequacies of the National Health Service. Significantly, these reviews discuss the fragmentation and doubling techniques through which this originally collaborative drama evolved in Wymark's work with students from Kingston Polytechnic, where she was Gulbenkian Writer in Residence. Documentary evidence, including contributions from the parents of the 'real' girl, who was eventually sent to Rampton, informs the drama. The problem of identity expressed in this girl's note, 'Dear whoever you are please find me and have me as your beloved'[15] is shown by the splitting of the protagonist, Verity, into five individuals, and the fluid assumption of different family and institutional roles, by the small cast. In spatial terms, a bare set and flexible symbolic use of chairs – for instance as trapping devices – highlight the sense of loneliness and oppression, whilst strong use of violent physical movement and non-verbal grunts expresses the frustration of Verity, who writes her transgressive polymorphously perverse desires through her body.

Wymark's other plays on psychological themes could be seen to be subversive in dynamic and radical in form. For instance, in the surreal play *The Committee* (Cockpit, 1981, as part of a programme entitled *Fireworks* commissioned by John Halle), a male, called Nanny, in female dress is interrogated by two mysterious figures, a formally dressed man in a suit and a severely clad secretary who is eventually shown to be wearing spangled circus clothes. *The Twenty-second Day* (1976) shows a girl's inner and external reactions to having been kidnapped from a psychiatric hospital by a male nurse. Fascination with the difference between the public and private self is also metatheatrically presented in pieces such as *Coda* (1967), where role-playing and games of various kinds play a significant part, or in *The Inhabitants* (1967), where a tape recorder/voice follows the inner voices of a man's thought. This staging of the split self[16] is also found in *Stay Where You Are* (1969), *Loved* (1978) and particularly in *Best Friends* (1981). The latter explores familiar themes of identity, female friendship, demystification of family relationships, sexism and the notion of female creativity. Employing the device of mixing the 'real' characters with those in a play that the protagonist Baba is writing, Wymark lays bare the process through which female fiction emerges by showing how Baba challenges and reworks the repeated experience of the return of repression.[17] The power of such semiotic incursions of repressed creativity is manifest in the interweaving of these fictional layers of characterization, for example the severally repeated 'I've got enough voices of my own. Inside. Laughing at me all the time. . . . And of course I have a preternatural gift for paranoia' (*Best Friends*, p. 19, pp. 38–9). This statement may represent the dynamic of the fragmentation and role play techniques that Wymark uses to show how the self-image is constructed by forces, often institutional, outside the private individual. The verbal and visual incursions of Baba's inner fiction into the world of the play, can be comically anarchic. The radio play *Child*, 1979, also explores role-playing and potential violence associated with mental handicaps and parenting; only finally is the 'child's' age shown to be forty-one. In 1987 Wymark's successful adaptation of Zola's nineteenth century novel *Nana* for Shared Experience, ran in the West End, although critics tended to misread it, emphasizing the sexual and comic elements of the lively production. Like Gems (*Sunday Times*, 4 February, 1984), Wymark has been selected for the *Sunday Times* 'Relative Values' series (*Sunday Times*, 14 August, 1988), in which successful parents and children are interviewed. Both dramatists, whose work has travelled from fringe to commercial or high culture venues, still consider that motherhood and dramatic creativity have similar qualities. The difference is perhaps that although the content of Wymark's plays is neither necessarily gender connected in the feminist sense, nor written from a particular ideological standpoint, her plays do more than reflect the *status quo*. Especially in experimenting with structure and fragmentation techniques, metatheatricality, carnivalesque intrusions and androgynous aspects, her writing seems to embody those qualities of l'Écriture Feminine, which break traditional forms and bear a kind of subversive drive, thus bringing the plays into the feminist/revolutionary mode and towards the female/ritualistic, as they seem to suggest that 'the artful process of meaning construction is in itself a site of struggle' (Erens, pp. 157ff).

Michelene Wandor is in a unique position, as a woman dramatist with both practical and theoretical credentials. She has produced significant critical writings on gender and theatre, and edited the first four volumes of the Methuen *Plays by Women* series, through which many of the texts discussed here have remained available, as well as the feminist play collection *Strike While The Iron is Hot* (1980). Associated from the first with the Women's Movement, she stated then, 'I can't separate the way I try to look at things from the way I write, so I'd say I'm conscious of trying to incorporate a feminist way of looking at things in my work' (*Time Out*, 21–27 October, 1977). Wandor's plays show allegiance to socialist feminism, and are inventive in form, exploring the relationship of the personal with the political context to an extent lacking in the work of more comprising, commercially successful women. She acknowledges, that her work is divided by the period when she undertook an MA in the Sociology of Literature (*Carry On Understudies*, pp. 186–7). During the first period she produced pieces such as *The Day After Yesterday*, 1972, about the Miss World contest, and the duologue on sexual politics *To Die Among Friends* (1974). On her return to dramatic writing in 1976, *The Old Wives Tale* was put on by Bargate and she began to work for fringe shows, including co-operative work with Caryl Churchill, David Bradford and Bryony Lavery for Monstrous Regiment's first cabaret *Floorshow* (1977) and *Care and Control* (1977), about lesbian mothers' problems with child custody for Gay Sweatshop. Fast flowing interchanges, fluid role exchanges and bare or simple staging are characteristic of *To Die Among Friends*, where duologues explore the struggle for identity through a range of relationships shown in the context of gender, class and other pressures. A surreal fantasy/satire *Whores d'Oeuvres* (1978) seems most consonant with l'Écriture Feminine. Here, two women are stranded on a raft in the Thames after a freak storm. Events break chronological form, including dream incursions and multiple role-playing, which lay bare the social construction of the female image, along the spectrum whore to madonna. A carnivalesque riotous and comical quality is evident in strong visual moments, such as the contrast between a series of pornographic poses and accompanying delivery of Lady Macbeth's 'Unsex me here' speech (Wandor, *Five Plays*, p. 79). Subversive use of coarse, sexual colloquialisms and rude rhymes, as well as a voyeuristic element, informs the audience's viewing of the raft – a tiny female sanctuary amidst the storm. Even so there is a clear indictment of sexism and the socio-economic underpinning of both prostitution and marriage. A further experimental venture, premiered by Mrs Worthington's Daughters (1979), after rejection both by BBC and National Theatre, was *Aurora Leigh*, a re-working of Elizabeth Barrett Browning's epic poem. Written in verse, the narration by Aurora metatheatrically enhances the split self-tension between woman/writer:

I perceive
The headache is too noble for my sex
You think the heartache would sound decenter?
(Plays by Women 1, p. 110)

The play celebrates Aurora's struggle through using 'clusters of feminine imagery, nature, embroidery in a subversive way' (p. 134), by turning it to active purpose. Sisterly generosity is opposed to traditional selfish competition for a mate, and Wandor, rather than allow the failed, philanthropic socialist hero Romney to obtain his bride only when symbolically castrated by fire in the Rochester tradition, provides a more egalitarian resolution than Browning. First performed in a fluid abstract set, a rehearsed reading at the National followed in 1980. Apart from recent radio drama, including successful adaptations of Austen, H.G. Wells, and George Eliot, Wandor has co-written with Mike Alfreds, a five-hour version of Eugene Sue's *The Wandering Jew* for the National, although this did not win critical acclaim.

Louise Page, slightly younger than the other dramatists considered here, was not included in the 1977 *Time Out* article. Her work, which has elements of reflection, revolution and ritual, is in some ways transitional. Reputed to admire the work of Howard Brenton and Edward Bond, she followed David Edgar's Birmingham University Playwriting Course. In an interview preceding the Watford Palace opening of *Diplomatic Wives* she stated that the term 'woman playwright' was a 'second division term', which should now be rejected (*Independent*, 27 July, 1989). Despite writing largely about women, revealing the social conditioning that may shape them and the emotional subtext that underlies ordinary lives, she claims that her concerns are wider than gender issues

> I don't believe in female separation . . . I can't write plays just to provide parts for women . . . I write about things I want to discuss . . . You have to compromise. It's no good writing radical feminist plays for the National Theatre because they don't get produced. My aim is simply to get my plays put on and I don't care if the director is male or female.
>
> *(Sunday Telegraph Magazine,* 'Make Way for the Ladies',
> 27 January, 1985)

This individualistic drive for success is mirrored in the content of some of Page's plays, in particular *Golden Girls* (1984), hence Wandor's assessment of aspects of her work as an expression of the bourgeois feminist dynamic (*Carry On Understudies*, pp. 180–1). Nevertheless, the formal variation of these plays, especially the strong emphasis on visual language, indicates that underlying the verbal surface content there is a subversive potential in her exploration of those themes shared with other women writers. Since 1976, her plays have mostly been performed in studio venues, and since she obtained the George Devine Award for *Salonika* in the Royal Court Upstairs in 1982, all her work has been commissioned, including *Beauty and the Beast* (1985/6), which then became the first joint publication by Methuen and the Women's Playhouse Trust.

Some of Page's early work centres upon medical or scientific themes, such as *Tissue* (1978), about breast cancer, *Lucy* (1979), about euthanasia, and *Hearing* (1979) about the isolation of deafness. A short but powerful play *Goat* (1986) embodies a critique of science in the nuclear age, through a monologue given by a woman scientist who is observing the animal's final deterioration due to its previous exposure to strong radiation as an experiment. It had been chosen as a scapegoat because of its bodily similarity to human beings – an irony drawn upon as the speaker's scientific discourse becomes fractured by a growing emotional panic. Gripping in performance, the play merges real and fictional time, and although slides of specimens taken from the goat are shown as a lecture-like distancing device, the tension is charged emotionally and intellectually by the woman's growing concern for the goat, which the audience never sees. Other plays, *Want Ad* (1977), *Flaws* (1980), *Housewives* (1981) and *Diplomatic Wives* (1989) deal with public issues such as journalism, bankruptcy and political involvement as they impinge on the personal. *Falkland Sound/Voces de Malvinas* (Royal Court, 1983) was based on documentary evidence, especially letters home from a young man – eventually killed on HMS *Glamorgan* in June 1982. Michael Coveney commented on a 1990 revival that it 'stands up well as a moving, elegiac testament of youthful disillusion in a cause', attributing this quality however, to the tone derived from the letters of the dead Lieutenant David Tinker (*Observer*, 13 March, 1990). Page's ambitious rewriting of *Beauty and the Beast* (1985) lacks the subversive attack of Angela Carter. In rather diffuse linear form, including animals and fairies in the dramatis personae, the fable explores parenting themes in parallel. Both Beast and Beauty, royal cousins, have adoptive/foster parents; the former's is a destructive fairy, the latter's a caring but impoverished merchant with other daughters reminiscent of Cinderella's sisters. Beast's real mother is a military, widowed Queen with no time to care for him. Beauty's father is a King who saves her by substituting her for the merchant's dead child. An elaborate plot ends in marriage and restitution for all but the doubly bereft merchant. Though open to Freudian analysis on the lines explored by Marthe Robert as an extension of the Family Romance,[18] the play does not reassess the notion of the family unit as such. Within this wide range of topics, despite lack of critique and a combination of reflectionist quality with chronological form, it seems that Page's plays tend more to experiment in technique than to develop ideological positions. In plays where what is being said could be said to be more revolutionary, Page fractures the time flow and sometimes also fragments the personae. In these more radically structured texts the images, paradoxically, tend to reflect this verbal content, pointing up the contradictions evident in the multiple discourses circulating within the play. Conversely, in her more traditionally structured texts, an emphasis on spatial relationships and visual details often acts as an ironic commentary upon or counterpoint to a play's verbal text. This difference is evident in *Salonika* (1982) and *Real Estate* (1984): both investigate the nature of mother/daughter relationships, which are shown to be problematic/selfish. In the first case, restricting yet unbreakable, and in the second tarnished by the need for both to be independent. *Salonika* is more revolutionary in its escape from spatial and temporal naturalism, merging the present in which an elderly widow Charlotte and her daughter Enid visit Greece to see the father's war grave, with the past in the shape of Ben, a soldier who drowned himself, who comes to life. Yet here the visual domestic details of knitting, tea-making and erecting deck-chairs seem to function as a physical discourse that coheres with the verbal dialogue and events. Subversive elements are verbally clear in the uncomfortable parent/child discourse, the unexpected love dialogue of the ageing lovers Leonard and Charlotte and the poetic speech of the drowned soldier. Even so, the strongest visual moments are body-centred and silent: the sight of a naked sunbather, the moment when the repressed daughter dances like Isadora Duncan and the emergence from the sand of the long-dead man. The sudden death of Peter, the strange young man, who apparently lives through selling blood and semen, may in its mystery suggest a waste parallel to the soldier's. Such waste in war is perhaps echoed in the restricted 'dead' lives the characters have led, revealed through dreamlike episodes of potential wish fulfilment and the final impasse; the women unable to separate, drink milk, a symbol of life, whilst the men are now either dead or sleeping.

In contrast, events in *Real Estate*, a more reflectionist piece set in a house and a wood, flow chronologically. Jenny, a pregnant career woman of thirty-eight returns to the home, mother and stepfather she left twenty years before. Deserted by her daughter, Gwen has toughened into a successful estate agent, and in ironic visual contrast to the verbal text that manifests her unmotherly behaviour, is her initial action of finding and keeping an acorn. 'The next time I find them they've withered', she says, putting it into her pocket as the first edgy conversation with her daughter develops (*Real Estate*, p. 5). Jenny throws her acorn away. Significantly, Gwen's final action as she leaves the house, taking the dog and her husband's tapestry, abandoning all her family – even her business – to the hands of her intrusive, alien seeming and more ruthless daughter, is to plant out this acorn that she has been nurturing. Throughout, the men are seen to be more active in domestic activities from tapestry to cooking – for instance Eric scraping cake mixture into a tin ironically accompanies Dick's graphic account of Gwen's miscarriage and curettage. Both the men put child care before any other relationship. Thus there is an ambivalence in Gwen's dawn escape through the woods that demythologizes the sacred notion of the maternal. Although both plays explore family relationships, through different modes, neither closure could be considered positively feminist, the tension between the content and techniques virtually cancelling out this possibility in both cases. Page uses temporal and spatial devices elsewhere in ways that might seem to be feminist/ revolutionary; for instance the consideration of body image and sexuality in *Tissue* (1978) and *Golden Girls* (1984). Despite, or perhaps because of, the juxtaposition of non-chronological scenes and the doubling of roles – one man and one woman play all the parts other than that of Sally, the breast cancer victim – the former play is very moving. Within a very simple set the action moves from present to past, apparently haphazardly covering the stages from suspicion to diagnosis to operation and after. Particularly significant are interspersed scenes in which, rather comically, women are heard assuming the dominant ideas of body image and sexuality as they grow up. Rhythmic vocal interchanges in some of the short episodes indicate the smoothness both of institutional medical procedure, which reduces woman to patient, and of mythologies of femininity and fear of illness. In this play, the subversive elements are both formal and verbal rather than visual: broken chronology, polyphony, fragmentation and doubling (heightened in the radio version by an inner and an outer voice for Sally), rather than visual. The ending is positive and life affirming.

In *Golden Girls* – a successful production in both RSC studios – plot chronology is consecutive and characterization naturalistic, yet the verbal discourses are more complex in their relationship and are more revolutionary than in *Tissue*. The strong element of writing-the-body in this play visually underlines/reflects what is said, and most significantly at key points merges fictional and real time as a factor in the critique of the way society constructs the conventional image of woman. The story line follows an Olympic team – three black and two white women – which eventually runs its race faster than the men, despite problems associated with selection and the sponsoring company, Ortolan, whose product is Golden Girl Shampoo. At the climax Dorcas is, at her moment of triumph, banned for life, since tests prove she has been taking more of a drug that she thought had been administered to the whole team, when in fact they have been taking a placebo. She has been so driven by the madness to succeed in carrying the baton – an obvious allusion to phallic power – that she must be shown to be wrong and punished. In the ambivalent final moments she is shown singing a psalm, 'her warfare is accomplished, her iniquity is pardoned,' in celebration of the evanescent seconds of the victory (*Golden Girls*, p. 108). Throughout, there are three major discourses: commercial, medical and that of competitive training, which, particularly through visual imagery, are shown to rob the women athletes of their bodies and their power. The most obvious instance is when, in the process of making a commercial, the stereotypically attractive model 'Golden Girl' runs ineptly across the back of the stage, whilst the team girls exercise energetically. This difference between the illusory trivializing association of the shampoo advertising image and the demanding reality of athletic endeavour is pointed up not only by the ironic humour of this visual contrast, but also after the later airport scene when the team has been posed for photographs with the Golden Girl. Here stage directions comment 'Without the gear she looks drab and ordinary' (*Golden Girls*, p. 74). Commercial success for the shampoo relies on the consumer feeling that using the product would bridge the gap – fill the lack – between the 'feminine woman' (model as signifier) and the 'successful woman' (athlete as signified). Workout scenes, where the girls train hard in a way that does not highlight their bodies sexually, are significant in their potential relationship to the notion of l'Écriture Feminine. The use of panting and running sounds, with discordant music, emphasizes the struggle both of the training and, in a wider sense, the attempt to write women's equality without words – by using the female body in a way that challenges man-made verbal language. Each team member also has a soliloquy delivered as she runs, which reveals what underlies her particular drive, and likewise uses sounds that are reminiscent of birth and struggle, as in Kristeva's theories: 'A panting, a breathlessness, an acceleration of verbal utterance . . . revealing within the interstices of predication, the rhythm of a drive that remains forever unsatisfied' (Kristeva, 1980, p. 42). These soliloquies, though verbal and interspersed with other sounds, show the desire to push forward and to break the limits of time and space through the female body, a notion that also echoes the Kristevan notion of 'Woman's Time'. A further breaking of dramatic conventions that separate the audience from the spectacle is also followed through in the fusion of fictional and factual time during the race, when – as in the RSC production – the minute clock onstage is seen to record actual race time, so that the spectator is drawn into the fiction as 'real'. Amplified beating heart and panting sounds blur the spectator's body with the spectacle in a way that suggests an Artaudian involvement rather than a strictly Brechtian detachment. This blurring makes the ability to judge Dorcas for her drug-taking as an extension of the will to succeed more problematic. Again, although the techniques used are innovative, and to some extent in visual terms lay bare the contradictory relationship between the social image and the female body, the play implies that rules should not be transgressed – that competitive behaviour, as in *Real Estate*, can distort the traditional norms of female gender values, an issue also explored in the plays of Caryl Churchill.

Diplomatic Wives premiered at the Palace Theatre, Watford in March 1989, concerns Christine, who has abandoned her own successful diplomatic career to marry John, a less able man, once her assistant, a widower with a son. A visit from the successful Dr Libby Webster, whom it transpires had also been a lover of John's when she had been a lecturer and he a student, provokes a re-examination of the past and potential future. Christine is at this crucial moment offered a diplomatic posting in her own right and has to decide whether to put her marriage before her career – and indeed she does, it seems, decide that the relationship matters most. Interspersed with flashbacks, the play's central image seems to be eating and drinking – with the main public 'party' functions taking place off-stage, whereas Christina is seen performing a range of domestically centred servicing activities. Reconciliation finally takes place as the women swim together in the pool – before Libby's departure – apparently satisfied with the compromise that they both, some days at least, think that they are doing what they wanted. Thus the closure can hardly be considered to be radical. Page is reputed to be one of the few women playwrights to have earned her living by writing since the age of thirty. The variation in her plays and her skilful experimental techniques makes it difficult to define the mode of her work. However, because her work is either revolutionary in form and reflective in content, or vice versa, but never both at once, it evades a clear ideological position on feminism or any other issue. As a dramatist who spans two phases in contemporary theatre history, this ambivalence is indicative of the dilemma faced by women dramatists hoping for performance as resources for major and minor venues dwindled in the 1980s.

3

Waving not drowning: The mainstream, 1979–88

Trevor R. Griffiths

Despite the difficult economic climate for the arts in the 1980s, the number of women writers staged by established companies and venues increased. The writers covered here are linked by having at least some of their work staged by established venues or companies or in the commercial theatre, albeit under a wide variety of circumstances, from the relative financial security of the RSC or the National to much less well funded theatres such as the Royal Court, the Soho Poly or the Bush, or innovative but financially undervalued touring companies such as Joint Stock. To reflect the diversity of mainstream women's theatre writing in the 1980s, I have covered separately West End transfers, which reflect the commercially successful side of women's writing; Caryl Churchill, one of the most challenging writers of the decade; Sarah Daniels, the 'acceptable' face of radical feminism; plays by other writers grouped on the basis of their shared preoccupations, either with mothers, daughters, and families or workplaces; and Timberlake Wertenbaker – like Churchill, an innovative explorer of non-naturalistic dramaturgy.

Although writers have adopted a wide range of stylistic devices, confessional and small-scale pieces have predominated: the naturalistic case study, albeit modified by years of epic practice and feminist insight, has remained a dominant genre. Economic factors, particularly the general reduction in funding levels, have led to a reduction in both cast sizes and production costs, thus encouraging the movement towards the small-scale and the minimalist, at the expense of a more epic scale and public settings. This may reflect a more general retreat from public feminism, as well as the need for a catching-up process in which issues that had been inadequately covered in previous periods were treated at appropriate length and in suitable depth. Many of the more interesting plays can be seen as reports from the front line of women's experience, examining adolescence and the family through the focus of mother–daughter relationships, using specific workplace or leisure activities as a microcosm of the symbolic order and often reworking stock (male) situations from female angles.

The range of topics and themes covered in these plays is wide, although the vast majority are implicitly or explicitly constructed as opposing dominant ideological positions. Many of the most successful plays are deeply concerned with role playing and anxious to challenge the idea of the psychologically realistic individual subject as an autonomous being whose activities are purely personal and authentic. This challenge is often expressed by the use of doubling, which is not only an economic necessity of much contemporary theatre but also part of a deliberate strategy aimed at deconstructing traditional ideas of character. One common thread that links most of the writers considered here is that they have chosen the path of what Sandy Craig calls 'political drama' rather than 'political theatre'.[1] In practice the success of *Trafford Tanzi* in the West End and the emergence of Sarah Daniels as the one lesbian dramatist whose work is staged by major theatres show that the issue is more than one of class, as gender expectations and sexual orientation can also profoundly influence audience response.

The West End

The few women who achieved West End transfers in the 1980s (and none of the successful shows originated in the West End), presumably represent the acceptable official face of female dramatic creativity. Pam Gems's 1978 *Piaf* and Robyn Archer's *A Star is Torn* (1982) subverted traditional biopic views of the female star as victim, and Gems's version of *Camille* (1984) rewrote the Marguerite Gautier story from a female viewpoint, but as with Nell Dunn's *Steaming* (1981), and Caryl Churchill's *Serious Money* (1987), their success with West End audiences may reflect at least a partial recuperation of their progressive elements by more traditional and reactionary perspectives. The other West End successes of the 1980s by women were *Trafford Tanzi* (originally staged 1978, Mermaid 1981), a battle between the sexes in the form of a male/female wrestling match, Denise Deegan's *Daisy Pulls It Off* (1983), a homage to the girls' school story of Angela Brazil, Sue Townsend's adolescent nostalgia *Adrian Mole* musical (1984) and Sharman Macdonald's *When I Was a Girl, I Used to Scream and Shout . . .* (originally staged 1984, West End 1986), a study of mother–daughter relationships and adolescent sexuality.

These West End successes all depended on an element of eavesdropping and voyeurism. This relates in most cases to the still widespread assumption that an audience should be united by the dramatic strategies of the performance in a common view of the events and characters on stage, and to the structural conditions of watching plays in proscenium arch theatres, which is inherently voyeuristic, although *Trafford Tanzi* is an exception on both counts. It is not perhaps surprising that the theme of men spying on women, which is at least as old as *The Bacchae*, recurs in graphic form in Wertenbaker's *Love of the Nightingale*, where it is treated very successfully, and in Churchill and David Lan's *A Mouthful of Birds* (1986), where it is less successful.

The element of voyeurism sometimes guarantees a good reception for a play, whilst at the same time comprising or problematizing its original design. *Steaming*, a rather sentimental piece of confessional consciousness-raising set in a public baths, appears to owe some of its success in the West End, on tour and as a film, to the 'legitimate' voyeuristic opportunities it offers to men to see women without any clothes on in public, talking about sex and swearing. While the presentation of a group of characters' insights into the ways in which they have been battered by patriarchy is important, the play traps itself and them into a set of false contradictions. The council want to close the relatively underused baths and replace them with a library, so the women who use the baths mount an ultimately doomed fight and then decide to occupy the baths. The women are present in the flesh as we watch, alive, naked, vulnerable and available to us as a community in a way that the absent, disembodied (apparently male) councillors are not. Men are associated with words, abstraction and control, women with bodies, the sensuous and emotion. The baths/library opposition is particularly suspect: there is a body/mind split, with women associated with the body and men the mind. Furthermore, Josie, who has turned to sex as a compensation for her inability to get a decent job as a result of her poor education, wants to improve herself intellectually, even taking informal lessons from one of the middle-class clients of the baths, but she is also their spokesperson at the council meeting because she was born locally and therefore can make an appeal to the traditional sense of community that the baths are supposed to represent. The potential role of a library in enabling her, and others, to fulfil themselves intellectually is simply ignored. Although the play closes on an image of apparent triumph, with the women's decision to occupy the baths, they are equally trapped by the baths: static, enclosed, with nowhere to go and with the heating and other controls in male hands. What they have learnt is still at the level of the individual and, although the characters' intercut confessional monologues are not the most sophisticated dramatic technique, they offer the most positive image of what remains an ultimately disappointing play.[2]

Whereas *Steaming* offers the female body as a passive object for consumption, *Trafford Tanzi* offers an active and positive image of the female body through its metaphoric treatment of life as a wrestling match between the sexes. First staged in 1978 as a touring production in clubs around Liverpool, Claire Luckham's play eventually arrived at the Mermaid in 1981. Staged in the round and set in a wrestling ring with Tanzi up against opponents who support patriarchy, ranging from her mother and a psychiatrist to her wrestler husband, the play culminates in a wrestling match to decide whether Tanzi or her husband will quit a wrestling career to become a housewife. Although there is nothing significantly new about its consciousness-raising elements, the play operates accessibly within both agitprop and sporting conventions, with the audience encouraged to cheer on one of the combatants on the basis of gender. Apart from the importance of showing a woman using her body effectively and efficiently outside the normal constraints of 'feminine' activity, the production also elicited a gendered response from couples who could be seen leaving the theatre arguing about their reasons for supporting either Tanzi or her male opponent.

The other West End successes of the 1980s offered audiences versions of their own negotiation of the rites of passage from childhood to adulthood and sexual awareness, and entry into the symbolic order. Sharman Macdonald's *When I Was a Girl*, which won her an award for most promising playwright in 1984, is a relatively straightforward account of a mother and daughter frustrating one another's desires at different times in their lives. Most of the story is revealed through flashbacks to the daughter's childhood and adolescence. The play's strength lies in its delineation of female sexual awakening in the flashbacks, rather than in the contemporary scenes, which lack social contextualization or plot development, so that it suffers from the absence of a sense of the world of work in the present or of school in the past.

School can be seen to some extent as a metaphor for any social institution and by extension the symbolic order itself, but despite the apparent differences between *Adrian Mole*, contemporary and male-centred, and *Daisy Pulls It Off*, which, despite its double-entendre title, looks back to a golden age of girlish innocence, the two plays ultimately offer very similar views of the family. The phenomenal success in various media of the Adrian Mole character owes much to Townsend's skill in capturing the associations of adolescent rites of passage. However, the theatrical version is little more than a compilation of major moments from the saga: the distinctive tone of Adrian's confessional diary with its unified point of view, from which we as knowing readers may extract contrary messages, is lost in the play, which emerges as a defence of family values with a traditional comic ending of reconciliation between erring wife and husband. But Adrian's mother is shown as having only a choice between the man who cuts his nails in the living room and the man who can't wash his socks. In her case two days in bed (for sex rather than because of flu as earlier) solves everything. Love conquers all and Adrian's marginalization culminates in his late arrival for the curtain call wedding of the elderly Bert and Queenie who met in an old people's home. It may not be quite the picture of the family that Daisy Meredith would recognize, but, for all its tensions, and for all its exposure of the contradictions of marriage, *Adrian Mole* may ultimately be as conservative as *Daisy*: everything ends happily with the grown-ups properly married off and love triumphant over domestic reality and institutionalization.

Although *Daisy* makes none of *Adrian's* apparent concessions to realism or contemporaneity, dramaturgically it works much better by adopting the device of characters narrating parts of the story in the third person, as in the fashionable novel dramatizations of the period (most famously the RSC's *Nicholas Nickelby*) and by having them introduce themselves and their social roles in an almost Brechtian way, 'Sybil Burlington, Vice-Captain of the Upper Fourth, and conceited, beautiful, only daughter of very wealthy parents' (p. 2).

Like Alan Bennett's *40 Years On*, which was enjoying a West End revival during its run, *Daisy* uses the device of pretending that the theatre audience is attending a performance of the school play, but unlike Bennett who used the format to offer a critical history of Britain through the Albion House school play, *Daisy*, offers a reaffirmation of traditional values: Deegan's girls may be pubertal but their sexuality is confined to innocent crushes on the most popular girl in the school. Again there is a marked contrast with yet another boarding school play staged in the West End at the same time, Julian Mitchell's *Another Country*, where adolescent sexuality has serious political overtones. *Daisy*, offers a fantasy of discovering origins, in which Daisy recovers father, family good name, wealth and property, thus conveniently obliterating such awkward issues as her apparent class origins. Like Adrian she seeks an identity, like Adrian she rediscovers it in a family. The case is made for meritocracy, but the girl who deserves because of her own merits is also allowed the trappings of class and power, the absence of which had originally caused her to be an outcast with a few (wrong thinking) girls. The general reception of the play by audiences and critics alike accepted it as a tribute to, rather than a parody of, the values and conventions it draws on, with only Giles Gordon discovering an Orton-like subversiveness in the play balancing 'the tightrope of homage to its subject with a knife in the back of its unimaginative and unsophisticated morality' (*The Spectator*).[3] The difficulty with what Gordon describes as 'elegant irony' is that audience reception can convert it back to the thing itself, and the pleasure in the text surely arises from its explicit offering of an order in the world, in which the outsider becomes an insider, the bad outsiders are reformed and everybody lives happily ever afterwards. Significantly the use

of an induction, in which the head teacher explains that the fourth form are
going to entertain us, an audience supposed to be made up of relatives and
friends of the girls in the school, with a play called *Daisy Pulls It Off*, and the
use of cast members to patrol the audience welcoming us in those roles, is
not followed up at the end of the play, where, although there is direct
address to the audience, there is no return to the frame offered by the
induction. We, the audience, have regressed from adulthood and parent-
hood to being treated as the girls of Grangewood and we remain locked in
the triumphant wish fulfilment fantasy of Daisy's triumphs and discoveries,
even if 'a look of displeasure appears on Miss Gibson's face' during Daisy's
final visionary speech, 'I ask you all to accept with open arms the scholar-
ship girls who come to Grangewood. They may have heaps to learn from
you about Grangewood's sporting and academic traditions, but my word,
have you a lot to learn from them' (p. 51).

Unlike Deegan, who has not yet produced another significant play,
Townsend was an established playwright before the success of *Adrian Mole*.
Her other plays, presented mainly on the fringe circuit, operate largely
within feminist agitprop conventions. Her interest is in the ideological
inhibitions that construct us as consumers and victims. She tackles important topics like agoraphobia (*Bazaar and Rummage*, 1982), illiteracy (*Groping
for Words*, 1983) and the institutionalizing power of hospitals (*Womberang*,
1980) through the adoption of revue-like techniques, but her work is held
within rather than developing those techniques and her recycling of jokes
and situations from play to play suggests that her works are generally best
approached as *ad hoc* interventions in specific areas. Perhaps the best of these
plays is *Womberang*, where the intimidating hierarchies of the hospital gyne
out-patients clinic are disrupted by an outspoken former agoraphobic who
incites her fellow patients to an understanding of the way they are socially
constructed as patients and victims. Just as the hospital waiting room allows
Townsend to introduce a cross-section of women, so in *Bazaar and Rummage* the rummage sale brings together a disparate group of social misfits,
and *Groping for Words* uses the schoolroom as a focus for a disparate group
linked as failures through illiteracy. In each play the exploration of issues
leads to a new confidence about facing them, despite a grim exterior world
marked by sexism, urban violence (real or imagined), and redundancy.

Townsend's Joint Stock play *The Great Celestial Cow* (1984) is similarly
concerned with questions of community and of growth through sharing
experiences. The use of doubling, which in her other plays tends to be
pragmatic rather than ideological, here takes on new resonances of a kind
that typify Joint Stock's work.[4] The play, which deals with people of Asian
origin in Leicester, was well regarded by white audiences but led to some
protests from Asian groups. Whites in the audience tended to find the
depiction of a British Asian community moving and illuminating, and
the use of a pantomime cow to represent a vision of a true community

memorable, while some Asians protested about the elements of caricature
in the play. The upbeat ending in which the virtues of family life in India
are associated with a naïve pastoralism is problematic, because it seems to
suggest implicitly that everyone would be better off at home. Townsend's
usual episodic style may have fuelled the resentment from the Asian community: the dramatic shorthand involved in her presentation of traditional
attitudes to, for example, the family, arranged marriages and the onset of
menstruation, inevitably militiates against 'in depth' characterization and
investigation, so that the play can seem like a package tour review of issues
from the women's page of an 'enlightened' newspaper. On the other hand,
the use of a predominantly female Asian cast led to some illuminating
juxtapositions when casually racist and sexist male Heathrow officials or a
racist female stall-holder in Leicester were played by Asian women, whose
reappearance in various roles, including the goddess Kali and various members of the family economically establishes a whole series of prismatic
contrasts between different attitudes to family and community. For some
audiences the declarative power of the play and its demonstration of
consciousness-raising in all the women of the community will serve to
break down stereotypes; for others the question is whether the issues are
confronted or whether the elements of cartoon characterization inevitable
in Townsend's vignettes lead to a reinforcement of stereotyping and a
trapping of the issues. Much of Townsend's work is family-centred, either
in terms of its investigation of the dynamics, contradictions and tensions of
family life or in its construction of alternative family/communal structures
that support the women and help them to realize a greater sense of self, but
its strengths and weaknesses are those of agitprop and consciousness raising.

Caryl Churchill

The most consistently successful dramatist of the period was Caryl Churchill, whose work at its best transcends the limitations of both naturalism and
agitprop to offer a genuinely challenging and entertaining vision. In her
best plays she brings two or more discursive structures into collision, trapping her audiences into working out the nature of the pressures and events
that are shaping her characters' predicaments and reactions, by an active
involvement in decoding, rather than simply interpreting information. As
the South American Woman in *Icecream* says, 'I know how to think it was a
coincidence. I went to university in Chicago. But I know how else to think
of it' (p. 50). Churchill's best plays are truly interrogative and require
precisely that complex seeing that Brecht demanded of his audience.
Churchill has tackled many of the familiar themes of British political
and feminist theatre in the 1970s including witches (*Vinegar Tom*, 1976),
terrorism (*Objections to Sex and Violence*, 1975) and seventeenth-century

revolutionary sects (*Light Shining in Buckinghamshire*, 1976), as well as more
unusual topics such as the nature of ideology and repression in the all male
Softcops, inspired by a reading of Michel Foucault's *Discipline and Punish*
(originally written 1978, staged 1984) and the Romanian revolution in *Mad
Forest*. Her work has explored sexual politics, especially in *Cloud Nine*
(1979), in which the links between patriarchy and colonization are mer-
cilessly and wittily exposed, and *Top Girls* (1982), a study of a 'successful'
career woman.[5] Churchill is a relentless experimenter, willing to tackle
topics from a wide variety of approaches, which have taken her, not always
with complete success into the realms of performance art and dance scen-
arios. Her later work, since *Top Girls* and *Fen* (1982), has resisted any
attempt to pigeonhole it as feminist but the preoccupations with the role of
ideology, mutual incomprehension and the relationship between social
pressures and individual desires remains as strong as ever.

 Cloud Nine is technically highly complex and concerned with many of
the themes that recur throughout Churchill's work: the nature and construction of time, the social construction of identity and of gender, the
difficulty of seeing the restraints and pressures that prevent us from achiev-
ing a fuller humanity. She uses time shifts, uneven ageing (the characters are
twenty-five years older in part two than they were in part one, but one
hundred years has passed), cross-race and cross-gender casting, doubling,
pastiche Victorian light verse and rhyming couplets as part of a consistent
strategy of upsetting and destabilizing conventional assumptions about both
drama and life itself. The main reasons for the cross-casting in part one are
clear, 'I had the image of a black man aspiring to white values and literally
being a white negro. And the idea of a woman who has taken on men's
values, a sort of man-made woman who has no sense of herself as a
woman.'[6] So in the opening tableau we have an economic presentation of
patriarchy and paternalistic colonialism. Churchill uses the kind of pantomime doggerel one might associate with a nineteenth-century author
such as J.R. Planché to perform the same kind of introductory explanation
as the induction in *Daisy*, but with even clearer Brechtian overtones in
which the dynamic contradictions that underpin the first part are made
explicit. Clive is a father to the family and the natives, his wife Betty, played
by a man, is 'a man's creation as you see/And what men want is what I
want to be' (p. 251). Whereas Betty is shown as wanting to conform to
Clive's values, Edward has a similar problem with an unacknowledged
discrepancy between his physical nature and his assigned social role: Clive is
trying 'To teach him to grow up to be a man' (p. 252) but Edward, played
by a woman, can only say 'What father wants I'd dearly like to be/I find it
rather hard as you can see' (p. 252). Victoria, the daughter, is played by a
dummy, Ellen and Maud (played by women), women without a voice,
assigned to their roles by paterfamilias Clive, who controls family and
society. The family's black servant Joshua, played by a white man, is

inevitably called a 'boy' and presented as having naturalized the paternalistic/imperialistic consensus within himself, 'As you can see,/What white men want is what I want to be' (p. 252). So, the discrepancy between assigned gender/race role and the actual individual assigned to that role establishes a counterpoint between the official position and the underlying physical reality at the heart of the play, as notions of 'femininity' and 'masculinity' are undercut by cross-gender casting. As the play unfolds, an almost kaleidoscopic polymorphous sexuality emerges, in which adultery, lesbianism and male homosexuality are revealed behind the facade of Victorian values. The first part of the play is very much concerned with what Churchill called softcops (education, the family, religion, the legal system), Althusser's ideological state apparatuses, operating in a family group that is itself, through Clive, part of the repressive state apparatuses. Everyone in the first part of the play, except perhaps the dummy Victoria and Maud, whose chilling comment to Betty 'you have to learn to be patient. I am patient. My mama was very patient' (p. 258) syntactically wraps up the perennial oppression of women, deviates from the norms, and most of them are unhappy precisely because of the extent to which they have internalized values they cannot wholly live by. Apart from the cross-casting, which clearly exemplifies this aspect of the play's themes, the most obvious way in which this is physically presented is through the doubling of Ellen and Mrs Saunders. Ellen's lesbianism is never acknowledged within the social group in the play, but she is siphoned off into a marriage of convenience with the homosexual explorer Harry Bagley. Caroline Saunders poses a challenge to Clive as the mysterious Other: 'You terrify me. You are dark like this continent. Mysterious. Treacherous' (p. 263).

It is possible to read part one simply as a virtuoso piece of comic writing in which the removal of various masks of polite behaviour reveals the sexual whirlpools beneath, and in which familiar targets such as Victorian attitudes towards black people, women and children are attacked in familiar ways. However, Churchill's dramaturgy is pre-eminently one in which we are asked to work out relationships between material that appears to exist within two different registers and to see how it connects, so that the result is prismatic rather than linear.

In part two of *Cloud Nine*, set in contemporary England, there is a greater openness about human relationships, which permits the possibility of certain kinds of fulfilment emerging, although it is still clear that the societal norm – the heterosexual nuclear family – is fraught with problems. Stylistically there has been a change, which appears to reflect a psychosociological improvement: many of the characters in part two address the audience directly and in their own words. In the first part direct address to the audience is confined to the exposition, channelled through the doggerel verse, and largely under Clive's control. The fact that the gay men and the women have found their voices and are less inhibited about the pursuit of their sexual identities is a

positive step, and so presumably is the problematization within the dramatic world of traditional male heterosexual attitudes.

Michelene Wandor has argued that, 'In the "historical" half imperialist
and sexual values parallel each other, with a clear cause and effect; in the
"contemporary" half . . . there is no . . . political analysis and therefore no
link between cause and effect.'[7] However, the precise analysis that we find
in part one is authorial: in neither part are the connections articulated by
the characters as part of their experience; they are presented in both parts as
so immersed in their own individual situations that they are in no position
to offer a coherent analysis. Hence the appearance of the ghost of Lin's
brother killed in Ireland, showing that the afterlife of imperialism is still a
factor in the equation. It has been marginalized compared to the first part,
but he is the inheritor of the Empire: bored, scared and ultimately dead,
with no idea of what he died for. As in epic theatre, the characters may be
trapped but we are in a position to learn: we understand that the fixed
positions of the official Victorian model of society are untenable, but if we
read the modern, apparently free, positions of the contemporary model in
the same light, we can begin to understand the underlying pitfalls.

This is where the play's title and the placing of the song Cloud Nine are
very important. As an expression 'cloud nine' has connotations of well-
being, elation and transcendence, which are reflected in the words of
Churchill's song. In the 1980 production at the Royal Court the song was
staged as an upbeat finale number, representing a utopian possibility that
the action of the play refuted by continuing beyond the end of the song. It
was a typically Churchillian trap because it looked like a conclusion but it
could not end the play because it offered no solution and could be seen as
just as much an ideological fix as the imperialist/sentimental songs of the
first part, eliciting an instinctive audience response, which is then challenged by the play going on. In the British, rather than American,[8] version
the song is a false ending, which demands that we practise complex seeing
and make connections which the characters cannot.

Similarly, Top Girls requires the audience to make connections. Although the play's willingness to confront the issues of 'bourgeois feminism'
has itself led some feminist critics, including Michelene Wandor, to see the
play as promulgating a bourgeois feminist line, it is actually an interrogation
of the bourgeois feminist stance. Top Girls begins with a gathering of
women from different periods and cultures (who cannot 'realistically' be
present in the same scene) to celebrate the promotion of Marlene the
central character within the Top Girls employment agency. In the first
scene Marlene is apparently emancipated from the entanglements of family
and children that have constrained the others but much of the rest of the
play is concerned with destabilizing this privileged position by trapping
audiences into semi-agreement with her and then encouraging them to see
her putative success in a far wider context, in which she is just as much a

victim as her sisters. It is an important interrogation of the traps that face 'emancipated' bourgeois women in contemporary society that is both funny and chilling in its brilliantly observed presentations of the everyday contradictions of life. Churchill's plays are clearly interrogative within the terms of Belsey's definition, but *Top Girls* also mimics in a number of ways the classic realist tendency to closure, which is also disclosure, except that the revelation that Marlene is in fact Angie's mother leads not to closure but enlargement of the debate. Churchill, like Brecht, suggests that what we need is a new way of seeing if we are to understand and confront the pressures the characters in *Top Girls* fail to understand.

The cast list itself is significant: all-female casts remain a highly visible dramatic strategy because historically, the vast majority of plays have concerned themselves with men or with male–female conflict. All the performers except the one who plays Marlene, play a number of parts; the characters in the first scene are not the obvious women from history that a 'successful' career woman might be expected to invoke. Amongst the women Marlene invites to her celebration are two fictional creations (Griselda and Dull Gret), a third whose status is controversial (Pope Joan) and two who are known through their writings, Lady Nijo and Isabella Bird. They were unlikely to have obvious connotations for the majority of the original audiences.

The mixing up of 'real' and 'fictional' characters reminds us that our view of reality is largely constituted through unchallenged assumptions about the way things are. Many newspaper critics, one of whose functions is to stabilize the position of their readers and guide them to form appropriate judgements, spent much of their space recuperating these characters in the first scene into a tidy narrative and telling us who they are. Similarly, a considerable amount of attention was paid to the overlapping dialogue because it is different from the ways in which even the most apparently naturalistic plays are written. Without orderly, turn-taking conversations, the whole normal pattern of dramatic dialogue is broken down. Even in epic theatres, the emphasis on rational analysis normally predicates orderly dialogue.

Marlene is the common link between scenes and locations and offers the most obvious point of entry into the play for the audience. She apparently offers a privileged discourse for us to identify with so that we are likely to attempt to invest Marlene with heroic status as well as recognizing her as the leading character. When the play then encourages us to scrutinize her actions critically we are acting out the trapping process: we have apparently been encouraged to value Marlene's success highly but then we are encouraged to see it in a far wider context in which she is just as much a victim of the system despite her putative success.

Perhaps the most obvious victims, however, are the various clients of the agency, played by the same actresses who played some of the historical victims, and the other women who work in the agency. When they talk about their economic prospects, we find that the promotion of one woman means that there is no room for anyone else to move upwards. These women have also adopted male linguistic registers and the scene serves to show how far they are merely mimicking established male attitudes and the extent to which they have been utilized by society to repress other women.

Rosemary Kidd, wife of the man beaten by Marlene, has conformed to another readily available stereotype, submerging her personality to male demands and is now reaping the rewards. Her confrontation with Marlene is very well structured to maintain our sympathies for Marlene: Howard, an off-stage character, is less immediately likely to attract our sympathy, Rosemary is fighting his battles and revealing that she has made the wrong choices as she becomes increasingly desperate in her comments. In contrast, Marlene has achieved success within a bourgeois feminist dynamic: adored by her niece, she has seen off the challenge of the respectable married woman, she has become managing director, and her position is 'self evidently' better than that of the women she invited to the Prima Donna.

However, even if we have been able to identify with Marlene up to the end of 2.1, the rest of the play destabilizes that position, particularly as the revelations of the final scene bring us face to face with the actual human costs she has ignored in her balance sheets. She can only succeed because she has Joyce at home to look after Angie. She readily sacrifices her own child, like Griselda and Nijo, and her true identity is revealed to us through Angie who, like Pope Joan's child, reveals her mother's predicament. In fact there is little difference between the status of Marlene and that of her fictional, historical and contemporary sisters. Dull Gret stands outside many of these parallels: like Angie she is taciturn where the others are articulate, but unlike them she confronts her situation. Gret faces the demons and in the last scene so does Angie in the final exchange with her aunt/mother, which ends with the word 'frightening' (p. 43). As that scene actually takes place chronologically before the scene between Angie and Marlene in the agency we know that Angie has not fully seen through Marlene. In fact her understanding is limited to knowing that the situation is frightening; like the other characters except Gret she has not fully articulated the need for radical change. But Gret, as Churchill presents her, is a far cry from the interpretation of Gret offered by traditional art history. Christopher Brown says that Gret personifies the sin of covetousness:

> . . . though already burdened with possessions she is on her way to raid the very mouth of hell itself. Behind her, to the right, a mass of covetous women are looting a house . . . Covetousness has led 'Dulle Griet' and her legions of women into the landscape of Hell.

Churchill, like Brecht in his notes on 'Alienation Effects in the Narrative Pictures of the Elder Brueghel': 'The Fury defending her pathetic household goods with the sword. The world at the end of its tether. Little cruelty, much hypersensitivity',[9] suggests that what we need is a new way of seeing if we are to understand and confront the pressures the characters in *Top Girls* fail to understand. Wandor has suggested that for all Churchill's 'formal and literary precision', sophisticated stagecraft and technique, and implicit declaration of 'the possibilities of liberation through the imagination', there may also be '. . . a thread of defeatism . . . suggesting that perhaps all individuals – men as well as women, oppressors as well as oppressed – are simply victims of a system beyond their control and beyond their power to change.'[10] The danger seems to be that when the dramatist refuses to offer easy analysis or solutions, investigation may be taken for acceptance and it is clearly the case that Churchill's trapping of audiences through ironic juxtaposition and stagecraft can sometimes allow space for the very people criticized to reclaim her work.

To a limited extent, this may have happened with *Top Girls*, which Wandor, among others, took for praise of bourgeois feminism, and perhaps more seriously with *Serious Money*, which attracted dealers 'in their hundreds, organising parties, taking the whole office, and having fun identifying themselves on the stage' (Neil Collins, *Daily Telegraph*, 8 July, 1987). In *Serious Money*, the manic energy of the markets in the City comes to dominate the play and whatever irony may be intended by the use of a free wheeling verse form, or by the film noirish narrator and flashbacks, is recuperable by those who can identify themselves onstage. It is an experience that is likely to confirm both pro- and anti-prejudices without necessarily moving anyone from a fixed position. Indeed, the use of a scene from Thomas Shadwell's 1692 play about the stock market may convey a pessimistic view of the inevitability of greed, rather than placing the action in an ironic context. The specifically feminist issues have dwindled into the 'heroine' Scilla (as in Charybdis?) investigating her brother's death, because she wants '. . . to get my share./They left me out because I'm a girl and it's terribly unfair' (p. 108).

Although some of Churchill's more recent work may have moved away from the sharply and specifically interrogative feminist mode of *Top Girls* and *Cloud Nine*, she continues to experiment: *Mad Forest* (1990) uses two families as the focus for a kaleidoscopic investigation of the Romanian situation after the overthrow of Ceauşescu, and *The Lives of the Great Poisoners* (1991) makes provocative juxtapositions between Medea, Crippen and the man who put lead in petrol.

Sarah Daniels

Much of Daniels's work is concerned with the family, as a site of ideological and gender conflict. Daniels makes no pretence at presenting both sides of an argument, and her work has often been attacked by male critics for its unwillingness to give men a chance but it has also been criticized by other women on the grounds of lack of stylistic control and for being ultimately escapist. Daniels's plays lend themselves to description in terms of single issues: *Ripen Our Darkness* (1981) is centred on patriarchal power in the family, *The Devil's Gateway* (1983) is about Greenham Common and the family, *Masterpieces* (Manchester 1983, Royal Court 1984) is about the corrosive effects of pornography, *Neaptide* (the 1982 George Devine award winner, not staged until 1986) is a lesbian mother custody case play, *Byrthrite* (1986) is a seventeenth century set treatment of witch-finding in the context of increasing male control of obstetrics, *The Gut Girls* (1988) is a sub-Shavian essay in historical reclamation dealing with the taming of independent late Victorian slaughterhouse workers by their social superiors and fear of destitution, *Beside Herself* (1990) is a child abuse play.

At her best Daniels can create telling theatrical images, such as the churchwarden's wife who finds herself in a heaven with a female trinity in the otherwise basically naturalistic *Ripen Our Darkness*, or the opening scene of *Beside Herself* between female archetypes including Eve and Lot's wife, and the use of an alter ego for the protagonist to represent the repressed memory of being abused. Equally her use of language can be incisive ('your dinner and my head are in the oven', *Ripen Our Darkness*, p. 33), but it can also be poor, as in the unconvincing seventeenth-century language of *Byrthrite* or the passages of social work jargon and dramatized Dale Spender, in many of the plays.

Michelene Wandor, in a review of *Neaptide* for *Plays and Players*, September 1986, deals at some length with the reasons why Daniels's work is problematic:

> My criticisms are that her sense of structure is unformed, that she veers in style between sit-com cliché, earnest naturalism and unintegrated polemic. In addition, I have been fascinated by the fact that her work unlike that of many other women playwrights . . . has been apparently selected as somehow representative of the new voices of women playwrights whose engagement with feminism is acknowledged.

In fact there is a crucial difference between Wandor and Daniels in terms of their being respectively socialist and radical feminists. As Lisa Tuttle points out:

> Many radical feminists tend towards a kind of essentialism, accepting the patriarchal concept of deep and significant differences between male and female, merely turning that idea round by claiming that there is something better in Femininity, a source of positive strength in women which is denied to men.

This in turn leads to separatism because 'it seems to imply that women are wasting their energies trying to fight male supremacy because it is

biologically ordained and cannot be changed.'[11] This can in turn lead to
the kind of selection process Wandor refers to in which radical feminist
work is more 'acceptable' than socialist feminist work, because socialist
feminism attacks entrenched attitudes to both class and gender, whereas
the essentialist reversals of radical feminism can be countered more easily.
Thus a male critic, Michael Billington, can praise *Masterpieces* on the
grounds that its 'supreme merit' . . . is that it makes me want to argue
back' and Milton Shulman can discuss it thus, 'Unfortunately Miss
Daniels has coupled her resentment against the sadistic exploitation of
women with her obvious loathing of men in such a way that she comes
close to inciting the very behaviour she deplores.'[12] In both cases the
argument has become essentially male-centred because the play itself is
pushing a reversal of everyday values in which all women turn out to be
good and all men turn out to be bad, which in turn lets all men off the
hook, as there is nothing a man can do to change himself. Moreover,
Daniels's position that there is a direct link from misogynist jokes to snuff
movies is established emotionally rather than logically and there are many
specific points where the links in the chain are only assumed, not proved,
thus offering opportunities for denying the validity of the analysis. Very
little of this need affect an *audience*, rather than a *reader*, as in performance
the writer's anger provides a kind of authenticating stamp, which can
leave very little space for criticism.

Daniels's plays, however, share certain common characteristics, which
give them a particular strength as well as providing some of the problems
mentioned by Wandor. The time scheme is often fragmented so that events
are not necessarily presented in the chronological order in which they are
supposed to have occurred. This device is presumably intended to de-
construct traditional ideas about chronology as causality. There is a stress on
the various apparatuses by which patriarchy polices the world: teachers,
priests, doctors, lawyers, psychiatrists and social workers, and their clients/
victims abound. Scenes of sisterhood and solidarity tend to be played in
'natural' outdoors environments, men are associated with unnatural environments, generally indoors and even underground, as in the Underground scene in *Masterpieces*. The world is presented as unremittingly
hostile, at both the personal and institutional level, to women who in any
way challenge the *status quo*.

One of the problems that arises from mixing apparently naturalistic
scenes and characterization with stereotypes and monologue is that the
dramatist inevitably lays herself open to accusations of loading the dice of
her play more than if she were using either a purely naturalistic or a clearly
non-naturalistic form. In *Masterpieces*, Rowena is a problem on the naturalistic level because it seems incredible that a social worker of her age has
never come across pornography before. Michelene Wandor argues that
Masterpieces:

. . . has a passive radical feminist dynamic, in which women remain irresponsible and unhappy. Even the values of the active, celebratory radical feminist dynamic are absent. Women are asserted as powerless, and, by implication, feminine in their place in the world – the heroine's final speech has shock value, but no social force. She announces that she will have nothing more to do with men – but since she is on the verge of a long prison sentence for manslaughter, the resolution has no material meaning.

(*Drama*, 152)

This significant criticism may have had some effect as, in the first edition and the Royal Court productions, Rowena listened to Hilary's recorded account of Ron's rape while sitting on a swing, with all its connotations of childhood innocence and irresponsibility. In the later edition she does not sit on a swing.

The suggestion of escapism is also present in *Neaptide*, in the eventual flight of Claire and Poppy to a better world represented by the offstage America. This is a legitimate fairy-tale ending and, in the context of production, it is a desirable one, but it also suggests that there is no point in fighting here and it displaces the struggle into a utopian realm, just as all the scenes of female solidarity appear to be set in a prelapsarian world. *Neaptide* certainly tries to cover too much ground and is uncertain in tone so that, for example, there are occasions when a character has to voice a sentiment which that character has no naturalistically plausible reason for holding. Also the sheer volume of plots is problematic and potentially implosive: Val goes mad as a kind of defensive reaction to patriarchy, the story of Demeter and Persephone acts as a mythical underpinning to the lesbian mother child custody case, the elderly mother has her consciousness raised, the lesbian pupils come out, so does the headteacher, and the school staff room contains enough minor plots for a series of *Grange Hill*.

Perhaps the most interesting way in which *Neaptide* challenges conventional ways of play-making is in its onstage presentation of children, five in all under the age of seven and all played by children. Ros Asquith wrote in *The Listener*:

It is . . . almost unique in its representation of the angsts of family life; there are five real children on stage and the mayhem over breakfast, or the exhaustion faced by a mother surrounded by sons tirelessly auditioning for the SAS is the stuff of everyday life that doesn't usually penetrate the TV soaps, let alone the National Theatre.

John Barber wrote in the *Daily Telegraph:*

Someone needed to tell the fervent author to cut out the unwanted characters and to drain of[f] the stagnant waters of cosy home chat . . . the roistering nursery mischief of no less than five toddlers. All this clutter of domesticity is aimed less at showing female servitude to the potty, the frying-pan and the ironing board, and more at coaxing the audience to laugh at the easily recognised drudgery of daily life.

Michael Coveney of the *Financial Times* wrote, 'Claire's flatmate is an educational psychologist who, quite unbelievably, tries to cut wriggling children's hair at the breakfast table and flicks milky cereal all over them'.[13] Both Barber and Coveney are reacting in a way that reflects their immersion in the business of being theatre critics rather than living life at the breakfast table. The breakfast scene is troubling precisely because it is an accurate presentation of all kinds of only too mobile contradictions: the need to get to work, domestic disputes amongst children, the linguistic slip that leads to a major philosophical point being raised just as you want to get the children out of the door. All this is introduced not for easy laughs but to indicate that the political, social, philosophical struggle, of whatever kind, is not a discrete matter but something that pervades a whole life. The personal is political and we do not laugh at the 'easily recognised drudgery', we laugh at the impossibility of the situation and at the gap between training as an educational psychologist and raw emotional actions and reactions. And while so many women's lives are dominated by children, the absence of children from the theatre militates against serious consideration of significant parts of their lives.

Ultimately, Daniels seems, rather like John Osborne, to be giving audiences 'lessons in feeling'. If there is no man with whom men can empathize as a way of entering the text, then men will have to resign themselves either to getting no pleasure from the text or try understanding and empathizing with aspects of female experience. The variety of male critical reactions to the plays suggests the power of her analysis: critics are after all, part of the apparatus by which a society reproduces itself to itself and to patronize Daniels (in both senses of the word) can probably be seen as a recuperative strategy. So Daniels remains an enigmatic figure: her dramaturgy is open to criticism, particularly for trying to pack too much into each play, but her polemic can be deeply moving and is usually controversial. However, the radical feminist dynamic of her plays may, ultimately, not be as unsettling as that of treatments of similar themes by other dramatists whose approach falls within the broad area of socialist–feminism, which may thus in turn account for her curious elevation as the acceptable face of feminism.

Family life, work and play

Given the traditional roles of women as homemakers, mother and wives, it is not unexpected that many plays by women focus on mother–daughter relationships, with the mother often seen as nurturer and role model but also as internalizer and policer of the patriarchal consensus in the family. Sisters also provide a convenient starting point for examinations of literal and metaphorical sisterhood. Most of the plays about family life covered here are small-cast pieces, which pursue their topics within broadly naturalistic frameworks, although there was a tendency towards the end of the 1980s, exemplified in the works of Lucy Gannon, Charlotte Keatley and Heidi Thomas to adopt a less naturalistic approach to language and to dramaturgy than can be found in, for example, Catherine Hayes's treatment of middle-class families or Andrea Dunbar's working-class versions. Dunbar, who died tragically young, wrote straightforward stories from a desperate northern landscape, which tend to remind critics of the young Shelagh Delaney, in part because Dunbar was only fifteen when she was first successful in the Royal Court Young Writers' Festival, in part because of her subject matter. The strengths and weaknesses of her work are well summed up in Rob Ritchie's introduction to her published plays. They are:

> . . . front line intelligence, rough and ready messages from someone living in the heartland of poverty and hardship. Sometimes the staff back at HQ, the decision makers, the audiences who come to see what is happening out there, express a weary impatience with the news coming through. Haven't we heard all this before? Where is the analysis, the break for fresh ground?[14]

The apparent autobiographical authenticity of her work (the heroine of *The Arbor* (1980) is called Andrea Dunbar) has generally been taken as validating the plays but, as Ritchie suggests, their importance lies in their declarative presentation of a set of issues and problems that the material success of certain social groups and regions has done nothing to eradicate. The basic dramatic method is naturalistic, although the later plays use antiphonal intercutting of two conversations to good effect. The plays all use a fluid inherently televisual style: *The Arbor* has thirty-four characters but was staged with a cast of nine, eight of whom each played three or more parts, with only Andrea not being doubled, *Rita, Sue and Bob Too* (1981) has a cast of six, each playing one part, and *Shirley* (1986) has three performers playing one part each and another four playing two or more. This pattern suggests directorial rather than authorial decisions. The characters are naturalistically incapable of articulating the nature of their experience, apart from a tentative condemnation of Margaret Thatcher from Bob in *Rita, Sue and Bob Too*, but the most positive values to emerge are a sense of female, and to some extent communal, solidarity at the end of all three plays. As in Bond or O'Casey the gestures are small but suggest a degree of faith in the possibility of human relationships, which is the only possibility of redemption. At the end of *Rita, Sue and Bob Too*, Sue's mother buys a drink for Michelle, Bob's former wife, who has been displaced by Rita, Sue's friend;

at the end of *Shirley*, Shirley offers her mother a cigarette, having refused her requests throughout the play; at the end of *The Arbor* Andrea says, 'I miss my mum and the kids and funnily enough, I miss my dad. And all my mates' (p. 42). The film version of *Rita* actually blends chunks of *The Arbor* into the original, but the greatest change comes with the ending, in which Bob leaps (literally) into bed with Rita and Sue. This looks like a male wish-fulfilment fantasy, but it could be argued that Rita and Sue have traded their sexual favours with great skill and enlarged their capital value. The question, as with all Dunbar's work, remains the extent to which audiences are being invited to join in a form of voyeuristic masochistic cultural slumming?

Catherine Hayes's *Skirmishes* (1981) is a naturalistic middle-class three-hander between a dying mother and her two daughters, which plots the contradictions and tensions of family life at a moment of crisis with unsentimental honesty, charting the powerful emotional undercurrents associated with the concepts of duty and familial love. It is particularly effective in the way that the sisters literally quarrel *over* the mother who lies virtually silent in bed between them, using eye communication to unsettle the daughter who has been sacrificing herself and her marriage to look after her, while the other daughter got on with raising her own family, and then intervening briefly but explosively to complicate the sisters' own resentments.

Hayes's *Not Waving* (1982), another three-hander, is also about family tensions, with an ageing and failing woman stand-up comedian suffering personal and career crises. The play reverses the conventional show biz motifs of the star who transcends personal problems so that the show can go on and of the youngster who goes on as understudy and comes back a star. Instead, in the first part the star reveals her major menopausal problems to her manager/lover and insists on going on, although the venue management do not want her to, and then raking over the coals of her estrangement from her daughter who arrives to tell her that *her* lover, the mother's former manager/lover, has just committed suicide. The second part shows us the comic's disintegrating and fragmented act. The play occupies some of the same territory as *Comedians* and *The Entertainer*, but with the emphasis on the family rather than on the decline of Britain or the moral and political role of comedy. The play ends with the end of the comic's act, in which she has attacked her daughter verbally, but there are no opportunities to see the daughter's reactions nor to see what happens next. Both plays cover important but familiar issues about the family, but there are potentially more interesting questions that the plays do not tackle in what happens to the comedian after her disastrous act in *Not Waving* and what happens to the carer after the death of the mother in *Skirmishes*. We are in the middle of the drowning (implied by the title's reference to Stevie Smith's 'Not Waving but Drowning'), but ending the plays where they do cuts off any further exploration.

Carol Bunyan's best work, like Hayes's centres on women characters, but absent men again exert a powerful influence. In *To Come Home to This* (1981) a home-making but sterile wife has sublimated her urges for meaning and excitement in life into secret drinking and competitive ballroom dancing, only to find that the drink makes her unable to keep her place in the dance team. It is a tale of the quiet desperation of a woman trapped into a situation that makes no sense, and in which there are no answers. *Waving* (1988) begins with two fifty-year-old women on holiday in Spain, contemplating their lives and their husbands swimming into the distance (again the title can be taken as referring to the Smith poem), and complicates the issue by introducing a wheelchair-bound seventy-year-old and her daughter in the second act. The play examines issues of women's tendency to sacrifice themselves in dependency in marriage, in caring relationships (the seventy-year-old is seeking ways of ending her dependency by killing herself), and in work (her daughter is enslaved to her boss) within a well established comic tradition of acute observation of the minutiae of everyday oppression.

Julia Kearsley's *Waiting* (1982) draws its inspiration from the Yorkshire Ripper case, examining the climate of fear in a community where women are terrified and men are suspects. Dismissed by many male critics as a tract or a thesis, and by some of both genders as too televisual and underwritten, others found it uncomfortable but challenging, covering 'Ripper territory in the geographical, emotional, and moral senses of the term', and showing how 'the local men, gelded by unemployment, instinctively use the fear of the Ripper as one more tool in the armoury they deploy to keep their women in place'.[15] Underlying the various critical views lay differing perceptions, considered or ingrained, about the nature of patriarchal power, which tend to bedevil any consideration of work by women playwrights, but particularly those which overtly examine issues to do with sexual power.

Kearsley's *Under the Web* (1987) is a northern mother–daughter play in which absent males figure large. Basically naturalistic, it deals with the threads that unite and also destroy families as Rose, separated from her husband and trying to construct a new life back in her mother's home grapples with the problems of trying to bring up her son, earning a living, keeping in shape and being a disappointment to her mother who idolizes her absent brother and then becomes dependent on her after a stroke. Once again it is the naturalistic authenticity of the writing that marks the play.

Ayshe Raif has earned a similar reputation as a meticulous observer of the pains and tensions of everyday life, whether those of actual isolation affecting single women in bed sits (*Another Woman*, 1983), or of the emotional isolation of couples in marriages blighted by unemployment (*A Party for Bonzo*, 1985) and the conflicts between mothers and daughters (*Fail Safe*, 1986). Her naturalistic style is sometimes seen as overly televisual but in *A*

Party for Bonzo the parallels between the sense of emptiness for the unemployed husband and for the childless wife are well handled.

Clare McIntyre's plays operate within the bounds of broadly naturalistic recreations of women's lives, but use monologues to allow access to the characters' interior fantasy worlds. One of her earliest writing efforts was *Better a Live Pompey than a Dead Cyril* (1981, with Stephanie Nunn), based on the writings of Stevie Smith, and much of her work relies on the detailed ironic observation of everyday anxieties that characterizes Smith's poetry. As Andrew Rissik pointed out in a review of McIntyre's *Low Level Panic* (*The Independent*, 17 February, 1988), her work fits into a developing genre concerned with 'the sovereign privacy of the imagination, the power of thought to redeem the wayward conflicts of day-to-day life through personal reflection and private interpretation'. But, as Rissik notes, the problem of this kind of writing, is that it can 'seem loose, inconsequential and disorganised'. Generally McIntyre transcends the limiting conventions of the mother/daughter/boyfriend scenario in *I've Been Running* (1986), where the daughter's convictions of inadequacy are staved off by compulsive jogging (a question of running to, running away, or running for) and also those of the aftermath of sexual assault and the effects of the pervasiveness of pornography on women's fantasy lives in *Low Level Panic* (1988). However, the characters in *Low Level Panic* have little existence beyond the bathroom in which most of the action takes place, and we know nothing of the material facts of their existence (jobs, education, etc). The bathroom is a useful setting for the making and remaking of identities through rituals of washing and applying make up, for introspection about one's body (one of the characters is convinced she has 'bunions and an unattractive clitoris')[16] and for daydreaming. But this stress on the validity of personal experience can lead to a retreat from the public world, which probably reflects in part the sense of stasis and inertia that resulted both from the external realities of the 1980s, when the possibilities of progressive changes on many fronts in the UK seemed remote, and also from some of the gains of bourgeois feminism, which led to a pervasive but premature declaration that we are in a post-feminist age. McIntyre's writing can be seen as replicating this stasis: by the end of *Low Level Panic* we are still in the bathroom, still fantasizing about men in exotic cars coming to whisk us off on white chargers. Of course, as Brecht argues, change does not have to come about on stage for an audience to see the necessity of change, but some kind of evaluation of the presented experience, either in the dramatic design or in the dialogue might be helpful.

McIntyre's *My Heart's a Suitcase* (1990) begins simply enough with two thirtyish women, Hanna and Chris, spending a weekend in a not yet fully converted flat belonging to Colin, a friend of Chris's. They end up sharing it with Colin's wife who has come to do some decorating, a down-on-his-luck business man turned vagrant, Chris's ghostly recreation of a hooligan who threatened her, and a Saint with a suitcase who earned her sainthood by endlessly carrying burdens back and forth across a mountain. The play justifies its title by being particularly concerned with how we cope with the emotional baggage we carry around with us, the extent to which we may surround ourselves with things as a way of avoiding moral issues, and the texture of quiet desperation in everyday life. But it leaves many avenues unexplored, such as the fact that Hannah suffers from dormant multiple sclerosis. The most powerful moments come in Chris's cascades of loathing and envy of the rich, directed largely at Colin's hapless wife. Although the final result is a kind of female Chekhovian version of *Look Back in Anger* mediated through *The Tempest*, the relationship between the inner and outer worlds remains unfocused.

Lucy Gannon used her professional knowledge of the downside of family life gleaned in a career in social work in her first play *Keeping Tom Nice* (1986), which presents a nuclear family disintegrating as a result of the strains of looking after the severely handicapped twenty-four-year old Tom. Its strength lies in an unsparing presentation of the emotional contradictions in the family as they attempt to keep Tom 'nice'. For example, the mother sprays air freshener to mask the smells of Tom's incontinence but nearly chokes him in the process. She takes comfort in televised ballet, representing the physical discipline her son cannot achieve and in ruthless gardening, a way of taming the nature of which he is a more disturbing example. The father's distress at his son's condition leads him to abuse him and eventually to commit suicide when a perceptive social worker realizes what is going on, while the daughter's conviction that Tom needs physical comfort leads her to an incestuous sexual overture. So, in many ways, the play occupies similar territory to Peter Nichols's *A Day in the Death of Joe Egg* and Dennis Potter's *Brimstone and Treacle*, but it also has points to make about the general structure of family life and the balance of competing demands and needs contained within the structure. Although the play operates convincingly as narrative, the rhetorical and metaphorical treatment of Tom is sometimes strained (he is seen as a Christ figure and the language reflects this liturgically), a problem which reappears in a more sustained form in Gannon's *Raping the Gold* (1988). We are in familiar territory for the 1980s: a northern town beset by industrial closures, long term unemployment and the destruction of the community, but the use of archery as a sustaining metaphorical device gives the play an unusual angle on the problems it deals with. 'Raping the gold' means hitting the centre of the bullseye, and it refers to the ultimate satisfaction of the archer, but it can also be taken to refer to the splitting of the family and the community that comes with recession. The play deals with reactions to recession and depression at both literal and metaphorical levels, with frustration, sterility and displacement activities. Gabby, the central character, has sublimated his distress at the failure of his factory into a Zen-like love of archery (and heightened prose), while his adolescent daughter Sally, the only woman in the play, sees hope for the future only in terms of getting out of the depressed (in both senses) town. Gabby's mystical attraction to archery contrasts with the teacher Stuart's desire to do something practical for the despairing young by agreeing to share the archery field with the cricket club. To Gabby this is a kind of rape of the last bastion of his self-respect, and with the merger the final meaning of his life, and his life itself, disappears.

While the play has some of the obvious attractions of introducing us to a subculture, many of the issues in circulation are not adequately focused through the archery metaphor. The phallic connotations of archery and the emotive connotations of 'raping' remain unexplored, despite hints that Sally's dead mother entertained gentleman callers when Gabby was away, the fact that Sally does not shoot, although she can do so, and the fact that Leon, Sally's unemployed would-be boyfriend, expresses his sexuality through masturbation, presumably an expression of the sterility of the environment. Equally unfocused are the class and race differences: Leon is black and his father worked for Gabby, but all three now sign on together. There are some parallels here with Nell Dunn's treatment of the potential displacement of the baths by a library in *Steaming*, although the argument here is more finely balanced within the play: the only ways forward within the play are the utilitarian proposal of Stuart, which cannot take account of the need for the mystic expressed by Gabby, and Sally's escape to college, like Phil in Debbie Horsfield's *Red Devils Trilogy*. The play ends with a biblical quotation by Leon, which aptly encapsulates the position of stasis it has arrived at, 'For with much wisdom comes much sorrow,/The more knowledge, the more grief' (p. 72).

Those final lines from *Raping the Gold* could be an epigraph for Heidi Thomas's *Indigo* (1987). Thomas, like Gannon, uses heightened prose but *Indigo* relies heavily on intercut monologues for its effects. *Indigo* works partly through presentation and recollection of versions of childhood and innocence, so it can be seen in Freudian terms as a reworking of fantasies of origin, an interpretation which bears much stronger fruit in Thomas's *Shamrocks and Crocodiles* (1986). Both plays are concerned with rites of passage and with questions of how we enter the symbolic order. The intricacy of the narrative in *Indigo* brings out the tensions and paradoxes of the triangular slave trade in the late eighteenth century, but its peculiar tone lies in the monologues which, on the page, lack the precision of detailed reference that saves heightened prose from being simply phrase making. Ide, the African prince, praises God in these terms: 'The sky is a sheet of semen, ruched by your sacred hands and held up high . . . Tongue my body with your thread of flame. Raise my head to your radiant heat' (p. 37–8). Like *Raping the Gold*, it is a very male-dominated play with the one female here carrying much of the metaphorical burden. Dragged along in

Ide's schemes, Mamila eventually becomes pregnant by the slave trader, who has himself been coerced into the trade by his father, and is then murdered by a foundling white child, the most obvious example of dispossession in the play, who sees her unborn child as symbolizing his own lack of belonging.

In *Shamrocks and Crocodiles* the death of a father brings about a scrutinizing of identities by his daughter and son, who eventually agrees to continue his father's shady enterprises. The funeral and its aftermath is intercut with scenes from the children's childhood. These include the daughter Christine confessing to a priest that she has seen her (clothed) father in a massage parlour, which is presented as virtually a fantasy of parental coitus. However the big scene is when Christine and her brother as children are discovered in bed together by a priest who has come to mediate in their parents' quarrels. Although their being in bed is innocent it coincides with Christine's first period, and the ensuing guilt sours family relations. It is a less ambitious play than *Indigo* with fewer passages of semidetached purple prose and works better for concentrating on the murky interactions of family life.

There were still relatively few plays about women outside their immediate family and domestic concerns in the 1980s. Although Debbie Horsfield's *Red Devils Trilogy* opened up a number of potential avenues, they were only followed up effectively in the latter part of the decade. The trilogy, is a kind of sentimental education for the four female Manchester United fans we follow from their early efforts to get tickets for the Cup Final, as each works through her own problems and establishes her own sense of identity, to a final reunion on the way to another cup match. Each woman's story is given more or less equal weight, and each ends well, with the women facing the future with a degree of confidence, despite the tribulations of variously marriage (and divorce), setting up in business, university and unemployment. The format is basically naturalistic, but in the later plays Horsfield handles a greater number of characters, makes an increasingly sharp use of juxtapositions between stories and shows an increasing ability to pick out naturalistic details with metaphorical overtones: in *Red Devils* itself the emphasis is on adolescent hopes and fears, with the narrowness of Alice's vision matched by the tightness of her jeans; in *True Dare Kiss* the initial juxtaposition is between the comradeship of supporting the team and the cutting of ties involved in Alice's marriage, but Nita's hair-dressing salon becomes a powerful centre of the play, with its continual creation of dream images and representations of women. Nita always puts the cheap hair conditioner in expensive bottles, so her decision to send it back in *Command or Promise* represents a powerful change of heart. Nita and Alice represent opposite poles with their fantasies of setting up in business and marrying happily ever after, but Nita not only makes her fantasy come true but is able to offer Alice the employment that emancipates her from the disastrous failure of her marriage. Phil, the one who gets away to university, and the punkish Beth represent other positions: Phil gets a first class degree and has a choice of journalistic jobs between *Cosmopolitan* and the (Manchester) *Evening News*; Beth is permanently unemployed, but ultimately finds herself in caring for a blinded Falklands veteran whom she teaches to roller skate. Perhaps there are sentimental elements in Horsfield's presentation of her characters, but the strength of the plays lies in the presentation of a group of women discovering themselves and learning their own importance to each other.[17]

Jacqui Shapiro has written a number of very different works, which show considerable promise and a refusal to be limited by naturalism. *One of Us* (1983) is a closely observed one woman monologue about racism spoken by a Birmingham Asian. *Trade Secrets* (1984) starts from the premise that all the men in the world have dropped dead so that all the fears associated with patriarchy can be forgotten by its four stock characters, before becoming an investigation of the effects of pornography, in a fragmented structure that mixes levels of reality without great effect. Shapiro is on surer, if slighter, ground with *Dead Romantic* (1984), which wittily charts the difficulties of contemporary dating and mating, and with *Winter in the Morning* (1988), which deals with life in the Warsaw ghetto, using the device of a cabaret within the play to cast light on the relationship between the reality of the incredible situation within the ghetto and the reality of theatre.

A number of writers have taken stock themes or devices, which have previously been largely the preserve of male writers and given them a specifically female inflection. Melissa Murray, whose verse drama *Ophelia*, (1979) offers a feminist reading of *Hamlet*, adds an extra dimension to the imprisonment play in her impressive *Body Cell* (1986) in which a woman in solitary confinement after political crimes attempts to find ways of coming to terms with her isolation. The body:tomb:cell equation characteristic of the solitary confinement genre gains strength from the addition of the womb as a fourth term, bringing a specifically female element to an otherwise familiar picture. Gillian Richmond's *The Last Waltz* (1986) similarly brings a female angle to the familiar story of the NCO who becomes an officer, by approaching the topic through two women whose initial friendship is followed across the vicissitudes of army life over a period of ten years. Much of the play's value lies in showing the effect on women of living within a tightly organized and hierarchically structured institution with rigid if often unspoken rules, which are constructed by and for men. Penny O'Connor's *Dig Volley Spike* (1988) uses the familiar device of the sports team to show us different approaches to the various challenges that confront women in the 1980s. Her volleyball team is drawn from the library of stock characters, situations and themes, the interest in the mechanics of the game is strong and the choreography of the sporting event is well handled.

Julia Schofield's *Love on the Plastic* (1987) is a witty, compassionate, but coldly angry look at the almost respectable end of the sex industry in the form of the hostess clubs in which business men buy female company, and more, on expenses. Its presentation of the underlying reasons for the women's presence in the clubs and their use of the only saleable commodity they have in a world dominated by the values of the marketplace is instructive, comic, moving and entertaining. Like many 'workplace' plays, its mix of characters is stereotypical, although the setting does mean that there are more female than male roles (eight to four) and the club format partly legitimizes the confessional soliloquies or monologues that form the bulk of the play.

Kay Adshead's *Thatcher's Women* (1987) also tackles the sexual subculture, specifically the growth in the 1980s of semiprofessional prostitutes from economically declining areas who ply their trade in London as a means of sustaining a family whose traditional financial organization, with male breadwinners, has been destroyed as a result of the Thatcher Government's policies. The play skilfully avoids voyeurism by placing sexual encounters offstage or under tables, or by showing only their aftermath, but there is a somewhat schematic element, both in the use of animal imagery (once again there is an undercurrent of essentialism in the tendency to equate women with nature) and in other aspects of the dramatic design. For example, Marje, the character who befriends a fox, symbolic of fierce independence and nature fighting back, on Wandsworth common, has a late long speech to a policeman who has been attempting to have sex with her in which she not only explains the underlying socio-economic realities that have led her to prostitution but also draws attention both to the significance of the women having worked in a tinned meat pudding factory and to her symbolic equation with the fox. Another long speech, from Lynda, who is becoming a self-made and self-satisfied small business woman, is more successful because the audience is aware of how she has achieved her success, and the evaluation comes from us, not the character:

> In years to come I'll register myself as a small business . . . a little office somewhere . . . find a catchy title . . . 'Escort Elite' . . . get a few names and addresses on my books, boys as well as girls . . . only the best types . . . you know, educated and well spoken . . . (*Ecstatically:*) I'll pay tax.
>
> Don't get me wrong. I've every sympathy with women like Norah and Marje, but I can't help thinking they bring a lot on themselves. I dragged myself up from the gutter – why can't they?
>
> (*Plays by Women* 7, p. 45).

Since Lynda has achieved her success as a result of participating in some highly dangerous bondage activities, the position is clear: she has achieved a kind of power but only at the cost of allowing herself to become a fetish and a sex object. As with other plays of the 1980s the casting of the original production ensured a greater voice for women: the three protagonists were the only characters who were not doubled: one other woman played the two London-based prostitutes and two men played the eleven male roles. Although the number of male characters easily outnumbers the number of female ones the actual cast was predominantly female. In such plays, as Martin Hoyle said in his review of *Love on the Plastic* there is often scope for the 'same sort of insider's shop-talk that illuminated a whole sub-culture in Wesker's *The Kitchen*' (*Financial Times*, June 26, 1987), but more importantly the smaller code – family, prison, army, sport, prostitution – stands for the larger symbolic order.

Timberlake Wertenbaker

Although Timberlake Wertenbaker is American by birth, and French educated, her work has all been created within the British theatre. Her most successful plays, *The Love of the Nightingale* and *Our Country's Good* (both 1988), offer an exhilarating contrast in their treatment of theatrical techniques and, despite the limiting economic and social pressures of the 1980s, she remains a dramatist who is willing to address major issues in a complex way. Unlike many of her contemporaries she has chosen to write about geographically and temporally distanced subjects, dealing like Churchill with issues of innocence and experience at the margins, and with the construction of normality and the sense of self identity, and in many of her plays there is an almost Faustian bargain in which knowledge is purchased at the expense of innocence.[18]

New Anatomies (1981), written for the Women's Theatre Group, is probably the most extreme example of her tendency to blur gender divisions. It is centred on the nineteenth-century traveller Isabelle Eberhardt, who adopted male dress and a male identity in her Sahara journeys, which were also a self exploration. In her 'Note on the Staging', Wertenbaker makes the point very clearly: 'Except for the actress playing ISABELLE, each actress plays a western woman, an Arab man and a Western man. Changes should take place in such a way as to be visible to the audience and all five actresses should be on stage at all times.'[19] Like Churchill's *Cloud Nine*, the play draws links between the colonial and the patriarchal mentality, but it also uses the contrast between European 'civilization' and the desert to chart the ways in which mental and physical boundaries are constructed. But it also presents the contradictions: Isabelle can only return to the desert and pursue her mysticism by agreeing to act as a secret agent, and she dies by drowning in a flash flood in the desert.

Similarly in *Abel's Sister* (1984), on which Wertenbaker worked with the disabled writer, Yolande Bourcier, the 'disabled' character reveals the

limitations and incapacities of the apparently 'normal' characters, and of the
ways in which we construct our notions of 'reality'. The theme of families
stifling their members is, of course, an old one, as the title suggests, and the
idea of twin main characters helps to thread it through the story, but the
point of the title is another of Wertenbaker's scrutinizings of received
wisdom: Sandra, the disabled character was apparently damaged in the
womb as a result of oxygen starvation whereas her twin brother Howard
was not; Sandra sympathizes with Cain.

The Grace of Mary Traverse (1985) is the most overtly Faustian of Wertenbaker's plays, using a sentimental education or female rake's progress, as a
dramatic design through which she can meditate on the nature of oppression. As with the majority of history plays, this one is determined very
much by its own period's preoccupations, so that the moment when Mary
Traverse finally makes her Faustian bargain with her Mephistopheles, the
aptly named Mrs Temptwell, comes after she has been refused admission to
the 'Universal Coffee House', which contains at that very moment, according to the Boy who bars the entrance, 'Mr Fielding, Mr Goldsmith, Mr
Hume, Mr Boswell, Mr Garrick, the Doctor, Mr Sheridan, Mr Hogarth
. . . And some foreigners, Mr Piranesis, Mr Tyepolo, Mr Hayden, Mr
Voltaire, Mr Liebnitz, Mr Wolfgang' (p. 70). Mary's exclusion from the
wisdom of the age at first hand finds a concise theatrical expression in that
moment. Offered the chance to explore the male world, Mary realizes that
'I have no map of this world. I walk it as a foreigner' (p. 71). This theme
recurs not only throughout Wertenbaker's plays but also in many of the
dramatists of the 1980s: inner and outer exploration feed on one another
both in plot terms and thematically.

Mary, as befits her name, traverses class and gender barriers in her quest
for experience and power. The play ends with Mary reconciled with her
father, and removed to 'A garden in the Potteries' (p. 129) together with
her daughter, Mrs Temptwell, and the other leading character Sophie. The
connotations of the setting in a garden and of the young child, who shares
her mother's name, are not unproblematic. Mary has made the journey
from the cloistered seclusion of her father's house through the Hogarthian
townscape, and found a kind of serenity in the garden; the child suggests
hope for the future and the possibility of learning from experience, but the
quest for knowledge ends with uncertainty:

> *Mary*: I'm certain that when we understand it all, it'll be simpler, not
> more confusing. One day we'll know how to love this world.
> *Mrs Temptwell*: Will you know how to make it just?
>
> (p. 130)

As the publisher's blurb on the first edition notes, the play 'explores the
moral cost of knowledge and the possibility of grace in an age of despair,'
but the key words are 'explores' and 'possibility'.

Exploration and potential are also key terms in relation to *Our Country's Good*, a major success at the Royal Court, in Australia and the West End. Its favourable reception owes much to what its director Max Stafford-Clark describes as:

> . . . the resonant chord it touched in London's beleagured theatrical community. A play that proclaimed the power and enduring worth of theatre, and that celebrated its centrality to our lives, was of importance in the third term of a government who deemed subsidy a dirty word.[20]

The play, based on Thomas Keneally's novel *The Playmaker*, concerns the first production of a play in Australia, by convicts from the First Fleet. That play, *The Recruiting Officer*, was performed in tandem with *Our Country's Good* at the Royal Court with the same cast. Wertenbaker presumably wanted to use the arrival of the colonists to explore relationships between the classes and the sexes, the colonists and the natives, which appear in Keneally's novel. The whole business of staging the play within the play gives room for arguments with obvious contemporary resonances about the philosophy of punishment, and the value of the arts in civilizing society. The play takes full advantage of familiar backstage situations to debate the aesthetics and politics of the theatre, and the original production used devices such as cross-casting, multiple doubling and onstage changes of identity to further the debate about the relationship between environmental and genetic influences on character and behaviour. The least developed part of the play involves an uncomprehending native Australian whose occasional appearances at least serve to remind us that the whole debate is taking place on white European terms while the native Australians remain marginal and irrelevant to the debate about the theatre. By the end of the play the innocent native, who had tried to ignore the settlers as a kind of bad dream, is dying of smallpox and realizing that 'Perhaps we have been wrong all this time and this is not a dream at all' (p. 51). The play's appeal to theatre goers is, as Stafford-Clark suggests, one that reinforces their *a priori* belief in the value of theatre in a (literally and metaphorically) hostile climate, and its value is in reinforcing those who already believe in the importance of theatre. These criticisms do not take away anything from the skill with which the debates are presented, nor from the acute observation of nuances of social intercourse, which one would expect from the writer whose translations of Marivaux have been the most successful so far. And, as Michael Billington put it, 'What makes this play work is its very assumption that drama has the capacity to change lives and liberate imaginations' (*Guardian*, 12 September, 1989).

The Love of the Nightingale makes some less rosy assumptions about the power of the theatre. Wertenbaker's gift for economical presentation is never more in evidence than in this play, which lasts under an hour and a half but contains the material of many myths, both ancient and modern, and finds a way of expressing their pith. It is a powerful reworking of the myth of Philomel and Procne, which includes a servant character called Niobe who carries some of the connotations of the classical Niobe and of *The Trojan Women,* and a staging within the play of the Phaedra story and an enactment of Bacchic rituals. Its use of the theatre within its design relates dialectically to that in *Our Country's Good,* where the theatre is regarded in terms of its power to transform the performers, rather than its audience. *Nightingale* is much more concerned with the making of myths, the power of language, gender roles and the role of fantasy in more negative terms. Here the power of theatre is questioned alongside a powerful exploration of the construction of 'proper' male and female roles and identities, particularly as they affect Philomele, whose powerful curiosity is accompanied by an innocent sexuality, which is the occasion of her brother-in-law Tereus's lust: Philomele is curious about the sexual act; Procne, who is about to be married, has a vague idea that the main organ is detachable; Philomele wants to watch Procne and her husband doing it, whatever it is. Philomele's incessant questioning, as she tries to make sense of life through language gives way to her eventual silencing when Tereus cuts out her tongue. This is a direct consequence of her rape by Tereus, in which he is reduced to cutting her hymen with a knife when he is unable to sustain his erection. Philomele is silenced when she threatens to expose his impotence, which she associates with his failings as a ruler, seeing the failure of the penis as a failure of phallocracy.

Once again journeys, here from rational, civilized, theatrical, Apollonian, Athens to emotional, wild, natural, Dionysiac, Thrace, provide the skeleton on which the exploration of the inner world can take place, and here there can be more of a conclusion, even if it lies in part in the imposed stasis in which the protagonists are translated into a different medium (as birds). Once again transportation leads to transformation, and the importance of, and the cost of the search for knowledge are foregrounded: Philomele's curiosity and her search for knowledge lead to her silencing by Tereus tearing out her tongue. But the final line of the play, and a fitting epitaph for the 1980s is 'Didn't you want me to ask questions?' (p. 49).

4

Sister George is dead: The making of modern lesbian theatre
Rose Collis

> I'm against all kinds of liberation – Women's Liberation, Gay Libera-
> tion . . . I think people should sweat it out.'
> (B A Young (*Financial Times* theatre critic)
> responding to a 1978 *Gay News* survey, March 1978)

For the first three-quarters of the twentieth century, Mr Young certainly
had his wish granted – at least in theatrical terms. Until the late 1960s/early
1970s the concept of 'lesbian theatre' was unknown and liberation and
theatre were rare bedfellows. Male homosexual characters had appeared
sporadically in post-war theatre, often veiled in a euphemistic code of
conduct and steeped in stereotypes: sexually repressed, veering to the
effeminate and certainly not 'glad to be gay'. Not until Joe Orton's *Entertaining Mr Sloane* (1964) and *Loot* (1965) were audiences presented with
sexually active confident male homosexual characters who eschewed the
characteristics of their prissy, tragic predecessors.

Lesbian audiences had to wait for another decade for a similar break-
through. In the meantime, anyone seeking lesbian theatre would probably
have been guided, discreetly, to a modest play that was basically a satire on
the middle class radio entertainment industry. The distinguishing feature of
Frank Marcus's *The Killing of Sister George* (1965) was that the central couple
consisted of a radio soap opera actress, June Buckridge, living with another
woman. However the 1969 film version, directed by Robert Aldrich,
purveyed an extremely influential damaging negative image: June Buckridge, the only character who is open and unashamed about her sexuality, is
not only punished but *seen* to be punished for this (pre-gay and women's
liberation) unpardonable crime: she loses job, lover and self-respect and is
left at the end of the film wallowing in a pool of gin-tainted misery and
desolation – humbled, shamed and defeated.

The modern Gay Liberation movement was also born in 1969, following the Stonewall Riots in New York, with the founding of the Gay Liberation Front and the Campaign for Homosexual Equality in Britain. This was also the era of Women's Liberation: women were starting to express their experiences, oppressions, and aspirations through an 'alternative' creative network, organizing autonomously in a variety of ways through, for example, consciousness-raising groups, magazines like *Spare Rib* and *Red Rag*, and the first women-only bands. Feminists started their own theatre companies, performing work devised, written, acted and directed by women, for women. Others worked within new or already established radical groups, often bringing music and drama together in didactic works of a polemical nature, committed to work that opposed an establishment based on discrimination on grounds of class, race, gender, sexual orientation or disability. Although many of these companies had gay men and lesbians working within them, they did not allow enough opportunities for feminists or gay men to explore their own concerns, so Women's Theatre Group (founded 1973), the first professional feminist theatre company, and Gay Sweatshop (founded 1975), the first professional gay theatre company, started work on productions that reflected aspects of women's and gay men's lives in a depth and manner that mainstream theatre had never attempted, or even seemed interested in attempting.[1]

No lesbians were involved with Gay Sweatshop until 1976, when writer Jill Posener, actress/director Kate Crutchley and designer Mary Moore were invited to stage Posener's *Any Woman Can* in their lunchtime season at London's Institute of Contemporary Arts. The play, written because Posener felt 'a deep frustration at not being able to express those things that were most dear to me. *Any Woman Can* was my coming out',[2] was originally staged for one night at the Leicester Haymarket as part of a Women's Theatre Festival, with Miriam Margoyles in the central role of Ginny, who spends most of her time on stage addressing the audience. The other characters – her teachers, friends, lovers – enable her to act out crucial episodes of her life: coming out, sexual experiences and relationships, as she recognizes and affirms her lesbian sexuality. After the ICA season *Any Woman Can* went on a national tour, sometimes as part of a double bill with Roger Baker and Drew Griffiths's ground-breaking *Mister X*, attracting both extremely positive and extremely negative reactions. Posener remembers instances where, after seeing the show, 'women would literally come up to us and say "I've never met another one"';[3] conversely Kate Crutchley recalls 'in Dublin, an arts centre got its grant taken away for putting it on. In Scotland, church organisations would chase it out of town and then students would find other venues for it' (Interview, *Gay Times*, January, 1989).

After this decisive break-through for lesbian theatre, the men and women of Gay Sweatshop worked together on a number of shows, before dividing into single sex companies in 1979. Women were increasingly finding that mixed companies did not always offer the best forum for exploring lesbian and feminist themes and by 1979 lesbian performers had started working either in exclusively lesbian groups or within feminist theatre and cabaret groups. In these formative years, lesbian theatre tended to be more concerned with contemporary political issues, rather than the-atrical sophistication. For lesbians as a theatre audience, there was a need for work that affirmed lesbian politics, lifestyles and relationships. For a time, it seemed that if a woman performer said 'I'm a lesbian' within her first speech, she was virtually assured of a standing ovation.

By the mid-1980s most companies felt sufficiently secure and confident to give a single writer the space and responsibility for creating a show, rather than relying on the principle of collective writing or devising of productions. The poet, dramatist, and critic Michelene Wandor worked in both modes, scripting Gay Sweatshop's devised lesbian-mother custody play *Care and Control* in 1977, and writing her own *Aid thy Neighbour* in 1978. This political comedy of manners, inspired by a London *Evening News* 'exposé' on lesbians and artificial insemination (a perennial topic of reactionary concern), involves two couples – one lesbian, one heterosexual – who are trying to have children and a gutter press journalist. The play's happy ending, with the lesbian couple being successful and the heterosexual woman realizing that she actually doesn't want a child, is an ironic reversal of 'normal' values. After the play's first production, at the New End The-atre in London, Wandor commented: 'There's still enormous resistance to anything with overt feminist consciousness, let alone a lesbian feminist one' (*Gay News*, June 28–July 11, 1979).

Hormone Imbalance, an all-lesbian company formed in early 1979, took their name from the traditional scientific myth that lesbianism and male homosexuality are caused by a 'hormone imbalance' in the body. Their eponymous first show adopted a revue style play-within-a-play format to explore the theme of control and manipulation. The Narrator declared 'One of the functions of lesbian theatre is to give us images we can all identify with'. In attempting to do this, *Hormone Imbalance* showed lesbians being controlled by a director as they struggle to put a revue together, lesbian characters in a short story attempting to free themselves from the control of its author, and the ultimate control of aversion therapy in a parody Tennessee Williams scene. Another scene showed an Ophelia actu-ally in love with her maid, but being forced into a marriage with Hamlet. Melissa Murray developed this scene into a full length verse play *Ophelia*, which the company performed later in 1979, another example of the complex seeing and deconstruction typical of feminist writing in general and lesbian writing in particular. Unable to secure funding, Hormone Imbalance was forced to close after *Ophelia*. Gay Sweatshop also lost their Arts Council revenue funding in 1980, together with other alternative companies, in what was widely perceived as a reactionary politically-motivated decision. Indeed, it seemed as though lesbian theatre began the new decade very much in the doldrums.

However, in 1981 the Brighton-based Siren Theatre Company produced their first show, *Mama's Gone A Hunting*, using the writing skills of Tasha Fairbanks and the musical skills of the three woman company. Siren's early work was didactic, but later grew more experimental in style and, to some extent, content. Their later shows include Fairbanks's lesbian double identity thriller *PULP* (1985), which 'combined glamour with sleaze in its parody of the femme fatale image of the Hollywood 1950s, alongside issues of betrayal, deceit, McCarthyism and espionage'.[4]

In 1982, the Women's Theatre Group, which had escaped the 1980 funding cuts, devised their first proper lesbian show. The entire company, including the stage manager and administrators, took part in the earliest workshops, in which particular themes – class differences, attitudes towards childbearing and pluralistic feminism – were identified. The performers, musician and director then did a series of improvisations to decide on the final characters and storyline, with additional contributions by the rest of the company. As director Libby Mason explained, a play produced by such an overwhelmingly collaborative effort 'makes it potentially a very difficult script to work on.' However, she also stated 'I do not believe that one writer *could* have produced a script like this; its idiosyncrasies are very much those of a particular group of women in a particular place at a particular time'.[5] The play traced the relationship between Sparky and Chum, two *very* different sorts of lesbians, from initial courtship, through living together and break-up to final friendship. Witty, pertinent, and often moving, the play also featured a musician, Joanne Richler, as a Brechtian Narrator commenting on the characters and their situations. *City Limits* called it a 'Woody Allen script for lesbians' (November 18–25, 1982).

Although devised in a manner that owed much to the late 1970s, *Double Vision* marked a new direction in lesbian theatre both in its portrayal of lesbian characters and in the complex themes it tackled: a new wave of formally and thematically ambitious work took lesbian theatre beyond political didacticism into hitherto uncharted areas of multiracialism, disability, soap opera and reclamations of lesbian history. In 1983 Hard Corps, a new unfunded company of lesbian actresses who had worked in both mainstream and fringe theatre came together during the Greater London Council (GLC)-funded London-wide lesbian and gay festival, September in the Pink, to stage Jill Fleming's *For She's a Jolly Good Fellow* and *Lovers and Other Enemies*. Fleming's irreverent and unabashed humour deservedly attracted the epithet Ortonesque. Hard Corps also reclaimed lesbian history with Adele Saleem's *John* (1984), an examination of the relationship between Radclyffe Hall and Una, Lady Troubridge, and Sarah McNair's *Les Autres (That Lot)* (1985) about the early twentieth-century lesbian community in Paris, as well as pursuing the comic strand in conjunction with lesbian comedy duo Karen Parker and Debby Klein in *For Ever* (1985), 'a revue centred around a lesbian feminist orgy'.[6] Even to see a lesbian production described in this way demonstrates how far writers and performers had come in shrugging off social, political and creative limitations to produce work that went far beyond Hormone Imbalance's intention of giving us 'images we can all identify with'. It is also remarkable that, despite the reactionary and conservative political climate, lesbian theatre continued to flourish through much of the 1980s, mainly in London. Certainly the GLC must take some credit for this, as one of the few funding bodies to put its money where its rhetoric was, in funding a substantial number of 'alternative' and community theatre projects, although this also contributed to its political 'murder' in 1987. Thereafter only the Drill Hall and the Oval House in London were seen to continue to support and produce lesbian theatre on a regular basis. The Drill Hall (formerly Action Space) hosted many lesbian and gay festivals throughout the 1970s and 1980s, including Gay Sweatshop Times Ten, and regularly included lesbian and gay shows in its annual programme. In the late 1980s it produced annual lesbian Christmas pantomimes and in 1990 staged the Parker and Klein show *Blood on the Lino*. In the 1970s the Oval House held annual *Gay Times* festivals of theatre, cabaret and music. Virtually every lesbian and gay theatre company performed there, from inexperienced fledgling groups to veterans such as the American group Split Britches. Sue Frumin, whose first play *Bohemian Rhapsody*, a medieval romp with music, was produced at the Oval House in 1980, had worked with the feminist music cabaret group Clapperclaw, which combined anarchic humour, socialist–feminist ideals and street band music in shows such as *Ben Her: The Epic Remake of 'A Concise History for Schoolboys Vol 1'*, featuring 'a cast of millions – all the women left out of history'. Frumin frequently reclaimed history and genres from a lesbian feminist perspective: *Rabbit in a Trap* (1982) is a feminist spoof mystery; *The Housetrample* (1984), inspired by the experiences of her mother, a refugee from Czechoslovakia at the beginning of the Second World War, is also a response to her own experience of anti-Semitism; *Home Sweet Home* (1987) for her own company Shameful Practice, combined the lives of past and contemporary lesbians; *Fanny Whittington* is a lesbian reworking of a familiar tale. Her most ambitious and accomplished play, *Raising the Wreck*, was produced in 1985 by a rejuvenated Gay Sweatshop with their first all-woman cast since 1979. *Raising the Wreck* is mostly set in a sunken galleon where four long-dead women sea farers tell a modern woman, apparently in no need of feminism, how and why they came to renounce the conventional roles that society tried to impose on them as working-class women, black women, lesbian women. A truly significant landmark in lesbian theatre, it combined a multiracial cast, a celebratory historical content, and a reaffirmation of women's, particularly lesbian women's, strength and determination in overcoming socio-political obstacles and disadvantages.

The Oval House also supported the work of Parker and Klein, who worked with Hard Corps, as a cabaret duo, and on shows such as *Devilry* (1984), a reworking of the Faust story, and *Forever* (1985), 'a satire on sex and fantasy'.[7] *Coming Soon* (Oval House, 1986), Klein's soap opera or 'Sapphic Sudsaga', inspired by Klein's love of such high camp soap operas as *Dynasty*, presents its main theme, sexual attraction, through supremely over the top, and therefore subversive, stereotypes, such as a psychosexual counsellor, her swinish twin sister and a lesbian sex-object body builder. Klein explained its ethos thus: 'If the play has any political message at all, it is: "Lesbians are glamorous, sexy, and sophisticated, and we know how to make fun of ourselves. Aren't you just a little envious that you're not one too?!"' This was lesbian theatre at its boldest, funniest and sexiest. Not surprisingly, given the worsening political atmosphere, it was also the least likely to win mainstream funding. Acknowledging the frequently unpaid work undertaken by lesbian casts and crews, Klein points out that without such self-exploitation 'there would probably be no lesbian theatre to speak of'.[8]

Frumin's and Parker and Klein's work illustrates the extent to which lesbian theatre was beginning to develop and deal with the multiplicity of lesbian experience and to recognize that not all lesbians were white/able-bodied/Christians/graduates. Jackie Kay, a black Scot, already known for her poetry and short stories, exemplifies another strand in this development. Her first play, *Chiaroscuro* (1985), which began as a thirty-minute performance piece for Theatre of Black Women, was expanded and developed through a Gay Sweatshop rehearsed reading and Theatre of Black Women workshops into a full length play, which toured nationally and in Europe for three months. The characters' identities as black women are as important as their lesbian identity, and *Chiaroscuro*, as Carole Woddis says, uses 'dreams, songs, poetry, naturalism' to confront 'the difficulties of communication in a largely white-dominated and heterosexual world'.[9] Kay's exploration of a multiplicity of themes in women's lives went even further in her next play, *Twice Over* (1988). The play was first performed under the insidious shadow of Section 28 of the 1988 Local Government Act, which prohibited local authorities from 'the promotion of homosexuality whether by publishing material for that purpose, by teaching in schools the acceptability of homosexuality as a pretended family relationship' or by 'giving financial assistance to any person for these purposes'.[10] The legislation's potential damage to the arts led to a vocal and effective lobbying campaign to prevent lesbian and gay theatre being abandoned by council funders. *Twice Over*, originally written for a teenage audience, seemed a likely target under the legislation, as it deals with a teenage girl, Evaki, coming to terms with her own perceptions and prejudices, as she discovers the truth about her dead grandmother's sexuality when sorting through her papers. In fact the play did not fall foul of the new legislation, which largely seems to be being held in reserve, and it established Kay as a writer of outstanding ability and maturity, able to explore themes of race, class and sexuality in a thought-provoking, perceptive, non-naturalistic and non-didactic style. Disability, however, remained a neglected area for lesbian writers until as late as 1985, when Maro Green and Caroline Griffin's *More* was presented as a 'work-in-progress' in Gay Sweatshop's Times Ten Festival. Developed by its writers, it was staged as a full production by the company in 1986. Centred on the passionate love story of Mavro and Coqino, it tackled the 'hidden' disabilities of anorexia, bulimia and agoraphobia, combining pantomime techniques and an ironic gallows humour. Director Kate Owen told *City Limits* (March 1986), 'It explores lots of philosophical themes to do with time and space, which are obviously linked to the hidden disabilities these two characters have'. Caroline Griffin explained the authors' intentions: 'I don't take for granted that the audience will be able-bodied: in writing this, I'm asking them to look at their own hidden disabilities or their known disabilities.' However, director and co-writer were quite clear about the play's ultimate content: 'It's a radical love story . . . about a lesbian relationship, which is really taken for granted'. Just ten years after Jill Posener's 'coming out' play, lesbian playwrights have taken enough risks, formed enough unfunded, self-energized companies and persistently defied and challenged the old stereotypes to the point of producing plays where a lesbian relationship could be 'taken for granted'. Against the odds, despite the lack of funding, of venues, and of mainstream press coverage, lesbian writers and companies have done enough crucial groundbreaking work to ensure that lesbians do not simply have to 'sweat it out'.

5

Black women playwrights in Britain

Susan Croft

we are mistresses
of strong wild air,
leapers and sounders
of depth and barriers
(Barbara Burford, poet and playwright *Women Talking*[1])

The major impulse behind this essay is to begin to record the work of black – Afro-Caribbean and Asian – women playwrights in Britain, thus drawing attention to the growing body of often very powerful work produced by them. While the work will be mapped thematically, indicating matters of common concern, a few plays will be examined in more detail. Although some areas – particularly family relationships, sexuality, identity and abuse – are similar to those explored by white women playwrights, as indicated in other sections of this book, there are also plays about women's history and mythology. The legacies of imperialism and post-imperialism both recent and historical, with the specifics of black experience provide a different context for these issues. Disability as a black woman in a racist society is inevitably different from a white woman's position. Plays may focus directly on black history, particularly black woman's history, especially of the generation who came to Britain in the 1950s and 1960s; and on the search for identity of the generation born in Britain.

To compensate for the dearth of critical studies and published material, I have listed as many plays as possible to facilitate further investigation. Women playwrights in general are less than visible. Despite their increasing numbers their work often remains unpublished, often receiving only a first production. As black playwrights' work is rarely produced outside of a few black touring companies, the situation for black women is often one of double jeopardy. Nevertheless, since 1982/3, their numbers have grown enormously – over forty have received full productions, and many more rehearsed readings and workshops. Groups such as Munirah, Options Ltd., and Theatre of Black Women have performed collectively devised work, whilst Black American and Caribbean women writers have been produced in Britain. Because much evidence remains undocumented, this essay draws on unpublished scripts, although where possible a contact point for their location is given in the Bibliography. The London bias reflects its theatrical predominance, but may have resulted in inadvertent neglect of productions in other areas.[2] Similarly the pre-eminence of Afro-Caribbean writers reflects their more frequent production.

The vocal emergence of Black theatre in Britain was a phenomenon of the late 1970s and early 1980s, although groups and individuals such as Barry Reckord and Errol John predated this period. In 1976, Naseem Khan's ground-breaking report *The Arts Britain Ignores*[3] discussed black theatre's problems; lack of training, venues, money and local institutional support: but showed that initiatives like the Temba theatre company were formally experimental as well as reflective of black life. In *Dreams and De-constructions: Alternative Theatre in Britain*,[4] in a small section 'Ethnic Theatre', she names almost twenty initiatives in Black (Afro-Caribbean) theatre, and details the growth of Asian theatre with the establishment of Tara Arts. During the 1980s new groups have replaced those mentioned by Khan, which have vanished, groups like Temba, Tara and the Black Theatre Co-op have consolidated their position, and funding bodies must perforce take Black Arts more seriously. Resourcing remains a struggle in a stark economic climate where commercial and marketing jargon controls the competitive funding arena.

In the earlier period, male writers involved with the companies included: Alfred Fagon, Mustapha Matura, Michael Abbensetts, Tunde Ikoli, Jimi Rand, T. Bone Wilson and, in Asian Theatre, Farrukh Dhondy and Jatinder Verma. Appearing only gradually in the early 1980s, women arrived in earnest from 1986 onwards as a result of their demand for a voice, and of the encouragement of new writers.[5] Most black women writers were at some point helped significantly by company or theatre developmental work – workshops, rehearsed readings, discussion, script surgeries or festivals. Such new writing theatres, black or feminist groups generated such work either as a central policy or in response to pressure. The Royal Court Young People's Theatre under the enlightened David Sulkin spearheaded the opportunities for young black women who joined the Activists youth theatre or writers' workshops. Jude Alderson, founder-member of the feminist punk band/theatre group The Sadista Sisters, led 'Talking Black' workshops, which encouraged Bernadine Evaristo, Patricia Hilaire, Yasmin Judd, Paulette Randall and Carol Williams into theatre writing. Others – winners at the Younger Writers' Festival – have followed, including Maria Oshodi, Jyoti Patel and Soraya Jinton. Mainhouse performances included Winsome Pinnock's *A Hero's Welcome* 1986 (first a reading, then a Women's Playhouse Trust production), and Jacqueline Rudet's *Basin* and

God's Second In Command. Despite such positive policies, elsewhere a danger of tokenism can reduce opportunities for new writers only to rehearsed readings and studio productions. For this reason, the Second Wave Young Women's Project under Ann Considine, when establishing a National Young Women Playwright's Festival at the Albany, Deptford, South London, in 1986, made mainstage production for the winners central to policy. The area's high Afro-Caribbean population and an emphasis on working with local women ensured a high number of young black women competitors and workshop participants in 1986 and 1988. Mainstage productions included Nandita Ghose's *Ishtar Descends,* Killeon Gideon's *England is De Place for Me,* and Shorelle Cole's *Blind Faith.* Other Second Wave activities range from supporting the Bemarro Sisters group, commissioning plays, to workshops and schools playwriting projects.

Black theatre groups originally working with male writers and directors are beginning to develop attitudes more responsive to black women's demands for participation. Black Theatre Co-operative staged Rudet's *Money to Live* 1984, Zindika Maccheol's *Paper & Stone* 1989, as well as the black American classic Lorraine Hansberry's *Raisin in the Sun* and a black production of white writer Ruth Dunlap Barnett's *The Cocoa Party.* In 1988 rehearsed readings of six new plays, five directed by women, featured work by Jenifer Ramage and dub poet Jean Binta Breeze. Temba has produced Saira Essa's *You Can't Stop the Revolution* and Trish Cooke's *Back Street Mammy*; and others have produced work by women such as Judith Hepburn, Petronella Breiburg and Peggy Bennette Hume. Asian theatre provided few opportunities, Tara's policy presents classics, and British Asian theatre as Star Productions has emphasized film, although women have written for Tara-in-Education. In 1988 Asian Co-operative Theatre, with actress Rita Wolf as a prime mover, staged a double bill of bilingual plays, Jyoti Patel and Jez Simon's *Prem* and *Heartgame* scripted from a Leeds Bengali Women's group by a white writer Mary Cooper.

Women's theatre companies, initially dominated by the white middle-class, began under pressure to address the issue of representing black women's experience; for example the Women's Theatre Group, working with a black company of performers and a commissioned writer working from the devising process have involved Pinnock, Randall and Sandra Yaw. Sphinx, which works in schools, Theatre Centre Women's Company, Women's Playhouse Trust, Red Ladder and Monstrous Regiment have all performed black women's plays. An especially significant influence was the 1980 West End production and publication by Methuen of the Broadway version of Ntozake Shange's *for coloured girls who have considered suicide, when the rainbow is enuf.* Receiving mixed reviews from the largely white male critics, it was a revelation for black women writers, then and later. Not only powerful, funny, joyful and angry; its original form, using music, dance and poetry was delivered by seven women who, dressed in different colours, assumed a range of identities. Bernadine Evaristo, co-founder with Paulette Randall and Patricia Hilaire of the Theatre of Black Women in 1982 states, 'You could say that she (Shange) was a sort of role model, or that the play was.'[6] The trio met at Rose Bruford College as part of an unusually high intake of black students, and were involved in the Royal Court Writers Workshops – devising and creating poems, the basis of *Silhouette* and *Pyeyucca* their first major works. Absorbing poetry drawn from the characters within a flexible structure, they evolved 'a rather surreal, timeless space which meant we were less restricted . . . our writing could be quite free'.[7] *Silhouette* is a complex wide-ranging exploration of black female and mixed-race identity, in which a slave-woman leads Pat, the central character, through a journey of self-realization to rejection of internalized white racist values. Hilaire and Evaristo cite as other innovative influences poets Alice Walker, Audre Lorde, Alexis de Veaux and the visionary black American playwright Adrienne Kennedy.[8]

This concern with experimenting with poetic language and form seems here, then, to have started not from theories about women's or black women's theatre, but from the women's practice as poets and the work they admired. As the Introduction to this book suggests, in relation to women's theatre in general, a pattern of work emerges, which moves from initially largely naturalistic – feminine/reflectionist – plays, through issue-based – feminist/revolutionary – work, thence towards an articulated need for a theatre language that would express women's exploration of their experience at a deeper level. This – female-ritualistic – performance language, confronting mythologies, desires, contradictions, memory and history would be more physical, allusive, visual and poetic.[9] In British feminist theatre this quest can be seen both in first decades of the century with the movement from the comedy of *How the Vote Was Won* and much of the work of the Actresses Franchise League, to more exploratory work such as Edy Craig's.[10] Similarly, in the 1970s there was a movement from more didactic plays such as those collected in Michelene Wandor's *Strike While the Iron is Hot* to experimental work by Bloodgroup or the Scarlet Harlets. In black women playwright's work, the issue-based style using more accessible forms somewhat resistant to experimentation can be seen in work by Theatre-In-Education groups such as Options Ltd, whereas Theatre of Black Women epitomizes the poetic experimental mode. A further strand allied to the former is the 'slice of life' approach, where companies have encouraged young writers to give immediate and powerful voice to their own lived experience; good examples are the black playwright Grace Daley's *Rose's Story* or the white working class writer Andrea Dunbar's *The Arbor*. Although in white women's theatre bitter ideological differences have arisen about the different approaches, black women's theatre, whether in companies or individual writing, has used the full range of modes within the same time span, developing alongside each other. Such mutual support is perhaps essential where an emergent interest is in competition with 'mainstream culture', and infighting would be self-destructive. This co-operation has been enhanced by the generous, empowering vision of black American women's culture as probably best examplified in Alice Walker's definition of 'womanist', celebrating the qualities of black feminism: 'Usually refering to outrageous, audacious, courageous or *willful* behaviour'.[11] All three Theatre of Black Women's productions explored new possibilities for poetic language, visual and verbal imagery and form with varying degrees of success. *Chiaroscuro,* their third show was commissioned from Jackie Kay, one of four poets published by Sheba in the 1985 collection *A Dangerous Knowing*, which also contains work by the established Grace Nichols, together with Gabriela Pearse and Barbara Burford – now also theatre writers. Burford's *Patterns*, written for the multiracial Changing Women theatre company in 1985, shows the growing consciousness of their racial, sexual and cultural differences in a group of garment workers trapped during a sit-in at their workplace. Stylized movement, symbolism and poetic dialogue evoking a parallel with the mythic Trojan Women, alternate with naturalistic present-day scenes, many developed from group devising. Caribbean folk tales of Anansi the spider formed the basis of Gabriela and Jean Pearse's 1986 children's play *Miss Quarshie & the Tiger's Tail*, whilst Kay's 1985 *Chiaroscuro,* non-naturalistic in form, was structured as a series of rituals, including dance, song and percussion. This play, just predated by Jacqueline Rudet's *Basin*, was one of the first to focus on black lesbian experience. The four women move into walking dance to 'name the nameless ones' (p. 60). Naturalistic scenes trace a growing lesbian relationship between Beth and Opal, their friends' difficulties in accepting it, questions of self-identity and racism. Whilst Kay, in her afterword to the play, acknowledges the problem of integrating the poetry, monologues and ritual passages within the hybrid form, perhaps too many issues are included. Gay Sweatshop produced Kay's second play *Twice Over*, which is more dramatically successful. Exploring Evaki's response to the discovery that her grandmother Cora was a lesbian, the play presents a variety of responses to the revelation. The dead Cora both overlooks the action and participates in flashbacks, in an accomplished presentation of the interaction of the past and present in the process of self-definition. Rudet's *Basin* similarly explores the reactions of a third woman to a lesbian relationship, and the significance of naming lesbian experience in the context of black traditions. Susan's 'there's a Dominican word for it . . . tell people we're zammies' (*Basin,* p. 129) implies a spiritual bond taken one step further, as does Opal's:

> I want to find the woman
> who in Dahomey in 1900
> loved another woman

tell me what did they call her
did they know her name
in Ashanti, do they know it in
Yoruba do they know it in patois . . .

(*Chiaroscuro*, p. 79)

Some plays extend the black individual's self-definition in relation with the past into an examination of history, for instance the Royal Court YPT devised *Women & Sisters*, scripted by Sandra Agard, Cassandra, Isaac and Marcia Smith, which centred on the antislavery campaign, especially the writings of Sojourner Truth. Others, by Judith Hepburn and Winsome Pinnock, respectively, are biographical, of Mary Seacole, the black nurse in the Crimean war, and of Claudia Jones, the 1950s political activist (*A Rock in the Water*). Shorelle Cole's *Blind Faith* draws on her father's experience of demobilization, to show a black soldier forced by his Second World War experience to re-evaluate and confront society's restrictions.

There is a genre of plays that looks at the experience of the previous generation that came to London from the Caribbean in the 1950s; ranging from themes of self-definition to those about the reasons for leaving home or the shock of the reality of arrival in contrast to the glowing 'motherland' images of the NHS and London transport recruitment campaign advertisements. Pinnock's accomplished *A Hero's Welcome* explores the lives and dreams of a group living on a West Indian island in 1947, and the desire to leave. Len, the returning wounded hero, intends to stay on and educate himself. Much of the play is about confrontations with reality and the betrayal of dreams of love or of leaving for England, through the intertwined relationships of the ambitious Minda, Ishbel and Sis, culminating in the revelation that Len's injury was caused by an accident in a Liverpool munitions factory, where white racism was a more immediate war than the one they were ostensibly fighting. But acceptance of the real is a positive force that unites Len and Sis in a commitment to changing their world, not escaping it. The portrayal of Minda also explores the way in which the sexually exploited may themselves turn to exploitation to escape poverty.

Relatively few black British plays focus on life in the islands after the exodus to England. Exceptionally, Gloria Hamilton, founder of Umoja Theatre Company, wrote *Mercy* and *In Nobody's Backyard*, about village life in Grenada under the harsh twenty-eight year Eric Gairy regime, then under the 1979 bloodless revolution's leader Maurice Bishop – later ousted and killed during the US invasion. She uses a mixture of naturalistic scenes, songs, story-telling, rap and rhyme in showing how politics impinge on the central character's lives. *Motherland,* devised then developed by Elyse Dodgson, co-ordinated by Marcia Smith, based on interviews conducted by girls from Vauxhall Manor School with their mothers and friends who arrived from the West Indies in the 1950s, is published with the workshop

exercises and interviews. Themes recurring elsewhere include housing difficulties, high rents for black tenants or 'No Coloureds' signs in windows,
the pressure on relationships caused by long working hours and isolation
from the community and racist attacks culminating in the right wing and
fascist-provoked sustained campaign of violence in Nottingham and Not-
ting Hill in 1958.

The struggle to maintain the family is shown in Lisselle Kayla's *When
Last I Did See You*, which contrasts Blossom's efforts in Jamaica, where she
supports unemployed husband and children through selling okra, with her
problems when alone in England facing her children's difficulties within
the new culture. As a comedy, the treatment of some themes, such as the
women finding solace in religion, is rather superficial. However, Killean
Gideon's first play *England Is De Place For Me*[12] manages to be both comic
and serious in comparing two couples in South London in the early 1960s.
Wilma and Dickie try to build a good life, and eventually fulfil their dream
of returning home whilst, after a difficult marriage, Rose eventually
divorces Winston, her poignant letter to her now absent friends contrasting
the dreams of England and home. Gideon skilfully turns the horror of a
racist attack on Winston into comedy through his exaggerated account of
the experience – actually brought about by his feckless womanizing. The
play also deals with male competitiveness, especially between generations,
whilst Rose's letters reveal her son's problems – left in Jamaica until the
money was there to bring him over, subjected to an interrupted education
and to the unjust Stop and Search Laws, he becomes a Rasta. Pinnock's
1987 *The Wind of Change*, commissioned by the Half Moon Young
People's Theatre for their community tour, is also effectively punctuated by
the letters home of Ruth, a trainee nurse who wants 'to be the best
Jamaican nurse since Mary Seacole' but is forced by the system to train at
the lower SEN grade rather than the SRN. Failed unjustly, like other black
girls, she learns to confront racism in hospital and the streets during the
1958 anti-black attacks. The play also deals with her relationship with Tina,
the white friend who champions her, but whom she must reject – as 'Nurse
Richards' little friend' Ruth is only 'allowed' to pass into the white world
on sufferance. She comes to feel that her struggles are not only for herself,
but for 'them bright-faced black girls who come up after me. This is what
give me the strength to persevere.'

A further category of plays about the immigrant generation explores the
relationship of black people who have lived in England to their home
country when they wish to return. In Rudet's *Take Back What's Yours*,
although Beatie longs for the idyllic Dominica of her past, where she
intends to marry Ronny, she is blind to the tensions that her dream of
family reunion will arouse. Winsome Pinnock's 1991 play *Talking in
Tongues* also explores the experience of a black British woman visiting
Jamaica and her sense of being deprived of the language to describe her

experience isolated between two cultures. In *Zerri's Choice*, developed by the Women's Theatre Group with Sandra Yaw, family tension bubbles to the surface on the evening of Zerri's return to Guyana after twenty-five years of putting her two daughters before her own needs. Despite the provocative subtext, evoked by food imagery as a sign of giving or withholding love, the largely naturalistic form, with a few flashbacks does not give enough scope for deepening the presentation of the daughter's fears and resentments – especially of the separation as symbolic of maternal death. This theme is also presented in Trish Cooke's *Running Dream*, commissioned for Second Wave. Moving between Dominica and England, and across three generations, the play shows her daughter and grand-daughters mourning the death of Ma Effeline with traditional rites; whereby the spirit rests for three days and nights, with special food prepared on the third for friends and relatives to celebrate the dead. Prompted by her mother's distant death to return to Dominica, Florence and her daughter Bianca are reunited with the half of the family she had left behind. Despite meeting her elder siblings, Bianca feels both alienation and resentment because her mother's migration had cut her off from part of her identity. Florence now dies, suggesting ironically that she has remained spiritually if not geographically close to Ma, but the play leaves pain and loss unresolved. Estrangement between generations is also explored in Pinnock's *Leave Taking*, through the tradition of West Indian ritual and magic, handed down through women. Enid Matthews is separated from her own generation and becomes alienated from the children for whom she has slaved and denied herself to create a better life. The flashpoint is her daughter Del's pregnancy, as she accuses her mother of being repressive, 'I'll never be like you. I'm going to have everything: life, love, sex – everything that you wanted, but were too frightened to enjoy' (p. 157). Inevitably, the family is a site for conflict in many plays about the search for identity; for example Rudet's *God's Second in Command* about a son who resists his father's conventional male values, and Jenny Macleod's *Cricket at Camp David* about family and racial tensions prior to a wedding, focusing on a desparate need for communication.[13] Family reactions to the discovery of sexuality is central to a number of black women's plays, some of which, like Grace Dayley's *Rose's Story*, examine the dilemmas of unplanned pregnancy. Running away from her ultra-religious home with her boyfriend Leroy, Rose becomes self-aware, angry and decisive; confronting family, friends and authority figures. As a first play, however, it centres on the protagonist to the detriment of full presentation of other characters; as 'Mai' wrote in *Spare Rib* (March, 1984), a more sophisticated analysis of the parents' vulnerable situation was needed: 'Rose had shattered their ultra-respectability, a protection they had made for themselves, using the ingredients of their own oppression'. The fierceness of Rose's character confronting authority figures is relieved when she reveals a vulnerable side in talking with her sister about the pain

of feeling that religion has replaced real family love. The prayer meetings
that pray for Rose's straying soul are also wittily observed. Another first
play, Christine George's *Family Bliss*, presented at the Albany Empire's
Basement Youth Arts Project includes the theme of unplanned pregnancy
in a plot that is rather overloaded with broken marriages, complicated
sexual relationships, generational conflicts and a death. Despite this rather
melodramatic narrative, George draws contradictory and complex characters well, producing very effective dialogue. The most subtle exploration of
this theme is found in Trish Cooke's *Back Street Mammy*, developed
through staged readings at the Half Moon and Second Wave to Temba's
1989 full-scale production. This evolutionary process is embodied in a
wide-ranging and complex staging of sixteen-year-old Dynette's awareness
of sexuality and confrontation with the dilemma of pregnancy. The play
uses a chorus commentary to underline Dynette's adolescent awakening as,
in the context of a Catholic upbringing, she is torn between her conflicting
desires and the opinions of friends and family. Despite her decision for
abortion, she speaks of her unborn child:

> She listens . . . she wraps herself round me and makes me know that
> whatever I decide is right . . . I've never been so close to anyone
> before in my life.

(p. 87)

Issues associated with health and disability are also found in black women's
plays such as Kayla's *Don't Pay Dem No Mind*, which was written for Hi
Time Theatre and presented at the 1988 conference on Black People and
Mental Health in Islington. It focused on the high number of black people
receiving treatment for mental illness or institutionalized – how white
society often defines black behaviour as aberrant or sick – through following Desmond Walker and the pressures that force him towards breakdown.
Maria Oshodi's 1989 play *Blood, Sweat & Fears* is about Ben, who suffers
from sickle-cell anaemia, a life-threatening hereditary condition confined
to people of Afro-Caribbean descent. Broader issues raised include the
strain of coping with invisible disabilities, others' lack of understanding,
society's fear of the sick and especially Ben's self-deluding pretence that his
condition will improve. Blending comedy and seriousness, the play moves
stylistically between naturalistic scenes with his girlfriend Ashley, through
the Star-Trek Burger bar with its Vulcan pies, Klingon burgers and 'cos-
mic' greetings, to broad caricature of the medical profession and expres-
sionistic scenes of Ben's delirium. Ashley, a proponent of self-help and
alternative medicine, is a strong influence upon the way Ben, unlike his
uncle, eventually comes to terms with his illness.

Society's assumptions about more overt disability are explored in Ruth
Harris' *The Cripple*, based on the life of Pauline Wiltshire, a disabled black
woman, and written for the actress T.M. Murphy for the Theatre of Black

Women in 1987. A simple but moving monologue conveys her struggle for
self-determination, refusing society's attitude that a disabled body entails
mental handicap, against the burden of maimed legs 'like heavy chains'.
Often as a by-product of working from a devising process – which, like a
consciousness-raising or therapy group, becomes a supportive space where
experience may be shared and validated – many black women's plays start
from women's relationships with each other. *A Slice of Life*, scripted by
Pauline Jacobs, devised by the four Bemarro Sisters from Deptford who
met through Second Wave, depicts post-school experiences and how
different life-choices influence their relationships, although all encounter
racism. Scripted by Deb'bora from devising, Akimbo Productions' *Where
Do I Go From Here* drew upon five black women's relationships with their
fathers, although the play shows the same woman at five different ages.
Drawing powerfully on autobiography in the portrayal of her father's abuse
of both mother and sister, it explores the writer's conflicting feelings for
'the invisible man called father.'[14] As in many black plays, music is central,
here produced and written by members of the band Akimbo. The subtext
or theme of the abandoning father, his absent presence or his displacement
of white society's harshness onto his family runs through other plays for
example *Rose's Story*, *Zerri's Choice*, and *England Is De Place For Me*.

Friendship across races is the theme of Christine Belle's *Word of Mouth*
and Oshodi's *The S Bend*, both first plays. The former, produced by Staying
Power, a Nottingham-based multiracial company, questioned the intrusion
of dominant culture and conditioning as barriers to interracial friendship.
Set in a launderette, the play's structure integrated poetry and song around
the wash-cycle as a metaphor for exploring the development of such
friendships. A naturalistic piece, *The S Bend* stages a friendship between a
studious young black woman, Fola, and white punk plumber, Mya. Both
find common ground in their parallel experience within their peer group.
Mya struggles to be accepted by male plumbers as an equal, Fola's West
Indian friends' values are different from her Nigerian culture. Another
aspect of the search for identity, the cultural conflict of being mixed race, is
explored in Adjoa Andoh's *Just My Luck*, and Cindy Artiste's *Face Value*. In
the latter, Sarah, a Citizens Advice worker wants to feel part of her client's
black culture. Discovering she is a quarter black, although appearing white,
she is received with unexpected hostility when she tries to ingratiate herself
at an antiracist meeting, and accused of appropriating experience not her
own. This provocative play challenges white liberal and left-wing audiences to question the motivation of their antiracist solidarity.

Artiste, like Bonnie Greer, Shorelle Cole, Cheryl Martin, and Deb'bora is
a black American writer working in Britain. Some of her plays, like *Dreams
With Teeth*, are set in America. This play, set in a 1970s University campus
follows the first four black women 'integrated' students, and despite a rather
pat resolution does confront the problems of their situation, as institutional

pressure isolates and alienates them in the all-white college. Greer's *Zebra Days*, produced by ReSisters, examines the collective past of black history, previously ignored by a young black British woman, through her meeting an older American. A numinous air of myth invests the older woman as a trickster and wise prophetess who produces history from her bag.

Lisella Kayla also crosses generations in her ReSister-produced *Don't Chat Me Business*. Here, Sharon an aggressive eighteen-year-old is assigned to working in a very respectable day centre with rules: 'No joking. No smoking. No untidy mess. No gum. No rum. No scum in de bath.' With humour, the play shows how, despite her attitude, 'stop chatting me business', two old ladies – bossy Miss Pearly who is in charge, and a resident Miss Cissy – manage, partly in rivalry, to bring the lonely girl to accept and return their affection. A relationship between three slightly dotty old people is also explored in Jenny Macleod's second play *Island Life* (1988). Plays about division between friends include Zindika's 1989 *Paper and Stone*, about quiet Brenda and tough Juliette for Black Theatre Co-op, and Ann Ogidi's funny, award-winning radio play *Ragamuffin*. The former blends naturalism with poetry, stylized narrative between Paper and Stone the two girls' alter egos, a capella singing, snatches of children's games and rhymes in exploring questions of identity and independence. Brenda realizes that her mother's religion and Juliette's toughness are both defences against past hurt. The second play examines the reaction of a group of Rastas when one of their number joins the police, thus raising questions about black people's relationship with white authority and institutions.

Although the politics of life in a racist society underpin at some level every play described, and are consciously addressed in many, relatively few plays are specifically sited in political struggle. Exceptions include Artiste's adaptations of Alice Walker's *Meridian* – about an activist during the 1960's American Civil Rights Campaign, Hamilton's Grenada plays, and Saira Essa's *You Can't Stop the Revolution* and Olusola Oyelele's *Many Voices, One Chant*, written and directed for Battersea Arts Centre as an award winning 'Young Director', both about South African struggle.[15] Their experience of apartheid and exile is expressed by South Africans Dorcas Faku and Diana Taylor one black, one white in *Wenanzi – What Are You Doing?* (1984). It draws upon poems, songs, family and friend's letters, accounts by women like veteran campaigner Helen Joseph and Dorothy Numzani Nyembi – imprisoned for fifteen years – and scenes improvised between them. Like the riveting *You Strike the Woman, You Strike the Rock*, toured to Britain by Vusizwe Players as part of the LIFT festival,[16] it voiced South African women's struggle and endurance.

Despite the influence upon British black writers of work from abroad in terms of role models and creating new possibilities of form and content, relatively little American work – in proportion to its quality and quantity – has been produced in Britain. Black Theatre Co-op produced Lorraine

Hansberry's classic *A Raisin in the Sun*, about the Younger family's struggle to realize their dreams in 1950s America, in 1985. This play is brilliantly paradied as one of George Wolfe's vignettes 'The Last Mama on the Couch Play' in *The Colored Museum*. Although Annie Castledine produced Endesha Ida Mae Holland's *From The Mississippi Delta*, about growing up in the Deep South, at the Young Vic in 1989, neither contemporaries such as Adrienne Kennedy, Aishah Rahman, Elaine Jackson, Kathleen Collins nor earlier writers like Zora Neale Hurston and May Miller from Kathie Perkins' anthology *Black Female Playwrights*[17] have been performed in Britain. However, dance drama and dazzling physical theatre that escapes categorizing, by American groups Urban Bush Women and Reduta Dux has been influentially present.

Contemporary West Indian work has introduced new, hybrid forms drawn from Caribbean and British traditions to create black boulevard farces in strong patois, as staged by Roots Theatre Company at Brixton Village, including Hyacinth Brown's *BUPS*. Both the Half Moon and Black Theatre Forum have produced Barbara Glouden's Jamaican pantomimes, *Flash Trash* and *The Pirate Princess*, attracting new black audiences by mixing traditional panto devices – the dame and principal boy – with reggae or ska music and Jamaican plots. Powerful populist theatre, extremely successful in Britain, created by Sistren, a collective of Jamaican women, most of them former street-cleaners, is based on workshops, improvisation, music, songs and sketches that confront the brutal realities of poverty in shows like *Muffet, Inna All We*.

British Asian women playwrights have been slower to emerge than their Afro-Caribbean counterparts and still number only a few. Factors include the social expectations of women in some Asian communities, although this is something that Jyoti Patel challenges:

> The only area (at school) where individuality and my 'lived culture' were recognised was in Drama . . . here I ran up against the stereotype categorisation of Hindu Asians; 'Hindu Asian girls don't do Theatre, it's against their religion. No one will come and see it anyway.'[18]

English language Asian theatre in general is less common than Afro-Caribbean, although traditional Asian forms of folk drama, dance and story-telling thrive as living cultural expression. Dance forms like bharata natyam, best known in Britain through Shobhana Jeyasingh, have been a site for tradition and experiment. Nevertheless, Asian Theatre companies now include British Asian Theatre, Tara Arts, Asian Co-operative Theatre, Hounslow Arts Co-op, Tamasha and others, although funding cuts continually threaten them, while the Royal Court, Theatre Royal Stratford East and the RSC have produced the work of Hanif Kureishi and Harwant Bains. Women's plays, though not numerous, do exist: Nandita Ghose, a winner of the 1986 Second Wave Young Women Playwrights Festival with the haunting and poetic *Ishtar Descends*, uses the Sumerian myth of the descent of the goddess Ishtar to retrieve her consort Tammuz from the underworld as a metaphor for the mental crisis of Ishtar, a contemporary young woman. Fasting, she talks to herself and an imaginary Tammuz, whilst details of an abortion and her lover's desertion emerge. When hospitalized she meets the other Ishtar, transformed into a bird.

> *Ishtar 2:*
> She made these movements, trying to brush away the thing that was hurting her, but it always came back . . . Sometimes she scratched her own face, was she mad? She was somewhere, where she couldn't get out. I wanted to help her, but I knew she was dead.[19]

Rather unfinished, yet a compelling piece, it bears the hallmarks of the experimental approach of Dartington College of Arts where Ghose trained. Her second play *Land*, presented at Oval House, about three young people's fight to save a piece of dockland from developers, is also poetic, but lacks dramatic development and effective characterization. Half Bengali, Ghose works as a workshop leader, story-teller and director, and was commissioned by Red Ladder to work with four Asian actresses for her third play. *Bhangra Girls* about four women setting up a bhangra band was evolved, exploring their differences and agreements over work, sexuality and finding their identity as British Asians – all positively imaged in the songs and music drawn from both cultural traditions.

Inevitably, many preoccupations found in Afro-Caribbean plays recur – especially self-definition in the space between parental and dominant white culture. Soraya Jinton's *Lalita's Way*, a winner of the Royal Court 1989 Young Writers Competition, deals with the pressures of an arranged marriage. In straightforward naturalistic style it shows how Lalita tries to avoid marrying Rajesh, as she does not love him. Comic touches include Lalita's attempts to deter his parents by being a terrible cook, loading their food with curry powder. Conveniently she escapes when she discovers that Rajesh already has an illegitimate child by a white woman. Mixed race problems are also evident in plays like Yasmin Sidhwa's one-woman show *Chameleon*, written with Euton Daley, a journey of discovery showing how the mixed-race are 'claimed and rejected by both sides'.[20] Meera Syal has performed *One of Us*, co-written with Jaqui Shapiro, a comic, forceful piece about a young Indian girl's ambition to be an actress. It was described by Naseem Khan as 'a comic Pilgrim's Progress'. Syal, who works as an actress has largely worked for television, including *The Leather Mongoose* for Channel Four.[21] *How's Your Skull? Does It Fit?* about an actress's attempt to avoid being stereotyped and sexually exploited was to have been scripted by Kanta Talukhdar for Hounslow Arts Co-op, but company disagreement led to two male members writing the play. Talukhdar has, it seems, written for television, and a new play had a rehearsed reading at Theatre Centre.

Although covering all forms of writing, Asian Women Writers Collective has encouraged playwrights: members like Leena Dhingra and Ravi Randawa have apparently written for Tara-in-Education, whilst Randawa was also commissioned for a new play by the Half Moon. Common Stock presented Ruhksana Ahmad's *Song for a Sanctuary* as a reading. Set in a women's refuge, written after the murder of Balwant Kaur by her violent husband it emphasizes the importance of mutual support there, and the terrible consequences of mistrust and misunderstanding.[22]

The most sustained body of work by an Asian woman playwright is that of Jyoti Patel, who works with Jez Simons, her former youth theatre leader on bilingual plays, mostly English/Gujerati, although they continually struggle to get their work accepted and sustained rather than temporarily feted as a novelty. Growing out of the dearth of apt material for the youth theatre Hathi, in Leicester, their first scripted play *Awaaj* (Voices) was given at the Royal Court Young Writers Festival as a one-woman performance, partly because of the apparent lack of bilingual actors. The central character is a girl who hears in her head one voice from the East, the other from the West, arguing about the symbolic issue of whether she should get her hair permed in the face of traditionalist family opposition. Undoubtedly these plays make particular but stimulating demands on actors – the authors point to the performance of Dhirenda as Rashid in their second play *Prem*, which was excellently reviewed. Audience members who do not know both languages are surprised at how much they understand, and how little they need linguistic skills to understand, and thus are challenged to consider the implications of biculturalism and bilingualism. In *Prem*, scenes between a Muslim boy and a Hindu girl stage the complexities of culture clash and religious prejudice, and are interspersed with fourth-century Tamil poems. Despite Patel and Simons' nightmare experience in working and constantly revising *Kirti, Sona & Ba* in rehearsal for the Leicester Haymarket, with little support from theatre staff, the performances received standing ovations, audiences in tears, excellent reviews and sell-out performances, bringing a new Asian audience to the theatre. Emblematic of three generations and hence different experiences, an African Asian mother, a runaway rebel daughter in her late twenties and a well-adapted bicultural Asian are involved in a five-day Hindu fast. Although comically exploring the tensions arising between mother and returning daughter, gradually tragedy overtakes them as long-hidden child abuse within the family comes to light, and the play's closure involves the mother's death:

> We tend to work by drawing people into our work and then hitting
> them with something. You get to like everybody, to relate to them
> and then have fun with everybody. Then when you realise that
> something's wrong you look back and think my God! what was I
> laughing at. That's our principal method of working.[23]

Most recently *Subah O Shaam* (Open All Hours) also mixes comedy and
serious issues in the life of interlinked characters, during one day in a local
Indian-run store. Shy Parminder, bullied by her brother, unsupported by
her religious mother, befriends and is welcomed by an old soldier, veteran
of an Italian campaign. Following the mother's unprecedented liberating
evening out with friends, valid communication with Parminder is restored.
Patel and Simons, now writing for television soap Eastenders, feel that this
experience has been their most instructive in terms of structuring skills,
which will inform their commitment to creating theatre which reflects
Asian experience truthfully for Asian audiences.

Recently, two British Chinese women playwrights, Lin-Shu Fern and
Su-Lin Looi, have appeared. The former's *Sale of the Century*, workshopped
in 1989, focused on issues raised by a London local authority's sale of
cemeteries, the 1997 change of government in Hong Kong and the plight
of Hong Kong prisoners of conscience – all refracted through the relationship of an elderly Chinese woman and her son. Looi's *All Sewn Up*, written
with Beth Porter for Eastern Actors Studio, explored the issue of what it
means to be Chinese in Britain today through the experience of three
generations of Chinese women meeting in London.

The emergence of so many new black women playwrights has been
encouraged by and thus further encouraged black women directors. Most
prominent are Yvonne Brewster, founder of Talawa Theatre Company, and
Paulette Randall; others include Pam Fraser Solomon, Gloria Hamilton,
Olusola Oyeleye, and Rowena Rolton McGann. Actresses like Joan Ann
Maynard, Decima Francis and Carmen Munroe have developed parallel
careers as directors. Projects like Second Wave Young Women Playwrights
Festival and the Albany Empire's Basement have also encouraged black
women directors, often from a youth and community drama work base, like
Deborah Rose and Wozzy Brewster. Among Asian women, Ghose and Patel
have also directed, while recently Sudha Kumar Bhuchar and Christine
Langdon-Smith directed their adaptation of the classic novel *Untouchable* as
the first project of the woman-founded company, Tamasha.

Paulette Randall, who has worked with Artiste, Cooke, Cole, Gideon
and Rudet helping their development, as well as directing Jamaican Barbara
Glouden's plays, says, 'I desperately want to remain as close friends as
possible with these women and that's rare. They're talented wonderful
people.'[24] She sees the current upsurge of new, black and especially
women's writing as a London equivalent of the Harlem Renaissance. As
almost all these writers have emerged over the past eight years, the extent of
their experiments with a range of subjects and stylistic approaches testifies
to a creative energy and burning response to the need to voice experiences
previously marginalized, to stage and explore issues confronting black,
Afro-Caribbean and Asian women in contemporary society. Black women
playwrights clearly intend to make themselves heard.

6

On the margins: Women dramatists in Wales

Margaret Llewellyn-Jones

Exploration of the work of women dramatists writing in Wales reveals in cameo the English context where larger theatres and companies encourage and support writers workshops. Overall, uneven opportunities are due not only to geographical factors, but because, as Elaine Morgan, the best known writer suggests, 'energies and resources which are bound to be limited in a small country are split between two languages'.[1] Paradoxically, according to D.I. Rabey and C.C. Savill, 'Wales can claim more theatre companies per head of population than the rest of Britain, but these are chronically under funded.'[2] A further restriction is the dearth of professional theatre outlets: the prestigious Theatr Clwyd in Mold often presents pre-London productions; the Grand Theatre, Swansea is seasonal, the Sherman has recently been severed from Cardiff University, Theatr Yr Werin and Theatre Gwynedd are associated with the Universities of Aberystwyth and Bangor, respectively, and the Torch Theatre at Milford Haven is listed as a repertory, touring and Theatre in Education (TIE) venue. Small town theatres, such as Harlech, mix professional and local performances. *Contacts* also lists a number of T.I.E. companies in the Welsh regions, such as Theatr Powys, the Llandovery festival, and a number of fringe and alternative groups mostly in the Cardiff area. Carl Tighe suggests that such groups thrive despite funding difficulties, but generally devise without writers, 'For complex reasons the only area which has done relatively poorly is . . . developing new writing for the theatre.'[3] As audience potential seems to be for 'mainstream' work, Tighe's reasons for underdevelopment of new writing seem particularly apposite to women as scarce opportunities may be

linked to relatively conservative form and content. Three theatre organizations with international interests are established in Cardiff. The Magdalena
Project is an international network investigating the work of women in
contemporary theatre.[4] The Centre for Performance Research, although
not specifically targeted at women's concerns, may include workshop/
lecture sessions relevant to gender and performance in its Conferences, as in
Points of Contact: Performance, Politics and Ideology at Lancaster University in April 1990.[5] Thirdly, Brith Gof, a major experimental 'site-specific'
performance company, is Cardiff-based. Approaches were made to all the
Welsh Regional Arts Associations, and all women writers and other relevant organizations they indicated, thus the following information is directly
based upon letters, telephone conversations, leaflets and scripts provided by
those who responded. Unfortunately, it has not been possible to cover the
extent to which women have been writing for the theatre in Welsh – and
inquiries have as yet yielded very little information – which is not to say
that such work is negligible. If Tighe's views are valid, this chapter's con-
centration on Anglo-Welsh writing may reveal only a partial view of the
situation because, he claims, cultural marginalization reduces such writers'
dramatic and ideological scope to a less inventive 'Home Counties-itis.'[6] A
striking characteristic of the work of Welsh women dramatists is the role of
writing workshops often organized – sometimes jointly with men – by
women who have already achieved some success; for example Playwrite
'89, organized by the Theatre Writers' Union, co-ordinated by Nicola
Jorden Davies (TWU) and Robin Hall, was based at small theatres –
Cwmtawe, Dylan Thomas, Penyrheol and Taliesin – and supported by the
regional Arts Association, the Welsh Academy and the Welsh Arts Association. This three-day event, leading to a Residential Weekend led by Sheila
Yeger and Peter Cox, began with a panel called Womenwrite, which
included dramatist Elaine Morgan, Jane Dauncey (BBC), Carolyn S. Jones
(TWU) and the Red Flannel video company (Pontypridd), followed by
play-reading workshops. Correspondence shows such writing courses provide encouragement and debate when prospects of full production and
publication seem remote.

A larger scale Annual Festival of new Anglo-Welsh Writing in Wales is
the 'Write On' series, run by the Made in Wales Stage Company – Artistic
Director Gilly Adams – which was set up in 1982 by Gareth Armstrong and
Hugh Thomas 'in response to the growing frustration of Welsh playwrights
and theatre workers at the lack of outlets for the home-grown product'.[7]
This Company premiers and tours a variety of productions, and has in
recent years co-produced some touring work with Theatr Clwyd, which
co-hosted the 1988 Festival with the Sherman Theatre Cardiff, host of
previous festivals, and hosted the fifth Write On Festival in October 1989;
Chapter Arts Centre, Cardiff, was the 1990 venue. The 1987 programme
devoted three workshop sessions to women's writing. In both 1986 and

1988 three of the plays performed were written by women, as were two in 1989, whilst three were directed by women, including Gilly Adams herself. In 1988 a joint Magdalena Project weekend workshop focused on the practical elements of women's theatre language.[8] Copies of some un-published scripts from the festival series were made available to me for this report, to facilitate discussion of their scope and style.

Morgan, an Oxford graduate, author of *The Descent of Man*, an influential feminist text of anthropological significance, is best known for her work in television from 1952. Most notable for the BBC version of Vera Brittain's *Testament of Youth*, she has dramatized documentaries on Gwen John and Madame Curie, written comedies and serials including episodes for *Dr Finlay's Casebook, Maigret* and *Campion*, and has had five plays performed on stage, one in the West End, though these were not considered to be 'Hits'. *Love for Liz* ran for a week at the Theatre Royal, Windsor; *Licence to Murder* on a nuclear theme, transfered briefly from Guildford to the Vaudeville; *What Got Into You?* is a two-hander written for a group touring South Wales valleys; *The Soldier & the Woman* adapted from a TV play and published by Samuel French, has had only amateur performances; whilst *Happy Ever After* is a panto-style play about the marital problems of Cinderella and the Prince.[9] In correspondence (November 1989), while admiring experimental forms generated by the co-operative approach of women's drama groups, she states that her '. . . own style was formed in a more structured medium', and she would not herself work in that way. Although not considering her style to be gender-specific, she prefers to write about trail-blazing women rather than 'best seller options', which function through gender stereotypes. Morgan has taken part in supportive programmes such as Playwrite '89, but her own scope has widened from Welsh settings. In an interview with Jorden Davies in the *New Welsh Review* (Summer 1989), she states, 'What interests me is what human beings all over the world have in common'.

Jorden Davies herself, as well as her workshop involvement, convenes a Swansea-based group of professional actors and writers. In recent years, her own plays have been performed at Theatr Elli, Llanelli and workshopped at the Sherman Theatre, whilst some are part of the New Playwright Trust's Library. She was runner up for the Drama Association of Wales 1989 One Act Play Competition, and reached the long list for the Radio Times Drama Awards, with *Green Grows*, a comedy about relationships. Jorden Davies' approach, based on realism, is not necessarily traditional, often centring on powerful women of middle age. The New Playwright Trust's script report on *After Eeyore* describes it as a feminist piece, 'blending naturalistic and poetic elements with a quiet humour.' The play centres on bereavement and a Sixth Form production of *Winnie the Pooh* as a metaphor through which it explores the nature of female unhappiness and its roots '. . . in the self-sacrifice demanded by the male archetypes which Chris-tianity and childhood stories almost invariably provide'.[10] The newly bereaved widow's retracing of her past from a crossroads point, ten years previously, enables her to go forward in to the present. However, in closure, the play affirms the value of motherly love. Selected from almost three hundred entries for the second annual London New Plays Festival, *After Eeyore* ran for a week at the Old Red Lion and then at Theatr Cwmtawe in 1990. In telephone conversation the dramatist spoke enthusiastically about the illuminating audience response to its tension between emotional intensity and humour. Jorden Davies is also researching the difficulties facing women dramatists as the basis for a Resource Guide on strategies towards publication and production – issues she has debated on TV in *Wales on Sunday*.[11]

Sheila Yeger, partly Russian, Polish and English, and living in Bristol, has been active at Theatre Writers' Union writing weekends in Wales, the Write On festivals and writing workshops for Made In Wales. Two of the plays from her 1987/8 workshop, written by Charmian Saville and Jane Buckler who had had very little prior playwriting experience, were performed in the subsequent festival, and Helen Gwynn's play, performed at the 1989 festival, emerged through Yeger's workshop in 88/89. Author of *The Sound of One Hand Clapping: A Guide to Writing for the Theatre*, Yeger herself has been writing for fifteen years, with thirty-five plays professionally performed, but very few published, most recently *Self Portrait* (1990), and *Variations* (1991)[12]. *Self Portrait* is about the Welsh artist Gwen John, which was commissioned by Theatr Clwyd and premiered there under the direction of Annie Castledine, for Festival 1 on 23 June 1987. It was then on the main stage at Derby Playhouse from 1 June to 23 June 1990 as one of Castledine's swan-song productions. In this impressive performance, aspects of form and content bore many of the qualities associated with the female/ritualistic mode and hence of a potential Écriture Feminine.[13] Indeed, in the introduction to the published text Yeger acknowledges that the present version:

> . . . has emerged out of several drafts and as a result of the very creative and exciting rehearsal processes leading to the first production . . . and to the care and commitment of Annie Castledine, who commissioned it, nurtured it, championed it.[14]

A range of traditional boundaries became blurred in this production – the auditorium had been restructured so that audience and actors seemed to be present at an Exhibition of John's works; on entering, spectators browsed around the pictures arranged in what became the main acting area, and during performance, actors browsed along rows of paintings lining the sides of the aisles. As the play is both biographical and autobiographical, its structure fades in and out of past/present and fact/fiction, with significant doubling of the roles played. For instance, the heavily patriarchal figures in John's life and the framing contemporary Exhibition plot line are performed by the same actor – who sports a series of phallic canes and an over-size paint brush. Spectators were both rapt and wrapped in a welter of pleasurable yet painful sensations[15] – in a very large recess high on stage, selections of John's paintings were projected while her story was intermittently told through scenes and extracts echoing her letters. Visual pleasure was heightened by a recognition of the staging of these pictures within the dramatic process, as the actors melted into the roles or tableaux. A sense of the fragmentation of female identity – especially of the protagonist – was intensified by the centrally placed repainting of the key self portrait actually undertaken by the Dorelia figure during the performance, as she stood next to a mirror. Piano playing on stage also accompanied many of the most emotionally acute passages of the play. John, powerfully played by Lucinda Curtis, was presented as an unconventional woman passionate in her relationships with women and men, who, having been moved through Catholic faith, is ultimately most possessed by her creativity, which drove her to lonely extinction, perhaps through sheer anorexic exhaustion. Strong performance elements include interplay between visual and verbal discourses, for example visual repetition of body movements across the past/present divide, especially at moments when the verbal text of the past has resonance for the emotional development of characters in the present. Paradoxically this apparently radical play, which celebrates women's creativity, lays bare the patriarchal pressures that attempt to stifle women and pushes against the traditional boundaries of the dramatic medium, nevertheless also reflects the more conservative view of the great artist as a suffering solitary – a point drawn from John's story and extended into the modern frame, where finally the novelist too, withdraws from love, even of woman, to create. Despite an uneasiness in witnessing John's despair when abandoned by her 'master' Rodin, and her transitional move from the love of man to that of God – surely a patriarch, even when represented by kindly nuns – the spectator participates in a complex experience, which is more comprehensive than a rejuxtaposition of the familiar Magdalen/Madonna role image, or a reclamation of an undervalued artist. It is typically frustrating that such a piece, reviewed favourably by the *Guardian*[16] and the Radio Arts programme *Kaleidoscope,* should have a short run in a beleaguered provincial theatre. Particularly committed as she is to workshops, Yeger's body of work merits consideration on its own terms and in its own right.[17]

Kathleen J. Smith, who is not actually Welsh, has lived in Wales for nearly thirty years and has had three stage, five TV and two radio plays produced, though none printed, and has also been involved in running writing courses. Her plays vary from a musical life of *Buddha,* to *The Bronte Story*, staged at the Theatr Gwynedd in Bangor to a more realist-style prison play for seven actresses – *Women Without Men* – staged at Bangor, Harlech and Newtown, and intended for the Pentameters Theatre in Hampstead.

Informative letters from Marged Pritchard provide an indication of the work of others like herself, who write plays in Welsh, although it seems that Welsh language writers have devoted more time to novels and short stories. The major exception is Eigra Lewis Roberts, as yet the only woman to win the drama medal at the National Eisteddfod twice, as well as the prose medal. Roberts writes mainly TV plays as well as the Welsh soap *Minafon*. Apparently a revolving stage was used by the then Welsh Theatre Company when it presented her *Byd o Amser*, (World of Time) about Ann Griffiths, a Welsh hymn writer of the eighteenth century Revival Movement. Pritchard suggests that, on the whole, women writing plays in Welsh tend to write about problems related to gender; the younger ones concentrating upon themes related to women in the context of social problems – the modern role of the Welsh language, anti-nuclear issues, rural community, the influx of the English and unemployment. This view that Welsh language writers are less reluctant than the Anglo-Welsh to embrace political issues is supported by Tighe, and by Rabey and Saville, who cite Mair Tomos Evans' solo piece *Yma o Hyd*, which dramatizes Angharad Tomos' imprisonment on nationalist charges.[18] Pritchard feels that Welsh women dramatists are also interested in human relationships and personality clashes. For example, two of her own plays deal with non-topical human situations: *Cylymau* (Knots) explores the loneliness of individuals on two levels – a comic chorus commentary from an elderly woman upon the tragic interpersonal tangles of the rest of the cast; *Goriad yn y Drws* (The Key in the Door), a generation gap play, centres on a young delinquent girl and a handicapped retired school teacher. Other plays include one adapted from a short story by Marga Minco depicting the plight of Jews in wartime Holland and *Dwy Ynys*, adapted from the author's own short story for S4C.

Unpublished scripts and Write On programmes provided by Made in Wales give an indication of the content and form of current Anglo-Welsh writing. *Iron Them Dry*, by Pat Lewis, one of the new plays given a rehearsed reading at the Sherman Theatre Arena in 1988, about a headstrong young girl growing up in a Welsh village, is framed by the moment before Penny leaves her family home on the way to her wedding. The story is told in flashback style with indications of realistic scenery. Despite the split between past and present time indicated through mirror image confrontation, by moving an orange (possibly symbolic of passion) and by the change from wedding dress to petticoat, the presentation of Pat's rebellious life is feminine/reflectionist touched with humour, rather than using the wedding as watershed notion as a deconstructive opportunity for a critique of gender relations or small-town morality. As this is not the final version, further analysis would be inappropriate.

Christine Watkins is a writer and performer in English and Welsh, who performed with a three-woman company Ar Fechniath at the 1985 Eisteddfod and was a founder member of the experimental theatre company Cwmni Cyfi Tri. Her *Adult Ways*, performed at the Sherman during the 1986 festival, breaks the realist frame through occasional direct audience address, and explores the difference between manifest and latent levels in communication through the relationship between a thirtyish female teacher and her pupils, male and female. Both humorous and poetic moments highlight the differences between dreams and reality as well as the split between public and private personae. Girls, ranging from dreamer to cynic to anarchist are more differentiated and interestingly presented than the boys, obsessed with teenage sexuality. The subversive characterization of the teacher – unlike the traditionally revered figure of Miss Moffat in Emlyn Williams' *The Corn is Green* – who is shown to be sexually active and fantasizing about a young male pupil, the presentation of the girls and a scene that is polyphonic in its effect, might suggest that this is a more feminist/revolutionary text. However, Veronica's reverse balcony scene fails to persuade her Romeo to elope to the anarchist struggle, Teresa's attempt to rationalize her life with a calculator leads to her apparently shooting someone – or the radio – offstage, and Carol's romantic dreams are debunked by washing a menstruation-stained sheet. The boys remain unenlightened and the teacher continues to fantasize as next week's lesson starts. Thus, despite some subversive strategies, a cyclical closure reinforces the notion that the characters are trapped within traditional life patterns and dominant ideology.[19]

Three other scripts, Paula Griffiths's *A Hanging at Hannika* (originally BBC Wales radio 1985) performed in the 1986 Festival, Charmian Saville's *The Consecrator* and *Burd Mary* by Jane Buckler, both from the 1988 Festival, have some features in common.[20] All are set in what seems to be the historical past, although the first two have mystical or even apocalyptic qualities. *Burd Mary* is specifically placed in the mid-eighteenth century, in a Forest of Dean charcoal-burning community. The narrative framework follows 'beautiful' Mary's relationship with Jon, a seasonal worker, by whom she becomes pregnant. Hoping to travel away with him to a more fulfilling life, when he is reluctant, she aborts and tries to bury the baby. Discovered, she is spurned by all – Jon, her relatives, all the women of the village, whether fertile or barren, and the hypocritical Preacher. Old, blind Alys says 'Women aren't all born with wings. We have to find them Mary. So you'll be leaving now. You've made the sky your own. So fly in it.' Stoically after the women attack, Mary leaves for her future elsewhere. Although framebreaking techniques are not suggested, the play is interwoven with songs and music, which are atmospheric or narrative. The author suggests that the music should be simple and work towards a stylistic similarity – often emerging from the physical action and groupings. As written there is a strong emphasis on the importance of visual imagery in terms of both proxemics and kinesics. The overall effect is of a subversively adapted folk tale that has strong symbolic and poetic potential – for instance in the repeated visual and verbal imagery of the bird, captured or free. A range of characters effectively show the complexity of women's attitudes to motherhood and the hypocrisy of male values. Although written individually, through a writer's workshop, the play's non-verbal elements in particular suggest that its feminist qualities are moving towards the female/ritualistic mode.

Significantly, for the 1989 Write On Festival, the play *Steady State* was billed as devised by the Company, written by Buckler and directed by Gilly Adams and Rosamunde Hutt. Apparently 'the starting point to this play was the precise visual image', a reaction to an environment created by designer Nettie Scriven, and evolved on improvisational lines post-Mike Leigh.[21] Possibly the evolution of this writer's work will embody qualities most relevant to the debate on a theatrical Écriture Feminine in the future.[22]

A Hanging in Hannika is a curious piece about a man's journey to Hannika – hermeneutic coding gradually reveals that there he is to be the hangman at the execution of two witches. *En route* he is dogged by a mysterious stranger – perhaps the devil, invisible to others, although not to the audience. Although the play has a realist narrative frame, the subtext suggests the relationship of self/other is the play's core, a fragmentation of the self, which is considered to be a feature of the interrogative text. Further, the protagonist, Jeffort, is an extremely self-repressive man, unable to respond to human warmth or even proffered sexual activity. His legal function could also be seen to epitomize the patriarchal symbolic order, as defined by Kristeva, whilst the play explores the tension between these dominant drives and the semiotic order emotions he denies. Gradually he reveals his loved daughter had gone to the bad and left home – inevitably he finds she is one of the witches awaiting execution. His alter ego helps him pull the lever, but he himself dies as the play ends, as if to indicate that full absorption into an extreme denial of human feelings is the moment of 'death' in the metaphorical sense. In contrast, the supportive relationship between the witches is sympathetically shown in brief interspersed scenes, as is the plight of Leonie the intrusive Inn maid. Although there is not necessarily a strong feminist focus, this element of warmth and supportiveness is shown as significantly different. Griffiths's style maintains the emotional and ideological tension through a balance between everyday diction accompanied by physical activity and occasional almost biblically charged language. Thus, there are formal elements that could be said to impinge on the qualities ascribed to the female/revolutionary mode, and content that does, to some extent, interrogate aspects of patriarchy.

Saville's *The Consecrator* is the most poetically intense of the scripts seen. Set on the Irish coast in an unspecified time, a boatload of refugees from a plague-stricken area seek to be taken into a community of apparently healthy survivors led by a woman farmer and a medicine woman, with a harsh male hunter figure. There are two women refugees: Kestra who has been raped and mutilated throws the other woman's baby overboard when it seems to be infected. A male seaman and a priest, apparently sent to renew the Church ritual, are also aboard. Within the play's chronological flow, a violent and symbolic quality, although it exposes the past cruelty perpetrated on the refugee and the brutal conflict on the boat, is ambiguous in its presentation of the powerful women who are the survivors, 'They accept us as leaders because we make their survival possible . . . We pretend no miracles/We have knowledge/we use it/Share it/Extend it/By experiment . . . We live with risks, voids/and no religion.' While attempting to heal the emotionally damaged female refugees, who discuss the possibility that 'God the Mother' is less harsh than God the Father, the survivors explain 'We speak through and for our community with no connections to ourselves as individuals.' However, whilst the refugees are still in quarantine, the male survivor Harse beats the solitary Kestra to death. The female Leaders feel that the newly arrived priest will be unable to adapt to new ways, so arrange for Harse to kill him as he reconsecrates the church and prepares to bury Kestra. The spectacle of Harse's necrophilia appals the female Leader, 'Trapped again/trapped and mutilated.' However, the medicine woman cautions to keep her head as there is likely to be 'A very red sky'. The title of the play seems ambiguous in its dedication to the murdered priest, and the apocalyptic ending emphasizing the need for tough and ruthless action by the female survivors is not appealing, even if the text could be said to have feminist and revolutionary elements. This play is apparently much harsher than Helen Gwynn's first play, *Echo Lady*, directed by Hutt for the 1989 Write On Festival, reported to be a rather poetic exploration of woman's affinity to earth and sky, through imagination and the supernatural.

Festival opportunities for presenting plays that range along this wide spectrum from the naturalistic to the poetic are clearly crucial for women. Although there are some tendencies towards the two more radical modes, tentative comparison with current work in England suggests that Anglo-Welsh women dramatists incline more towards the more conservative feminine/reflectionist approach, in which the formal elements of naturalism and consequent movement towards closure reinstate the dominant ideology. This factor may predominate because these new writers are most influenced by television, where realism is dominant. Tighe implies that new Anglo-Welsh writing that manages to be staged is 'linked to scaled down versions of TV naturalism, with strictly linear plots, and a very keen avoidance of theatrical and political controversy.' Tighe's claim that 'Wales has no theatre history of its own' is based upon historical and geographical factors, the post-Bosworth departure of the gentry to London, the sparse population, the language division, poor transport and the growth of Methodism. These aspects may mean that writers have less frequent access –

either as spectators or contributors – to experimental live theatre than those who live elsewhere in Britain, and may explain why the Anglo-Welsh writers are 'at the mercy of prevailing middle-class taste, fashion, ambition, language and politics'[23] – and are polarized towards the interests of the Cardiff area, which is likely to provide the greatest potential theatre audience. A curious absence, within the work encountered, is any sense of strong issues, setting or form that might seem peculiarly Welsh or even Anglo-Welsh. In some cases there is a tendency towards the poetic and conventionally symbolic and ritual mode, which could perhaps be associated with the cultural history of Wales, where strong oral tradition and overtones of religion have always been influential. However, there does not seem to be as strong an emphasis on national cultural history as in plays written in Scotland, or indeed Ireland. Possibly more culturally specific issues are found in Welsh language plays, although Rabey and Saville suggest that the most regressive Welsh theatre looks back, whilst progressive groups reject 'retentive celebrations of the past, in favour of displaying the arrogance to discover and confront new images and arguments which explode through expectations'.[24] Apart from references to Brith Gof and the Cardiff-based Moving Being, it is difficult to trace evidence of companies who, according to Tighe, 'in a country where audiences are radically divided on linguistic and geographical and social lines to an extraordinary degree, have found ways of exploring themes and narratives through the language of image, sign and gesture, frequently dispensing with "words" altogether.'[25] Such an approach would seem promisingly akin to that of the female/ritualistic mode apparently absent here from most women's work. It is also difficult to know how far the operation of amateur dramatic groups, a strong feature of local life in South Wales after the shrinking of professional theatre in the 1840s due to the rise of Methodism, still give local 'amateur' writers performance opportunities of the kind my father, a member of the Guild of Welsh Playwrights, certainly enjoyed in the late 1940s and early 1950s, when social and artistic activity was often focused within a small community due to economic factors related to the Second World War.[26] There is some community–centred cross-cultural professional work in progress, such as Taleisin's events for Asian, Welsh and English speakers, but women writers are not specifically targeted. Radio, in Wales as in England, has for some time been a major outlet for new playwriting, whilst those who work in Welsh have benefited from the development of the television channel S4C. However, the more establishment nature of such outlets, and the major funding source, the Welsh Arts Council, makes it less likely that they will support the most radical work.

A survey of the range of material offered in the major Welsh venues for the summer of 1990 supports the rather depressing theory that there is no real market for innovative, political, or challenging material.[27] Mainstream Box Office constraints and tourism may explain, for instance, preference for the mythic presentation of Wales in *Under Milk Wood*, before an implicitly political piece written on some issue such as unemployment, for example the powerful naturalistic *The Scam*, by Peter Lloyd, directed by Gilly Adams for Made in Wales at the 1989 Edinburgh Festival. Women writers may well have chosen to avoid stereotypical and romanticized views of Wales, but the absence of broader political and cultural issues of this kind, which do impinge on gender is odd.

On the whole, given the relatively small amount of information available, it would seem that Anglo-Welsh plays presently written by women are not predominantly concerned with issues of gender – or cultural identity. Further, although there is a pleasing development of support for new writers there is no strong evidence at present of a coherent philosophy or innovative stylistic approaches that could be clearly related either to the notion of a female language of theatre in terms of performance strategies or to a consistently feminist consciousness in overt content. As elsewhere in theatre at the moment, there need to be many more opportunities for staging new and more radical work, and in particular means of publishing or at least keeping centralized records of work written by women in Wales – in English and in Welsh.

7

Irish women playwrights since 1958
Anna McMullan

Since the indefatigable effort and enthusiasm invested by Lady Gregory in the founding of Ireland's first national theatre in 1898,[1] women have formed an integral part of the backbone of Irish theatre. Lady Gregory, Mary Manning and Countess Longford wrote for the theatre in the first half of the century and, in the immediate post-war years, the plays of Maria Laverty, exposing the appalling conditions of Dublin's poor, were popular at the Gate Theatre. Deidre O'Connell, Shelah Richards, Carolyn Swift, Mary O'Malley,[2] Phyllis Ryan, Mary Elizabeth Burke-Kennedy, Lynne Parker and Garry Hynes are among the many women who have founded, directed and, in some cases, written for their own companies or theatres in recent years. Yet the dominant image of Irish theatre remains that of a male-authored literary drama – from the texts of Yeats, Synge and O'Casey to the work of the present generation, which includes Brian Friel, Thomas Murphy and Frank McGuinness. However, women are challenging the canon, both through their involvement in non-traditional forms of theatre, and through the emergence of a small but growing number of prominent individual writers.

In an article in *Theatre Ireland* in 1989, a number of women writers, actresses and directors in contemporary Irish theatre declared themselves wary of their work being categorized as 'women's theatre'. The article concludes, '. . . they do not think there is any way of maximizing women's participation in Irish theatre that would not ghettoise them'.[3] However, this participation tends not to be widely recognized,[4] either because the writers' play texts have not been published or because they are working in alternative areas of theatrical activity, such as community theatre or Theatre

In Education, which are undervalued because the dominant critical and cultural consensus works towards a privileging of the literary 'authored' text.[5] Moreover, while there has been a distinct increase in women's participation in all areas of theatrical production, including textual production, since the 1970s, the key positions of power in the major theatres, in the arts councils and in the publishing houses in Northern Ireland and in the Irish Republic[6] remain largely in the hands of men.[7] A study of women's contribution to Irish theatre therefore involves not only an acknowledgement of the work of individual women in the corpus of Irish drama, but a recognition of the power of patriarchal values in Irish society.

Women in Irish society

Irish women come under pressure from both Catholic and Protestant ideologies to retain the domestic role as their primary function. The Reverend Ian Paisley has insisted that the divinely ordained role of a true Protestant woman is to provide service and succour to her husband,[8] while in Catholic iconography, women are offered as role models both the Virgin Mary, infinitely forgiving and supportive, and Mother Ireland, a grieving mother whose land has been plundered and her sons taken.[9] Whether Catholic or Loyalist, the role of the woman is to serve and to suffer. While her image is sublimated, her voice is suppressed.

Nevertheless, there has been a growing feminist awareness in Ireland since the 1970s that has led to a challenging of these stereotypes. This is most evident in the Irish Republic because the last four decades have brought about enormous economic and social changes. For this reason, the context material will deal mainly with conditions in the twenty-six counties. The focus of the material on the six counties will be on the post-1968 'Troubles'.[10]

The 1950s and 1960s

As in Britain, there was little feminist consciousness in Ireland during the 1950s and 1960s. In the 1937 Constitution, the Irish State enforced by law the teachings of the Catholic Church, which emphasized the woman's duty to uphold the family. Contraception, divorce and abortion were illegal. There was a marriage ban on women working after they married. Single mothers and women living apart from their husbands had no right to social welfare, 'A subservient role for women was locked into social structures by state services which mirrored the teaching of the male-controlled Catholic Church'.[11] However, the late 1950s marked a development in governmental policy towards modelling the Irish Republic more on her Western capitalist neighbours. This marked the beginning of considerable socio-economic changes within Irish society and life-styles.

The major political development of the 1960s was the organization in 1968–9 of civil rights marches on behalf of Catholics in the six counties who were being discriminated against in terms of housing, jobs and political representation. These peaceful marches were violently met by the police and Protestant activists. British troops entered Northern Ireland in August 1969 to 'keep the peace', and were initially welcomed by the Catholic population. This soon changed, however, as the British Army became identified with protecting the Protestant majority. Because of the political sensitivity of the situation, it was some years before dramatists were prepared or allowed to overtly explore 'The Troubles' in the theatre. It was not until the 1970s and the 1980s that women's voices entered the debate, clearing a space within the cross-fire for women to place themselves on stage and on the agenda.

The 1950s was quite a fallow time for new writers in the Irish theatre, but the 1960s saw the emergence of a new generation of playwrights concerned with exploring the changing tensions and contradictions in Irish identity – from the male point of view. These dramatists – those at least whose work was produced and published – were almost all men, among them John B. Keane, Thomas Murphy and Brian Friel. Women were putting their energies into founding and directing companies. In 1951, the establishment of the Lyric Theatre in Belfast provided an outlet for new writing and for the performance of poetic drama, particularly that of Yeats. Mary O'Malley played a major role in establishing and running the Lyric, both as a private company up until 1967 and thereafter as a public theatre, and directed many of the plays which were performed there. A few plays by women were included in the programmes, including Lady Gregory's *The Rising of the Moon*, but new plays by women writers were very rare. Those that were performed at the Lyric during this time were adaptations of well known works, such as the performance during the season 1958–9 of an adaptation of Joyce's *Finnegan's Wake* entitled *The Voice of Shem* by Mary Manning.

In Dublin, in 1953, Carolyn Swift founded the Pike Theatre with Alan Simpson, and Phyllis Ryan founded the company, Gemini, in 1959. In the early 1960s, Deirdre O'Connell, an American of Irish parentage who had studied under Erwin Piscator in his Stanislavski Studio in New York came to Ireland and opened her Stanislavski studios in Dublin in 1963. She went on to found the company Focus with Mary Elizabeth Burke-Kennedy in 1967.

The 1970s

During the 1970s, the first steps towards an improvement in women's rights and conditions in the Irish Republic were made, economic conditions in general improved and a growing feminist consciousness among some sectors of the female population[12] led to the establishment of organizations such as the Commission on the Status on Women, set up by the government in 1970, Cherish, founded in 1972 to defend the rights of all mothers, regardless of marital status[13] and Irish Woman United, founded in 1975. The marriage bar was removed in 1973. The introduction of equal pay in 1974 and the Equal Opportunities Act in 1977 improved women's economic and working conditions.[14]

In the 1970s, a small number of women began writing for the theatre, including Margaretta D'Arcy, Siobhan O Suilleabhain, Geraldine Aron and Edna O'Brien. Margaretta D'Arcy is by far the most radical of these. Her theatrical collaborations with John Arden drew on Brechtian techniques to call for revolutionary change, and she has frequently come into conflict with political and artistic authorities in Ireland. Her recent work with Galway Women's Entertainment rejects even more radically the framework and forms of traditional theatre.

Margaretta D'Arcy was born in Dublin in 1922 and worked in small experimental theatres in Dublin from the age of 15. She then went to London and worked as an actress in London theatre clubs and regional companies. In 1955 she met John Arden, with whom she has collaborated in the writing of several plays. D'Arcy and Arden settled in Galway and established the Galway Theatre Workshop in 1976. D'Arcy's commitment to theatre is inseparable from, and has been deeply influenced by, her political commitments: to feminism, to socialist revolution and to the ending of British imperialism in Ireland. She was imprisoned in Armagh gaol in 1978 and in 1980 as a result of her support of the H-block campaign. D'Arcy's play, *A Pinprick of History*, performed at the Almost Free Theatre in London in 1977, reveals the opposition encountered by the Galway Theatre Workshop when they toured *The Menace of Ireland*, a series of plays about repression and imperialism in Ireland.

Among the best known of the plays on Ireland by D'Arcy and Arden is *The Non-Stop Connolly Show,* begun in 1969, completed in 1974, and first performed in a 26-hour performance at Liberty Hall in Dublin over Easter 1975. The play centres on the Irish trade unionist and socialist revolutionary James Connolly. In 'A Socialist Hero on the Stage',[15] D'Arcy and Arden discuss the conception of the play. The figure of James Connolly focused the conflicts between capital and labour, between revolution and reform, and between socialism and republicanism that recur throughout their dramatic works. While the conflict between capital and labour was taken for granted in the movements within which Connolly worked, D'Arcy and Arden wanted to explore the conflicts within the Left between the reformists, associated with Home Rule, and those who, like Connolly, believed that the entire structure of capitalism must be changed. The play draws on a number of popular dramatic forms, and includes songs and emblematic backcloths which provide a Brechtian commentary on the action.

The Ballygombeen Bequest deals with a land dispute in rural Ireland, between the English landlord, Major Baker-Fortesque, and the local tenants, the O'Leary family. When the O'Leary's insist on improvements, Baker-Fortescue tries to have them evicted and the struggle over possession of the small-holding carries echoes of the struggle between Michael Collins and Lloyd George over the signing of the partition treaty. The play was based on an actual current local dispute, and was first performed in 1972, but had to be withdrawn because of a libel suit. During performances, actors and actresses distributed leaflets naming the landlord at the centre of the dispute and urging the audience to protest. The case was settled in 1977, and a new version of the play, *The Little Grey Home in the West*, was published in 1982.

Vandaleur's Folly, staged in London in 1978 by the 7:84 Theatre Company, who then toured the production, also deals with the issue of land – a central one in Irish history. It is set in an agricultural co-operative that was set up in Ralahine, Ireland, in 1831, by John Vandaleur. The experiment was highly successful until Vandaleur, who had retained ownership of the collective, lost it in a gambling match. The play was written, according to Margaretta D'Arcy, '. . . in order to demonstrate the impossibility of reformist policies succeeding so long as the basic reason for the reforms is to keep the ruling classes in possession of their wealth and political power . . . John Vandaleur's dream of communal harmony imposed from above, by the very ruling classes against which the violence of the underprivileged was directed, could not and did not succeed'.[16]

While men are the main agents in the above plays, the role played by women is acknowledged, and their experience is represented. D'Arcy has also suggested that women could play all of the parts in the plays, in order to undermine the assumption of sexual, economic and political power by men, and to foreground the repressed and oppressed presence of women. D'Arcy's more recent work with rural women in Galway will be discussed in a subsequent section.

Siobhan O Suilleabhain, from West Kerry, writes in Gaelic.[17] The majority of her work is written for Irish radio and television, the main performance outlet for Gaelic writers and local theatre groups. She deals with issues and concerns of particular relevance to the *Gaeltacht,* the Gaelic-speaking areas of Western Ireland, including the high emigration rate. Her work explores the experiences of rural Irish women, with an emphasis on accessibility and entertainment.[18]

In 1975, Garry Hynes founded the Druid Theatre Company in Galway City, with Marie Mullen and Mick Lally. Druid Theatre has remained one of the most vital companies in Ireland, and Garry Hynes has become a director of international repute. She has directed for the Royal Shakespeare Company, and her own play, *Island Protected By A Bridge of Glass*, won a

Fringe First Award at the Edinburgh Festival in 1980. She was appointed Artistic Director of the Abbey Theatre in Dublin in 1990. Although her work has not foregrounded feminist issues, on her appointment to the Abbey, she called for more women's voices to be heard.[19]

Druid Theatre gave three plays of Geraldine Aron, now living in South Africa, their first production in Ireland: *Bar and Ger* (1978), *A Galway Girl* (1979) and *Same Old Moon* (1984).[20] Of these, *A Galway Girl* is most centrally concerned with women in rural Ireland. The play explores the particularly harsh plight of the rural working class Irish wife who tries to keep family and finances together, while her husband proves the power of his virility by drinking and gambling, and the integrity of his soul by reading poetry. The lack of communication between husband and wife is emphasized by the form of the play, which consists of monologues delivered to the audience, with very few exchanges between the characters. Despite the aridity of her marriage and its incompatibility with her naïve and rather snobbish views of an ideal family and social life, Maisie stands by her husband and her faith till the end. As Dermot comments, 'Isn't the Catholic faith a wonderful institution the way it stops our wives abandoning us? . . . I'll tell you something, I'm still her ould fella – for all her airs and graces' (p. 11). Yet the play is uncomfortably poised between a critique of the conditions and attitudes that stifled Maisie's life, and an almost sentimental recognition of her tenacity and self-sacrifice in having stoically weathered an unfulfilling marriage. This tendency to lament the sacrifice of Irish women in accepting their tragic lot does little to promote active change.

The criticism in Edna O'Brien's *A Pagan Place*,[21] adapted from her novel, is sharper and more cruel – the play is a surreal black comedy. Here again, however, women are portrayed as victims rather than agents, and the only hope lies in escape. The central figure is a young girl, Creena, who becomes a missionary and escapes from Ireland, after having been raped by a young priest and subsequently beaten by her father. The hypocrisy of Irish rural society is exposed, as the professional roles of doctor and priest are used by men to exploit the naïvety and ignorance of the females in their physical or spiritual care. Those women who, unlike Creena, remain in Ireland seem to be in grave danger of becoming mad (like her schoolteacher), ill (like her friend) or pregnant (like her sister).

The 1980s

The 1980s ushered in a recession as far as women's rights in the south of Ireland are concerned. On 26 June 1986, the majority of Irish people voted against a proposal to introduce divorce legislation. The laws against contraception and abortion were also tightened. A prominent feminist writer, Nell McCafferty commented:

The nineteen eighties will go down in history as a lousy decade for
Irish women. During what have become known as 'the amendment
years', church and state fought for control of our bodies and our
destiny. The Catholic Church won handily, and the Irish Constitution contains written prohibitions against abortion and divorce.[22]

Nevertheless, the 1980s have seen an increase in women writing for the
theatre, in both mainstream and radical forms. A recognition of the oppres-
sive and repressive nature of Irish patriarchal attitudes and institutions can be
found in the work of Jennifer Johnson, although she works within largely
traditional theatrical forms. Johnson also writes novels, but her theatrical
background, as daughter of Shelah Richards, actress, director and television
producer, emerges in several of her plays. *The Nightingale and not the Lark*,[23]
premiered at the Peacock Theatre, Dublin in September 1980, is set in a
room at the top of an old hall in a provincial town in Ireland used by touring
theatre companies. The play focuses on the aging Mamie, the caretaker of the
hall, who is wrapped in her memories and reflections on the past, in her love
for her republican father, to whom she was an idealized 'Cathleen Ni
Houlihan', and her bitterness towards the husband who abandoned her, was
killed by a Nazi bomb in London, and who now literally haunts her.

The Porch, first presented in the Gaiety Theatre Bar in June 1986, also
centres on the figure of an old woman, Maud. Both plays expose the extent
to which these women have been repressed by arrogant and contemptuous
husbands or fathers and ignored by the world as non-entities, so that they
retreat into a world of memory or fantasy. Johnson laments the way in
which Irish women's lives have been thwarted by unhappy or sterile
unions, and emphasizes the distance between the sexes and the stifling of
genuine emotional responses.[24] She uses humour, particularly in *The Porch*,
and explores the subjectives of her two central women characters. The
form remains within the framework of naturalism, although this is undermined by the emphasis on memory and imagination, so that the apparently
real confines of the stage become increasingly indistinguishable from or
contrasted with the inner world of the main character.

Mary Halpin's *Semi-Private* was voted winner of the Irish Times
Women's Playwriting competition in 1982. *Semi-Private* is set in a
gynaecological ward of a Dublin hospital. It consists of a series of interchanges between an unlikely combination of patients – a *nouveau-riche*
housewife, an outspoken working class shopgirl, a nun and a hard-line
feminist. The play is in the tradition of light comic entertainment, and
tends to rely on and indeed reinforce female stereotypes.

Many women in Irish theatre during the 1980s were working in fringe
venues or in non-traditional forms of theatre. A major outlet for feminist
work has been the Project Arts Centre in Dublin. The Project premiered a
one-woman show by Nell McCafferty called *Worm in the Heart* in 1985.

This presented a young feminist activist and exposed the sexism she had encountered in her involvement with left-wing Irish politics. She is certainly no victim, but, as she prepares to give birth, she is increasingly drawn to the memory of her mother, devoted entirely to her children. The play emphasizes and reflects upon the differences between the two generations.

Several women continue to work outside the established boundaries of theatre: children's theatre, puppet theatre, cabaret, community theatre or Theatre In Education. Annie Kilmartin's Moving Theatre Group, and the Raised Eyebrow Theatre Group, brought theatre to women whose concerns are rarely voiced in the major Dublin theatres, patronized largely by a fashionable, middle class audience. Carolyn Swift has written scripts for radio and television, children's theatre and puppet plays. She recently presented a one-woman play about Lady Gregory at the Peacock Theatre in the 1987–8 season. Prisoners from Mountjoy Gaol formed the company Exit, which presented Miriam Gallagher's *Fancy Footwork* in 1983. Two of Ireland's three excellent theatre in education companies were founded by women: Emilie Fitzgibbon founded the company Graffiti, and campaigns vigorously against the marginalization of theatre in education, and Brenda Winter, a former actress with Charabanc, founded Ireland's newest TIE company, Replay, based in Belfast.

Mary Elizabeth Burke-Kennedy, Anne Hartigan and Marina Carr have produced innovative work for the Dublin theatre in the last decade. Their work comes closest to what may be described as a female/ritualistic aesthetic. Burke-Kennedy was co-founder of the company Focus with Deidre O'Connell in 1967. She then founded Storyteller's Theatre Company in 1983. She has written several plays for children, but now writes also for an adult audience. Her play *Women in Arms* was performed at the Dublin Theatre Festival in 1988. *Women in Arms* tells the story of four of the major female figures from the Ulster cycle of stories in Irish mythology: Nessa, Macha, Deirdre and the proud warrior queen, Maeve – all strong, influential women who have left their mark on Irish myth and history. The play therefore reclaims active images of women, in contrast to the passive icons that tend to dominate Irish culture. The tradition of oral story-telling is an important element in the play. Actors and actresses address the audience and shift in and out of roles. They also move together to recreate landscapes of lakes and trees. This fluid association of character and landscape breaks the strong Irish tradition that links land to individual, male possession or dispossession.[25]

Anne Hartigan was involved in the creation of a new Irish company, Moveable Feast, which emerged as a result of an experimental workshop that she organized at the Tyrone Guthrie centre at Annaghmakerrig. The workshop, led by Robert Gordon, explored ideas about contemporary sexual attitudes, which developed into a performance piece, *Beds*, presented at the Dublin Theatre Festival in 1982. The form was experimental, fusing mime, dance, speech, drama and music in a series of linked actions and images that evoke the flow of life through birth, marriage, lovemaking and death, creating the rituals of daily life as movements to and from the stillness of the bed. Another play by Hartigan, presented at the Dublin Theatre Festival in 1989, *La Corbière*, deals with the tale of a group of French prostitutes brought to the Nazi-occupied island of Jersey during the Second World War and lost at sea when their boat hit the rocks off La Corbière lighthouse on the return journey. Although the play exposes the degrading treatment of the women by the men, the text is also a rhythmic, poetic celebration of the women through the eyes of the sole survivor, Marie Claire. Hartigan embraces a theatrical language that recalls Kristeva's theories of the maternal 'semiotic' rhythms[26] that rupture the patriarchal Symbolic laws of identity and representation. Individual sounds and individual identities rise and fall back into the engulfing presence of the sea (homonym of the mother in French), represented visually through the use of muslin and, aurally, through close repetition of sound.

Marina Carr is one of the newest female voices in Irish theatre. In *Low in the Dark*[27] produced at the Project Centre in 1989, she uses the conventions of the 'absurd' to comment on gender construction, and the repression of women. One character is constantly having babies, which are always declared male (whatever their sex) and another character refuses to emerge from her veil of curtains. She, however, is also a story-teller, and the play in general, both comments on and subverts women's exclusion from representation.

Margaretta D'Arcy remains a pioneer in continually challenging the established forms and limits of theatre. Since the beginning of the 1980s, D'Arcy has rejected writing for the theatre and she now works directly with rural women in Galway, helping them to find their own voice through drama and drama-related community projects. Galway Women's Entertainment was set up to provide a forum for local Irish women, to 'explore mainly through stories and through developing the more ephemeral senses, possibilities of other artistic techniques, challenging time, challenging logical plot-structure, challenging the accepted boundaries of artistic disciplines by means of radio, video, parties, excursions.'[28] Women's Sceal radio was launched, broadcasting for local women and invited guests, poets, musicians or anyone who wanted to share information, stories or air their views. Margaretta D'Arcy stresses that all views are welcome, reflecting all aspects of the community. She is particularly interested in alternative media, like radio and video, which can be shared by members of the community who are at once producers and public, thereby rejecting the dominant approach to the creative arts as a commodity to be marketed by the producers and consumed by the public. Her work is by the community for the community, particularly the rural women whose voice is almost wholly neglected within the institutions of Irish culture.

The theatre has become an important forum for exploring the conflicts and tensions within individuals and communities in Northern Ireland.

Women have made an important contribution to this debate. Indeed, women have been active on both sides of the political struggle, although even more of them, like the women in Anne Devlin's *Ourselves Alone*, are 'waiting on men'. Following an incident in Belfast, in August 1976, when a mother, Mrs Ann McGuire, was injured and her three children killed, Betty Williams and Mairead Corrigan, Anne McGuire's sister, brought Loyalist and Catholic women together under the banner of the Peace People. For a number of years, women's voices were strongly raised in support of peace, although their movement ultimately foundered. The demise of the Peace People underlines the danger of simplifying the Northern Irish question and calling for peace without considering the underlying causes of the unrest.[29] Nevertheless, in a land dominated by the rhetoric of heroism and struggle, women can offer a different perspective.

Anne Devlin has written and adapted plays for radio, television and the stage. Her first stage play is *Ourselves Alone*, produced at the Liverpool Playhouse Studio on 24 October, 1985, and at the Royal Court Upstairs on 20 November 1985.[30] This play centres on a family where the father is 'a big fella in the Provos' (p. 23), and the brothers are also involved in IRA terrorist activity. Although Josie, one of the daughters is admitted as a courier, most of the women play a passive, nurturing role. Women are seen as victims of a male ideology of violence, symbolized by Auntie Cora, blind, deaf, dumb and without hands since she was storing ammunition for her brother, Malachy, and it blew up in her face.

Conflict is presented not only between Catholic and Protestant 'tribes' but within each rank. Frieda describes her brother's political career, 'He joined the Officials when they split with the Provos, then the INLA when they split from the Officials; the last time he was out on parole he was impersonating votes for the Sinn Fein election' (p. 22). The father of her protestant lover, John McDermott, was 'thrown from the deck of a ship' by his workmates, for trying to set up a union. The women in *Ourselves Alone* are weary of this battlefield. Frieda declares 'I was thinking of leaving the tribes behind. Both of them' (p. 80). Josie has 'lost the killing instinct' (p. 63) and is more concerned about the baby she is carrying, whose father is Joe Conran, an attractive Englishman who has recently been admitted to the IRA. In their different ways, they resist the scene of violence and the shadow of the 'dark figure which hovered about the edge of my cot – priest or police I can't tell', and reclaim the right to create rather than destroy relationships, intimacy and life:

Josie: I'm tired. Tired of this endless night watch. I've been manning the barricades since 'sixty-nine. I'd like to stop for a while, look around me, plant a garden, listen for other sounds; the breathing of a child somewhere outside Anderstown.

(p. 77)

The play does not engage in direct political analysis, but expresses a plea for hope and freedom on a personal and national level. Indeed, Devlin's characters may not have found a balance between personal need and political vision, but her play articulates the very difficulty of finding such a balance in the emotional and political maze of life in the six counties. It underlines the difficulty of separating Irish politics from personal loyalties and emotional commitment: Joe's betrayal of Josie by informing on her organization and her family and by abandoning her is both personal and political. At the end of the play, she is reclaimed by 'The Tribe', represented by her father, Malachy. Philomena Muinzer suggests that the mythology of the Tribe, the notion of an innate, primarily male drive towards violence and betrayal tends to lead to a situation of stalemate and political fatalism, a denial of 'logic, ideology, or modern political causality in favour of an unconquerable primal force' (p. 56). It is true that the portrayal of women as victims of this male violence may be seen as fatalistic, but Anne Devlin's plays, and others in this section, work against the mythology of heroism promoted by both sides and thereby contribute towards dismantling the myths that obscure the political, social and economic issues. The plays of Christina Reid and Charabanc also celebrate the resilience, fortitude and, above all, the sharp and vibrant humour of the women of Northern Ireland.

Christina Reid's plays focus on the experience of women from the Protestant community. She was playwright in residence at the Lyric theatre from 1983–4, and at the Young Vic from 1988–9. She emigrated to London in 1987 and her recent plays include the experience of the exile, at once rooted in the complex, closely knit and self-enclosed community that has been left behind, yet also possessing a much wider experience and perspective.

Tea in a China Cup, first produced by the Lyric Players Theatre in Belfast in 1983, is set in Belfast and spans more than three decades, from 1939 to 1972, in the life of a working-class Protestant family. It opens with the grand-daughter, Beth, going to buy a grave for her dying mother, and discovers that the strictly segregated northern Irish society is reflected in the graveyard:

> *Clerk*: . . . The new cemetery is divided in two by a gravel path. Protestant graves are to the right, Catholic graves to the left. Now what side would your mother want?[31]

In a series of flashbacks, the play explores the stereotypes perpetrated by each community about the other, which help to maintain the suspicion and lack of communication between them. The play both celebrates the earthy humour and vitality of characters such as Beth's grandmother and great aunt Maisie, and reveals the stubborn pride of the Protestant family who see the beginnings of Catholic prosperity as a threat, and seek desperately to keep up a respectable 'Protestant' appearance with very little means. Both

Beth and her mother, Sarah, marry spendthrifts, who drain them financially and emotionally. Sons are lost in the cause of a mythical loyalty to 'the Crown'. The play comments both on the sectarian and the sexual divide in northern Irish life. Men and women rarely meet in the same space, the women congregate in the home, the men in the pub. However, the play offers some hope on a personal level for Beth as, after her mother's death, she contemplates the future on her own terms.

Joyriders, commissioned and produced by Paines Plough at the Young Vic Theatre in London in 1986, is set in the former Lagan Linen Mills, where a Youth Training Programme is in operation. Many of the members are from the notorious Divis flats, which have been described as the worst housing development in Western Europe. The resort to violence is linked to cramped living conditions and economic hardship. The play explores the social divide between the working class young, and the middle class social worker in charge of the programme, who attempts to defend them against the snobbery and condescension of the authorities, and to alleviate the lack of hope in their lives. The latter is emphasized, however, when the army shoots down a defenceless young girl, one of the members of the pro-gramme, as in the final scene of *Shadow of a Gunman,* which the young people watch at the beginning of the play. As in her subsequent plays,[32] Christina Reid tries to shed fresh light on the conflicts of Northern Ireland by showing how the sectarian conflict is bound up with questions of economics and class.

While her characters and dialogue are largely naturalistic, Reid has made increasing use of songs, and other anti-illusionist devices. A recent article by Diderik Roll-Hansen on *Tea in a China Cup* outlines dramatic strategies that have remained characteristic of Reid's work, such as her 'flexible post-Brechtian handling of the 'changes of time and place', both delicate and spirited, and her command of an urgent, free-flowing theatrical form. We move swiftly from scene to scene, quite often in defiance of chronological time'.[33]

Charabanc is a Northern Irish Touring Company of women performers. It was founded in 1983 by five women actresses who had been out of work for almost a year: Sarah (Marie) Jones, Carol Scanlon, Eleanor Methven, Brenda Winter and Maureen Macauley. There were and are still very few good roles for young women. These women decided to make their own work and started to explore the issue of unemployment. Some of the actresses came from families where the women had worked in the Belfast linen mills and they decided to base a piece of theatre around the women mill-workers' strike of 1911, which became their first show, *Lay Up Your Ends.* They spent six months researching the period and talking to women who had first-hand experience of working conditions in the mills. This became a pattern that they repeated in preparation for subsequent plays. Martin Lynch was then invited to join them as script co-ordinator and Pam

Brighton, who had directed Peter Sheridan's *Diary of a Hunger Strike* for Hull Truck Theatre Co., as director. The collective then spent two periods at the Tyrone Guthrie Centre at Annaghmakerrig, during which they worked out a script on the basis of improvisations. The piece dealt with the working conditions at the mill, family responsibilities of the women, their marital relationships and attitudes towards the strike, raising issues of trade unionism, class and sectarianism. The five actresses played a spectrum of characters, male and female, rich and poor and the show exudes energy, verve and a characteristically vibrant, tough, satiric sense of humour.

Subsequent pieces, several devised by the company or written by Marie Jones, have focused on issues of concern to the Northern Irish community. *Oul Delf and False Teeth* (1984) presents the community around St George's Market at the time of the election of 1949 where it seemed that there was a chance to stem the policies of sectarianism. *Now You're Talkin* (1985) is set in a reconciliation centre where five women, two protestants and three catholics, one of whom is an ardent Sinn Fein supporter, have come for an encounter weekend with an American evangelist. The women end up barricading themselves in the centre, protesting against other people's solutions. *Gold in the Streets* (1986) is concerned with Irish emigration to England and explores the lives of three women from different times – 1912, 1950 and 1985, who have been driven out of Northern Ireland by sectarian bitterness and harassment. *The Girls in the Big Picture* (1987) centres on rural life in the province in the 1960s, while their next piece, *Somewhere over the Balcony,* presented in 1988, explores the deprivation and discrimination suffered by the residents of the Divis Flats in Belfast.

Charabanc is committed to presenting plays that reflect Northern Irish society, and to community touring. The majority of their shows involve careful research and interviews with local people. Their form remains within a broad framework of community theatre. Many of their pieces are devised by the company or written by Marie Jones,[34] who has also written for the TIE company Replay, although Charabanc has also presented Darragh Cloud's *The Stick Wife* (1988), and Neil Speirs's *Cauterised* (1989). Charabanc deliberately avoids adopting a particular position in relation to the political debates in Northern Ireland, in order to reflect all sides of the Northern Irish community. This is indeed a continuing problem in the attempt to represent the struggle in Northern Ireland. To achieve consensus among the audience, the deepest roots of the conflict are frequently left undisturbed.

The conflict in Northern Ireland remains unresolved but the 1990s appear to be offering more opportunities for women than ever before. The repressive climate of the 1980s in the Republic is being challenged. Contemporary theatre, established and alternative, in Ireland as a whole, seems to be entering a particularly creative period. Emilie Fitzgibbon writes, 'The possibilities of growth and development are all there; the changing fashions, the production talents, the inventive minds are all vital and energetic in their potential'.[35] Women's energies and voices have contributed to the reshaping and revitalizing of Irish theatre and it is to be hoped that lack of support and funding will not prevent them from continuing and expanding that process.

8

Transformations and transgressions: Women's discourse on the Scottish stage

Susan C. Triesman

Country: Scotland. Whit like is it? . . . How me? Eh? Eh? Eh/Voice like a choked laugh. Ragbag o' a burd in ma black duds, a' angles and elbows and broken oxter feathers, black beady een in ma executioner's hood. No braw, but Ah think Ah ha'e a sort of black glamour. Do I no put ye in mind of a skating minister, or, on the other fit, the parish priest, the dirty beast?
(La Corbie In Liz Lockhead's *Mary Queen of Scots*[1])

Truth happens to me
at the top of my voice
these days.

(Joan Ure[2])

Women dramatists in Scotland work from the twin sites of gender and national culture to cross discursive patriarchal modes, inflecting, and some-times transforming, the meanings of both. Their compelling exploration of the female as an issue at the centre of all human concerns is problematized by Scotland's recurrent identity crises and the concomitant over-assertions of the ugly macho values, which have been taken up as signs of 'the Scottish' by the media. Their work does not present a monolithic front: there is no single female discourse and there are varying levels of political consciousness about feminist issues. However they are all concerned with expressing women's experience, 'You just have to express women as truth-fully as possible, and that's an affirmative thing in itself . . . because of the *starved* way a lot of women in Scotland feel about their experience.'[3]

These writers also deal with the outcast, the marginalized, the invisible, the abused; the classic experience of the Other, where otherness becomes a multiple oppression crucial to character structure. Transcending that other-ness to produce a woman inscribed as a subject within history requires

courage and passion, producing a transformative and poetic theatre prepared to run risks and quarrel with itself if need be. It is a theatre marked by
strong celebratory and comedic properties, ready to wrest familiar narrative
forms from the dominant culture to make the familiar strange so that
questions can be asked.

Prior to the emergence of this new women's theatre in the late 1970s,
women writing for the theatre in Scotland received little encouragement to
stay with the medium. Ena Lamont Stewart's classic *Men Should Weep*
(1946), was acclaimed for its powerful interweaving of sexual politics with
the humiliations of poverty under the relentless pressures of capitalism
when it was revived by 7:84 in 1982, after decades of neglect. Naomi
Mitchison also wrote occasionally for the theatre: her *Spindrift* (1951, with
Denis Macintosh) shows the painful life choices of a West Coast fishing
community living on the margins of survival, with the women having even
less control over their lives than the men, as they have no source of
economic independence. Netta Blair Reid's *The Shepherd Beguiled* (1957)
was not staged until 1982 when, in Theatre Alba's production, it proved to
be a powerful and poetic drama, capable of dealing with the Scottish psyche
through intense symbolism and an accumulated 'glamourie o' words'. The
rediscovery of such writers as Ena Lamont Stewart and Netta Blair Reid
has helped to create an inheritance that embraces both naturalism and
modernism.

Ada Kay's important *The Man from Thermopylae* (1961) assaults the
patriarchal ideologies that dominate women, perpetuate war and reject
creative values. The play's central ironic device, that one Spartan survived
the massacre at Thermopylae and chose to go home, makes the audience
question how history is constructed, and by whom. The comic is woven
closely with the tragic and the interaction of different systems of signification shows a very sophisticated understanding of both theatre and culture.

In the 1960s and into the 1970s, even the most prolific women playwrights did not have serious *careers* in theatre. While Jessie Kesson worked
mainly for radio, Joan Ure's plays 'have a delicacy and an irony whose very
fastidiousness may have prevented her work receiving more attention'.[4] A
theatre culture relying heavily on two-dimensionality, the rural romanticiz-
ing and sentimental reductionism of the kailyard play and, latterly, on what
Joyce McMillan has called the Slab Boys Syndrome,[5] did not really have
room for her experiments with a whole variety of European forms from
Pirandello to the Absurd. When Ure handles the past, she reclaims women's
lost history, as in *Go West Wild Woman* (Castle Douglas Unity Players, 1974),
which presents the survival strategies of the impoverished and of the
egalitarian evangelical movement of Elspeth Rule, using multiple viewpoints
in a 'historical fantastical' play so that the audience have to provide their own
conclusions. She herself identified the major problem in Scotland as the
divorce of intellect from imagination ('the suspect stepbairn'), with John

Knox the culprit, 'the reformed church in Scotland reformed magic out of existence. With the last witch went the last shred of imagination in the flames.' She links this life-denying culture with sexism: if Jane Austen had lived in Scotland, she says, they would have had her buttering bannocks.[6]

In the 1970s, the discovery of oil in the North Sea, political talks leading to what it was hoped would be devolution and the slow permeation into society of issues raised by the Women's Movement, created an optimism and a sense of possibility. The Scottish Arts Council began to fund commissions for playwrights and, although there were heavy macho plays to go with the dangers of life on the rigs, there was some room for manoeuvre. It is no accident that the first women writers to break into this culture, Marcella Evaristi, who is a committed feminist, and Liz Lochhead, who already had a considerable reputation as a poet working from the viewpoint of women's experience, have also proved to have great staying power.

Marcella Evaristi's recognition of the need 'to bear witness bravely' to women's experience, even when painful, has led her to develop a savage wit that scours the complacency of male chauvinism. The voices may not all be people we approve of but there is a need to understand how they come to be as they are. If radical theatre is about 'exposing absences in our cultural expression', it is also about women constructed as absence by that denying culture. 'Good art,' says Evaristi, 'gives people back their dignity. Which is exactly what our politics should look to'.[7] This involves a combination of feminism and socialism traversing theatrical forms and, especially, transgressing some of the constraints of comedy of social manners to reveal their hidden rules.

Dorothy and the Bitch (1977) takes the dark spirit of the end of Dorothy Parker's life to create a monologue of the bleakness of non-authenticity. Parker has degenerated, through self-created illusions and men's uses of them, into a whisky-soaked cynicism, driven by despair: she is fully aware of the total lack at the centre of her existence. *Scotia's Darlings* (1978) explores another lack: the emptiness of a Yuppie culture that rejects the whole background of nationality. *Hard to Get* (1980) prises open the relations between men and women through two couples who want both love and independence. The real discourse is the silencing and subjugation of the women's needs when they conflict with the needs of the dominant male. The play moves into increasingly dangerous areas uncovered by marriage from a light-hearted opening showing the courtship and bedding of the couples. The actual bed, as a learning arena, and the power of the language are potent signifiers. The women in this play at least have access to the idea of discourse, but the three girls growing up in *Wedding Belles and Green Grasses* (1981) live in a culture that requires them only to marry. Their patriarchal silencing is reinforced by the concept of chance, of the real decisions having nothing to do with them, like the children's game with cherry stones that spell out fate in the play.

The concept of cultural constructs as prisons is central to *Commedia* (1982/3), where the constraints of Italian Scottish culture are added to gender oppression and ageism. The play brings together two opposed theatrical genres, farce and naturalism, to create a heady mixture. Fascism, terrorism, death and the male gaze are explored from a woman's point of view. In claiming the right to be the centre of the narrative of her own life, and of the play, woman as subject subverts male signification systems and enacts – literally for the character and symbolically for the audience – an alternative, female, desire. The invisible becomes visible. The double oppression of macho Scottish culture and its pressure on gender is brilliantly taken on in *Terrestrial Extra* (1986). The symbiotic relationship of image and language in male discourse is ruptured when Eek and Um, two creatures from outer space, arrive by accident in Scotland, speaking a bizarre, rapid-fire language of their own. Through vivid verbal images that express their sampling of the local culture from sex to an Orange March, the aliens' nonsense reveals the non-sense of male discourse. They represent women's alien experience of their own culture as a result of their disenfranchisement by patriarchal discourse. Um, amazed by her body, announces 'I'm a democracy' in a most Cixous-like manner.

Evaristi's recent work has started from questions of art. *The Hat* (radio, 1989), a surrealist fantasy dealing with the real pain of loss, which uses linguistic playfulness to act as a release, enacts the serious question of woman as muse, her creative potential taken over to help male artists. *Visiting Company* (1989) moves cunningly from the awful stereotype of a Tory lady mouthing her husband's speech to a meeting of Conservatives for the Arts Alliance, to real sympathy when she realizes the horrors of the sexual politics of her marriage, and turns away from her husband's control to sign a petition against Clause 28.

Liz Lochhead has taken a trajectory from writing for revues in 1975 to becoming Writer in Residence for the Royal Shakespeare Theatre in 1989, in recognition of the quality and courage of her work. With a training as a visual artist, acknowledging developments in women's expressivity in dance and Performance Art, she has also found modes of verbal utterance that have revitalized Scots as a theatrical language whilst authenticating women's experience. Her plays deal in what Foucault described as the instability innate in the procedures of mastery in patriarchal society, unleashing links between desire and power, creating discourses that reclaim the repressed and deny prohibition and exclusion. Hers is, increasingly, imagistic work, where the play of significations across the central image precludes single readings. This is a passionate process that launches the audience into contradictions, into the questions that appear in the interstices of a complex intertext. This does not necessarily happen at a conscious level, but the audience is itself repositioned as subject in relation to its engagement. The text continues to cook, as it were, after the performance.

Indeed, for Lochhead texts continue to cook as long as they have a production life: by 1986 when John Carnegie directed *Blood and Ice*, probably her best known play, for Winged Horse,[8] it had undergone six sea-changes. *Blood and Ice*, which is about Mary Shelley, the creation of *Frankenstein*, and relationships between the Shelleys and Byron, explores the psychosexual roots of creativity and the contradictions inherent in an attempt to live liberated personal lives in an unchanged society where women were still hostages to biology, as Mary's many pregnancies and the death of the children make very clear. The whole question of giving birth to creativity is central to Lochhead's work. The play takes place inside Mary's head and has a structure akin to dream work, where the play becomes a place of proliferation and transformation of desires: symbols operate on the edge of danger, ready to slip out of control, just as the Creature – Mary/Lochhead's art – has a life and desires of its own. On the connotative level, the intertextuality brings the work of Wollstonecraft, Godwin, Shelley, Mary Shelley and Byron into a round dance with the ideas of the sexual revolution of the late 1960s, when one might argue that patriarchal politics also undermined the basis of supposed equality. The question of human responsibility is crucial to this process. In living out Utopian ideals, what does the Shelley ménage create? Byron suggests, by inference, the bloodshed that followed the French Revolution, the perversion of basic humanity. The fluidity of the form of the plays makes room for harsh facts and also for images of possibility, of the pleasures of creation, fantasy, desire as art.

In *Dracula* (1985) Lochhead again works through layers of fiction, including the major fiction that women have no right to sexuality, which transgresses male systems of control. The play reclaims the complex fascination with female desire that permeates Bram Stoker's original novel from horror movie stereotype. The referents in *Dracula* create an extraordinary texture of meaning, from Lucy's anorexia to the fear of menstruation/ creation that appears in all the bloody imagery. The fact that Dracula's home is the meeting point for all the armies that have ever passed through Europe connotes the conflation of sexual repression with the authoritarian personality's displacement of sexuality onto death. The repressed returns with a vengeance, erupting through discursive containment to examine the distortions produced by Victorian society. What happens to the young women in *Dracula* is made easier by the absence of any parents. In fact, there is a stunning lack of fathers in women's plays in Scotland, an absence that stands as an analogue for the loss of heritage through cultural imperialism: fatherlessness and loss are a pervasive feature of a mystification of patriarchal control.

In *Mary Queen of Scots Got Her Head Chopped Off*, a 1987 collaboration with Communicado, the key issues of nationality and what its history bequeaths to us are brought together with a questioning of gender division.

Fragmentation, contiguity and ambiguity are played across Mary, the body of the nation/woman, to examine the key concern: why are the kids at the end of the play as bigoted and sexist as they are? The reasons are embedded in two male repressions: John Knox's refusal to acknowledge the female in himself, and the Scottish lords' inability to accept that power is held by a young, sexual woman. Meanwhile in England, Elizabeth is having to behave like a man to keep her throne: Mary remarks that it would be easier if they could marry each other. The actresses playing Mary and Elizabeth also play each other's servants, emphasizing their strange symbiosis. Mary is a cultural construct inhabiting an impossible territory of absence, the sign of 'woman' alienated from herself with no real choice but self-destruction, in a country where even the image of the Virgin Mary has been ripped from experience by Knox. All the modes of pain and pleasure, and actual theatricality, are held together by the splendid invention of La Corbie, the ragged and sardonic black crow/Scotland, who has the capacity to move with her singing.

The kids at the end of the play reappear at the centre of *Jock Tamson's Bairns* (1990), a theatre piece that moved performance language in Scotland to another dimension, bringing painting, music and dance together with more traditional theatre skills, enacting a ritual of deconstruction and renovation on a central myth of Scottish culture – the Burns night. The silent figure of the Drunk Man/Burns is an open book on which the national culture might be inscribed: there are many analogies here with the ways in which gender inscription is enforced. The Bairns, a community of the dispossessed, frequently split into mutually uncomprehending gender camps to emphasize the alienation involved in the process. Lochhead provides the ground for the expression of small human dramas and an ironic voice within an abstract/ surrealist frame in which the central dramatic/emotional events are expressed through dance and music. Actors and audience alike need to decode the given amidst multi-layered images: a form of theatre Lochhead had been working towards for ten years, transformational generative theatre, where transcendence of the mundane is wedded to what Gerry Mulgrew of Communicado calls artistic orienteering, the radical integration of all the arts in creative meanings at every level, a free play of desire.

Sue Glover and Rona Munro emerged as writers in a cultural climate that had changed drastically from the 1970s: the failure of the 1979 Devolution Bill and the rise of Thatcherism, accompanied by years of recession, led to a feeling that Scottish identity was again being repressed. It was no longer Scotland's oil. On the other hand, a visit from the Women's Theatre Group had triggered the establishment of Mother Hen, a co-operative touring company that devised all its own shows, in 1980. Despite a hostile climate in Scottish theatre, the company had some success, and its pop group, Polly and the Phones, broke away to develop something of a cult following. Jules Cranfield, who founded Focus Theatre Company (Scotland), a group with

clearer feminist aims in 1982, was also one of the founders of the Women
Live festivals (1982–4), which first gave space to Rona Munro.

Sue Glover's work focuses on difference, transgression and the outcast as
images central to women's experience. *The Seal Wife* (1980), a reworking
of the old legend, deals with the limitations of the rational in love, the
fascination with difference that later wants to tame otherness, the very
image of sexuality as chaos that is implicit in the boundary-crossing capacity
of the seal people, and builds to the inevitability of death. Two sisters who
scavenge the beach reinforce the image of marginality – they 'always kept
hoosies without fathers', but there is a sort of optimism at the end as Alec
understands enough about his seal baby to become furious at the idea of
registering it: how do you register the child of your fantasy, of your inner
drives? The audience also brings the mass media images of seal culling and
man's wanton destruction of the earth as a powerful intertext to the story.

In *An Island in Largo* (1981) she explores narrativity to present transgression as the central drama, through a sort of magic realism. The play is based
on a real person, Alexander Selkirk, the original of Defoe's Robinson
Crusoe. His inscription as an outcast starts early, and is causal in his aban-
donment on the island. Even on his return with plunder from the Third
World, puritanical Scots life cannot accommodate him, nor he face it. We
see how difference is constructed, how authorship is attributed to its victims, how – as a strategy for survival – it produces worse extremes. The
power of value judgements is linked to the theme of exploitation and the
experience of the Other is placed in a global context.

The Straw Chair (1988), also based on a true story, offers an archetypical
experience of woman as other, removed from history and silenced, the
woman herself construed as a sign of transgression. Lord Grange abducted
his young wife who would not divorce him, announced that she was dead
and buried a coffin full of stones. She was moved violently from island to
island until she arrived at Hirta (St Kilda), the rockiest and furthest away,
preventing her from ever communicating with the outside world. Set on
Hirta, the play shows how the very act of utterance can be sabotaged by
male power that defines women physically and symbolically as being
beyond the margins. Language becomes a way to recreate her own realities
when out of her normal context, but this takes on a quality of obsession, of
madness. The final image of Lady Grange 'writing a letter' without paper
and locked in a silence of desolation, is very hard to take. *Bondagers* (1991) is
a major achievement. The dynamic of the music of the language, the
integral chorus and dance sequences, power through the lived realities of
the particular serfdom of the nineteenth-century female farm labourer. This
lost history explodes into a vision of woman *as* local culture, with fierce
pride in her work and status. A powerful web of individual experience of
work, sexuality, madness, and the instability of the class system, produces a
powerful insight into collective life.

Rona Munro has also experimented with forms of expression that are rooted in the local but also capable of handling world politics, relating gender, imperialism and military violence. Her work consistently refuses to concede perpetual strength to patriarchy, opening up other symbolic orders. *Fugue* (1983) operates a multiple counterpoint of personality inside the head of a woman. Existential questioning and psychological delving combine to create a thriller, where fear is almost consciously sought to counter the entropy of the mundane, to the point where the woman must reconnect herself to a vital female principle.

Piper's Cave (1985), a complex as yet unstaged attempt to address the issue of male violence, drawing on the fable of the piper who took his harmonies into the hill, uses a beach as a liminal symbolic space at the edge of the known, a place where things might be remade. *The Way to Go Home* (1987) also deconstructs the myth of male violence, stripping away the glamour of the male genre of the chase/thriller movie through a female perspective to reveal the horrific details of blood spilt and peoples crushed beneath. This tightly timed trip through the poisons of cultural and gender imperialism, in which the scenes are given precise times of day through a period of about 28 hours moves the action on with great urgency. It also allows time for jokes against the odds, and for us to discover what kind of human beings the two Scottish women protagonists are. *Bold Girls* (1990) which won the Susan Smith Blackburn Award for the best play by a woman in the English-speaking world in 1991, also presents women trapped in a brutal patriarchal culture, using the ingrained black humour of life in Northern Ireland to subvert the law of the (absent) father in West Belfast. In de-sentimentalizing working-class popular comedy, and inter-cutting other levels of both the inner and material lives of the protagonists, Munro explores the relativity of truth for women coping with the everyday realities of life in a war zone.

Anne Downie is best known for her two novel adaptations, *The White Bird Passes* (1986) and *The Yellow on the Broom* (1989). In *The White Bird Passes*, a version of Jessie Kesson's semi-autobiographical novel set in North East Scotland in the 1920s, she contrasts the oppressed, dependent women's experience of poverty with the sturdy independence of an old tinker woman. The play is both a forceful reclamation of the past and a moving and funny testimony to the resilience of the human spirit. Marginalization from mainstream society links both Downie's adaptations: *The Yellow on the Broom*, taken from Betsy Whyte's well-loved elegy for the end of a way of life among the travelling people, uses the idea of telling stories round the fireside as its frame. This episodic structure, developed by song, enables the audience itself to become a repository for the memory of this different life. Her bingo play, *Waiting on One* (1987), also involves the audience actively, through playing bingo themselves and through various Brechtian devices, such as a Christmas in July pantomime, which presents the topsy-turvydom of capitalist logic. The play affirms the positive side of bingo – the hassle-free atmosphere for single women, company for the lonely – but does not delve into the darker side of gambling.

Two important new writers, Ann Marie Di Mambro and Paula Macgee, set up Annexe Theatre in 1986, using the Strathclyde University Drama Centre; Macgee is still deeply involved with its policy of encouraging new writers. Di Mambro's great strength in constructing narratives and creating credible characters was clear from her first play *Hocus Pocus* (1986), which deals with the failures of the church and the ways in which it aggravates women's problems. *Visible Differences* (1986), a Theatre in Education play toured as part of Theatre About Glasgow's anti-racist year, brings together a fascist thug who has broken up a multiracial festival, and subsequently blinded himself breaking up a phone box, with a young Sikh who manages to reason him into acknowledging that difference alone is not a cause for contempt. A similar theme emerges in the monologue *Joe* (1987). An elderly Scottish–Italian woman visiting her husband in hospital talks through her experiences of being an immigrant and the prejudice she encountered. Their neighbours, the Patels, now suffer similar prejudices: 'How many times they write "Wops go home" on the shop window? Used to be Wops, now it's Wogs. Makes you think, Joe, after 40 years they change just one letter.' In *Sheila* (1988) two working–class painters educate a very empty-headed young student. Its social comedy mode allows the men revealing comments about gender, but the lack of explanation about Sheila's background to explain her vacuousness is problematic. The monologue *The Letter Box* (1989) presents a chilling portrait of marital violence, through the voice of a battered wife who has been thrown out of the house trying to calm her small daughter through the letter-box. Even more chilling is her attempt to cover up for her husband and make sure the child tells no-one. In *Tally's Blood* (1990) di Mambro returns to the Scottish–Italian experience, this time from the perspective of an Italian woman who has to find a way to overcome her prejudice against the Scots. Reviewers found the play too soap operatic in structure, thus raising the question of the extent to which a patriarchal narrative form may undermine a reversal of viewpoint or, conversely, whether accessibility is in fact a good way of quietly involving your audience in issues they would not otherwise address with ease.

Paula Macgee uses a wide variety of forms from the naturalism of her investigation of a Catholic upbringing, *In Nomine Patris*, to the episodic construction of the 1986 TIE play *Spacemen and Party Frocks*, or the cartoon/grotesque juxtapositions of images of breasts and food in her truly televisual TV play *Breast is Best*, triggered by a real incident in, of all places, the health food café of the avant-garde Third Eye Centre in Glasgow, when she and a friend were thrown out for breastfeeding their infants. *Daddy's Wedding* is a rare Scottish exploration of a father–daughter relationship. The daughter wonders if the ten years of bitter silence that have frozen and controlled the household will spread over into her wedding celebrations. When the car with the wedding dress in it is stolen, and the father accuses the mother of stupidity, she breaks her silence to give him an ultimatum: change his behaviour or be left alone after the wedding. The car, joyously, is returned with good wishes for the wedding from the thieves and the father, unstereotypically, gives a good caring speech on the day.

Aileen Ritchie's plays, mostly written for Clyde Unity, a company with sexual politics at the root of their work and the only Scottish company staging plays about homosexual experience as a matter of policy prior to 1990, have accessibility to a community audience as a key priority. She is mining a rich seam of women's and sibling friendships in texts, full of lively demotic language in a line of descent from Ena Lamont Stewart. She deals with a need to re-evaluate women in terms of their construction in the family, and a consideration of personal histories as repositories of the effects of gender battles. *Can Ye Sew Cushions?* was an angry response to the stage adaptation of *The Gorbals Story*, which glamorized the violence of the hard man and denied the woman's point of view in the book. *Shang-a-Lang* is an interrogation of friendship. Senga and Tam have been left alone when their mother goes off with a lover. Senga and her friend Kirsty are part of a gang that follows the Bay City Rollers and can dive into their routines at a moment's notice. Senga's developing need for independence is, unfortunately, crushed at the end of the play, when Tam's needs override hers, and she stays to look after Kirsty, who is now pregnant by Tam, rather than leaving for London. *Asking for It* (1989), a Traverse play, places women from the same deprived background in a Yuppie flat in the city in the course of a night on the town. It is an uneasy play, which first asks the audience to make value judgements about the women, and then to learn the different truths about the total oppression of their lives and the ways in which hardness is a shell developed for self-protection.

There are some positive factors, which have made the climate in Scotland less hostile to women's writing since 1980. An increase in the number of women working as Artistic Directors and Administrators made the first approach to a theatre a less alienating experience. Scotland was also unusual in having a preponderance of women newspaper critics, so that new plays by women are received without that coy 'edge of the unfamiliar' attitude that undermines much reviewing elsewhere. Stewart Conn at BBC Radio, Tom McGrath in Edinburgh, the Scottish Society of Playwrights, and the Edinburgh Playwrights' Workshop have given support and feedback and helped form networks among authors. The infrastructure has become firmer: the cultural climate of the 1990s embraces Women's Studies, political groupings like Women's Forum and A Woman's Claim to Right, local government women's committees, the Scottish Arts Lobby/Scottish TUC working party on women and the arts, and two organizations working in arts and media: Women 2000 and Women in Profile.

The availability of commissions for stage, radio and TV has allowed consistent career patterns to develop and allowed a distinctive women's voice to be recognized as a vital aspect of Scottish culture. There have been setbacks: the hot-housing of new writers has sometimes destroyed their self-confidence by exposing unfinished work to the critics. The talented Catherine Lucy Czerkawka's experiences during the preparation of her *Heroes and Other* for the Scottish Theatre Company, when she found her work being unacceptably changed by the director, helped to drive her from the theatre and clarified the need for control over working practices. Economic necessity may also lead established writers to take on too many commissions each year, not leaving enough time for reflection, or for the longer gestation period for full length plays.

Nevertheless, there is now a body of important plays that deserve a place in the repertoire of the whole United Kingdom, but this will not happen until more Scottish plays have been published and the Scottish theatre has been recognized as a national, not a regional, theatre.

9

An alphabet of apocrypha: Collaborations and explorations in women's theatre

Susan Croft and April de Angelis

A is for apocrypha

A writing or statement of doubtful authenticity, spurious, un-canonical.

(*Oxford English Dictionary*).

Anonymous was a woman, it has been said: in the case of collaborative work it may be that she was women. An unstable beast to accommodate, perhaps refusing definition, the multi-authored text has been central to the development of women's theatre and performance. The script may be collectively devised; improvised and then scripted by a writer; there may not be a recorded script; if there is, mere words may not convey the essence of the final performance; women's experiments in physical or visual theatre have been sparsely documented, though some videos may exist. If such material is available in manuscript, it is even less likely to be published than scripts by a single woman playwright. An experimental or devised piece, very personal to the experience of the creators may be irrelevant for future production, but the problem of recording still remains.[1] Although companies working in other non-traditional experimental modes have begun to address this, women's theatre has often lacked the resources and will to document work. Hence, collectively created scripts which were, and to a lesser extent continue to be central to the development of such theatre, rarely exist, neither do notations of key works by women performance and visual theatre artists. This essay therefore draws upon a number of other resources including personal testimonies in attempting to explore these significant areas of work.

Approach

Enjoying relatively little critical attention, often presented as a narrow area of concern, thus easily marginalized, women's theatre is in fact a vast, diverse area encompassing a multitude of approaches, forms, politics, processes and visions. To avoid imposing false cohesion, wishing to reflect the vitality of debate, and to embrace differences and contradictions, we have alluded to as many companies, artists and works as possible. The Alphabet formula allows us to be inclusive and eclectic, colliding interviews, facts, quotations and speculations without imposing a limiting uniformity of discourse.

Audience

Angela Brinkworth, founder member in 1982 of ReSisters Theatre Company, spoke in interview of their debut, *The Self-Defence Show*:

> We got our audiences primarily through word of mouth – we had no money for publicity, telephone calls, etc. Gradually we got bookings in community centres, employment centres, women's events, women's centres. We did what what self-defence classes did, we validated other women's experiences by sharing our own. We had tremendous feedback . . . We also had after-show discussions, which were often very painful. I wrote a poem *No, I'm Not a Mother* about my experience of abortion after being raped. One woman said 'Haven't you thought there might be a woman in the audience who might get very upset about this.' I felt guilty and then I thought – it's OK for them to be upset – I'm not going to protect them.'[2]

Feminist theatre in the 1970s and early 1980s aimed to create and respond to an audience that felt free to challenge, question, add to or deduct from the constantly evolving show. Excisions could cause disagreement about what was to be seen as offensive – theatrically or politically – in terms of representation of class, race, sexuality or disability. New personal and collective demands were made on actresses by this continual process of self-questioning and debate, while for audiences of women, a public arena and dialogue space was created, where for the first time they could express their opinions, responses, anger and grievances about highly volatile personal subject matter from abuse to motherhood, body image to racism. Small companies found it hard to cope with the needs their work released; ReSisters stopped having formal post-show discussions because of the virulence of some remarks addressed to them.

. . . Accessibility, Anger, Art, Adaptation, Arts Council, Agitprop . . .

B is for bodies

Problems associated with representing women's bodies on stage have been addressed by many women's theatre groups. Difficult questions were raised

through engaging with controversial material, which explored women's
sexuality, cutting into new territory like problems of its presentation,
which avoided collapsing into stereotyping. How could issues about the use
of women's bodies in our culture be tackled without collusion, compound-
ing the usual objectification? How could actresses challenge the need to
conform to a male image of beauty if they were to get work in an industry
that prioritizes attractiveness? Other women have been frustrated by what
they feel is a puritanical streak in the Women's Movement and women's
theatre, which denied women the right to dress up their bodies to look
'sexy'. Much experimental work in the 1980s began to address these issues
of inherent conflict:

> The second room was the womb of art;
> An artist, who's a man, is sitting on the floor and
> holding an easel or a mirror. He can only stare at
> what he sees. All he sees are women . . .
> Either butch or fem, the women the warrior sees are
> warriors . . .
> The women the artist sees on his right are all enslaved or
> imprisoned . . .
> On no side, from no perspective do men and women mutually see
> each other or mutually act with each other.
>
> (Kathy Acker, *Lulu*, 1981[3])

> *Dirt* would be about performance, the sex of theatre and the theatre
> of sex. The intention was to research prostitution and develop a
> common viewpoint, but the issues constantly gave rise to problems
> of interpretation. The need to express a 'correct' viewpoint in
> terms of the women's movement was important, but within it were
> many conflicting attitudes. The material was dense, contentious,
> the desire to use new media at times got in the way of clear
> expression.
>
> (Stella Hall on Bloodgroup[4])

The re-writing of women's bodies is an element significant for a possible
theatrical 'Écriture Feminine', discussed under the heading Deconstruction.

C is for collaborative

Comments made about collaborative works may be made about women's
works in general. Kathleen Betsko has said that her mass reading of such
plays for *Interviews with Women Playwrights*, gave the impression of 'non-
plays' (spurious . . . uncanonical[5]), as their approach rejected traditional
'well-made' forms, while the refusal of a single authorial voice redoubled
their unacceptability within the traditional critical canon:

There is no reason to think that the form of the epic or of the poetic
play suits a woman any more than the sentence suits her. But all the
older forms of literature were hardened and set by the time she became a writer.

(Virginia Woolf[6])

Context

Cathy Itzin's *Stages in the Revolution* documents the emergence of women's
theatre groups from the post-1968 socialist theatre movement. Listing
changes reveal a development pattern: shows by CAST (Cartoon Archetypal
Slogan Theatre) are in 1966–7 listed as 'by CAST with Ronald Muldoon'
and 'by CAST with John Arden and Margaretta D'Arcy', indicating a collaborative process. From 1968, the first wholly-devised group shows are listed:
agitprop players produced six issue-based shows, and the Pip Simmons
Group two, while after 1971 occur 'Albert Hunt et al' and 'Hull Truck with
Mike Bradwell'; then plays listed as 'by the company' include those for Belt
and Braces, 7:84, Sal's Meat Market, Gay Sweatshop and Red Ladder. Although theatre venues and arts centres are still listed as producing single-
writer works, almost every contemporary radical group produced devised
shows. This context of creative collectivism is paralleled in the evolutionary
pattern of women's productions. Although Women's Theatre Group
(WTG) produced six shows between 1974 and 1978, writers are not credited
until October 1978 for *Hot Spot* by WTG with Eileen Fairweather and
Melissa Murray.[7] Monstrous Regiment have followed a similar traceable
movement from the collective, to the individual writer with the collective,
to the individual writer.[8] This movement is also traceable in political theatre
in general, although WTG have now returned to commissioning writers to
work with the company, particularly to give black companies a stronger
voice. Like Theatre of Black Women and Theatre Centre Women's Company, they have encouraged black writers previously involved in devising/
performance: Adjoa Andoh, Sandra Yaw, Lennie St Luce, Bernadine Evaristo and Patricia Hilaire. Gay Sweatshop developed in the opposite direction
– from Jill Posener's *Any Woman Can*, to 'by the company with Drew
Griffiths' to devising. Collective devising by women was essentially political
– born of egalitarianism and a dearth of scripts – particularly concerned with
consciousness-raising for both group and audience. Where the upsurge of
'angry' playwriting in the late 1950s and early 1960s had been essentially
male, with rare exceptions like Ann Jellicoe and Shelagh Delaney, the
Women's Movement later began to validate women's experience, giving
them confidence, opportunity and the development of skills – the collaborative process becoming a starting point for many writers recorded here. Although, like the Movement, the 1970s women playwrights tended to be
white and middle class, the return to devising variants by WTG, for instance,
is a policy giving more women, especially minorities, a voice, 'And

undoubtedly, I thought, looking along the shelf where there are no plays by
women, her work would have gone unsigned.'

(Virginia Woolf, of 'Judith Shakespeare'[9])

Collaboration

> How better to enter a new territory but together? How could the
> strange landscape be mapped singly when no apprenticeships had been
> served? The Women's Movement had accentuated the personal as
> political . . . Mined through self-analysis in a collective context, the
> examination of the marginalized but massive catalogue of women's
> personal experience to be discovered as political through sharing,
> identifying, recognizing, naming, (entailed that) consciousness-raising
> was done in groups.[10]

Presenting this experience was inevitably through a collective voice:

> The energy of similarity, shouting into the silence, 're-placing' our-
> selves was powerful and shared. In re-writing ourselves on stage, in
> re-writing the world, new methods were forged from desire and
> necessity . . . we were not ready to abdicate (our potential) once again
> to the expert, to single authorship (male) . . . As a product it was not
> finished. Its voices often refused the normal hierarchy of importance.
> Upon occasion it spoke of archetypes and not individuals. It was ill-
> resourced and lacked 'polish'. As to the process, often valued above
> the product, it was often stormy and explosive; the material emotion-
> al, uncharted, the structures untried, unordained.[11]

Clean Break

Founded in 1979 by Jennifer Hicks and Jacqueline Holborough after meeting in Ashcombe Grange prison, the group aimed both to inform the public
of the experiences, conditions and lack of resources for women prisoners
and to counteract the damaging effects of thwarted creativity, through
providing active opportunities. Linking women's confinement within and
without prison the work celebrates the liberation sparked by sharing personal stories. Despite eleven highly productive years none of the group's
scripts or other material has been published.[12]

**Comedy, Collectives, Career, Confrontation, Critics, Cabaret,
Contradiction, Contract, Consciousness-raising, Copyright, Community,
Children . . .**

D is for dreams . . . desire . . .

In *Pyeyucca*, something I wrote from improvisations on the floor, we
had two characters, Laura, a very contemporary Black woman, and

her alter ego, Pyeyucca who spoke poetry through the piece. She
would say things to influence Laura – she's Laura's imaginary friend.
She plays with her, she's very wild, very free. That's cut out of Laura
by parents and school. Laura becomes very rigid . . . Pyeyucca . . .
tries to get back into Laura through poetry and song. By the end of the
play, Laura's body begins to crack, her emotions are alive, her awareness of sexism and racism have grown, she brings to life all the things
that have been suppressed in her by the society she's living in.'
                    (Bernadine Evaristo of Theatre of Black Women[13])

Whereas during the 1970s, born through the socialist alternative theatre
movement, much collaborative theatre had been in the 'upfront' feminist/
revolutionary mode, the 1980s saw the emergence of more poetic, experimental and visual theatre female/ritualistic forms.[14] These, rather than
directly raising consciousness, attempted to explore the contradictions between the conscious and the unconscious, as in the work of Changing
Women, Hard Corps and Monstrous Regiment at this time.[15]

In the Performance Art world also, feminist sensibilities grew, coupled
with a desire to create new performance forms. A 1980 series of articles in
Performance Magazine examined the absence of women in the medium's
history, and the presence of male – often sexual and masturbatory –
imagery in the 1970s. New developments in performance and visual theatre
were then influenced by the art world of happenings, environmental theatre, Grotowskian experiment, explorations into ritual, surrealism, social
and political ideas including anarchist politics and Situationism . . . a world
strongly male-dominated. Writing of her training at Leeds School of Art,
working with influential artists such as John Fox of Welfare State International and Jeff Nuttall and John Darling of the People Show, Geraldine
Pilgrim, later founder of Hesitate & Demonstrate, said, 'The ultimate put-
down was for one's work to be called feminine.'[16] Gradually women in
performance art did develop their own visions. Twin strands thus contributed to the exploration of a new female theatrical language: the new
reflection on gender within performance art and the socialist feminist companies starting to experiment with different physical, verbal and visual
form. This movement towards the more visual and experimental theatrical
languages, drawing on dreams and contradictory desires was informed by a
growing fascination in feminism and on the left with psychoanalysis and
issues around sexuality and eroticism. Thus, in the 1980s, debate moved
from politically 'correct' behaviours and slogans towards exploration of
material from dreams and the unconscious, which informed the development of new structures that challenged traditional forms.[17] Women's use of
these forms, which inherently resist mainstream critical analysis with their
frequently collaborative creative process, compounded their marginalization, their status as apocrypha.

Deconstruction

Critical theorists in semiotics, such as Roland Barthes and Michel Foucault have had a major influence on the development of feminist film theory, where writers like Laura Mulvey, Annette Kuhn and Teresa de Lauretis have examined representations of women, starting from the visual image and how women's role as signifier generates meanings.[18] The influence of their theoretical studies of classical and experimental film texts by women, which challenge traditional readings, may be traced in theatre, especially the performance art area, in certain one-woman shows. These, for example Annie Griffin's *Almost Persuaded*, may employ techniques of dislocation of image, music and text to comment on the fragmentation of women's self-image and desires. Griffin here uses the cultural icon of the country and western star, while in *Blackbeard the Pirate* cross-dressing confronts the dual male/female image. Like doubling, such theatrical techniques are amongst those that both problematize the stereotypical presentation of the female body and are associated with women's search for especial performance strategies and language.

Theories of deconstruction developed by Jacques Derrida and those psychoanalytic theories extended from those of Jacques Lacan by French feminists like Julia Kristeva, Luce Irigaray and Helene Cixous, have certainly had some impact both on British novelists and other feminist critiques of female representation in literature. These are only just beginning to affect theatre criticism and creative practices, but even the theatricality of much of the language employed by such deconstructionists suggests that the collision of theory and practice could provide powerful possibilities associated with the challenge of experimenting with form, language and the construction of meaning. The possibility of what a theatrical 'Écriture Feminine' might mean informs much of the discussion in this book. The notion extends further than the written text, to the kinetics of the medium; visual presentation, performance, gesture, movement, voice, structure, use of time, space and the relationships between them. The potential for imaging new ways of working is suggested by the near homonym of the words jouer and jouir – the former meaning 'to play', the second approximating both to enjoy and to orgasm – and the slippage in English between to play and the play.[19] The notion of play, central to deconstruction, challenges the fixed relationships between the sign/signifier and the signified of semiotics, asserting that any text is not a self-enclosed model, but that meaning is always deferred by the play of signification. The playfulness of this concept suggests new forms in theatre, which rather than recreating the traditional well-made play with its one climax, similar to the single male orgasm, opens up the possibilities of multi-orgasmic theatre, playing with and subverting the unified authority of the single authored theatre text. The link with jouissance and the erotics of writing created by l'Écriture Feminine is clear:

In the infancy of the work of art, there is the staff, its terrors, its questions, its who–will–I–be?, it's dark rooms full of demons . . . Enter then the Others! I have the honour to be the stage for the other . . . Free of "I" they enter and enchant me. At last, theatre! The theatre is a palace of other people. It lives on the desire for the other, for all the others. And on the desire for the desire for the others: for the audience, for the actors.

(Helene Cixous from *Incarnation*[20])

. . . Disability, Diversity, Demystification, Director, Difference, Devising

E is for Experiment, Entertainment, Ex-centricity, Equal Opportunities

F is for funding

We missed funding. We applied too late to the GLC, they were on the way out, and stressed that they couldn't fund us unless we had a black performer . . . We missed being funded as a lesbian group . . . the Arts Council . . . judged us by their criteria which had nothing to do with us . . . Funding's been a nightmare. The funding bodies make incredible demands on companies without giving them the resources to fulfill them – you can't develop without money. It merely eases their conscience.

(Siren Theatre Company[21])

. . . Fringe, Friendship, Fear, Family . . .

G is for Greenham, Gender, GLC, Growth, Group Dynamics

H is for humour . . .

Question: How many feminists does it take to change a lightbulb?
Answer: That's not funny!

The stereotypical image of the Women's Movement as humourless seems in itself laughable to those women involved in collaborative theatre, where humour is a vitally important tool and area of exploration. In the 1990s the roles available to funny women are infinitely diverse; French and Saunders, Victoria Wood, Rose English and others have gone far beyond the old male dichotomies, which defined women according to their sexual 'attractiveness' as busty blonde or frustrated old maid. Humour as a way of taking back power, relieving pain and refusing to be the butt of male jokes now provides a collective sharing of anecdote and experience in women's theatre, where taboo subjects can be aired; menstruation, food, hip size, orgasms – 'Mummy, what's an orgasm?'; 'I don't know. Ask your father'.

Groups like Beryl and the Perils, Bloomers, Cunning Stunts and Spare Tyre pioneered a new physical comedy for women, providing a rich history as recorded in *The Joke's On Us* by Morwenna Banks and Amanda Swift in 1987, and opening up possibilities for individuals and groups to be funny in ways previously unacceptable. Some, still uncompromising, have entered the mainstream, whilst such humour has fuelled the work of playwrights including Sharman MacDonald, Liz Lochhead, Claire Dowie, Claire McIntyre and Marcella Evaristi, some of whom have worked as stand-up comediennes. This early work helped create a climate, language and aud- ience vital to later developments:

> Today's recipe is for Auntie Josephine's Revenge Pud . . . I don't think you'll have any problem getting the ingredients and you may feel like being adventurous and adding a little something of your own!
>   9 oz finely ground broken glass
>   For the ashtray he smashed on my head
>   10 oz marinated fag ends
>   For the one he stubbed out on me in bed
>   A chopped durex found in his pocket for the
>   contraception he didn't use
>   A shredded pawn ticket for my wedding and eternity ring
>   256 crushed valium for the anti-depressants the doctor
>   gave me because of him . . .
> Now I have gone over the top with the valium, but it's never in short supply and so easy for us women to get hold of . . .
>   (ReSisters from *The Refuge Show*, 1984)

. . . Hierarchy, History . . .

I is for Image, Identity, Identity Politics, Informal Networks, Interviews, Improvisation . . .

L is for list . . .

The following is a composite list covering British feminist theatre com- panies, projects and some individual performance artists. Women perfor- mance artists have not been included unless their work focuses in some form on women's issues. Plays produced by collaborative work processes, individual plays produced through workshops and published performance texts and documentation are listed in the Bibliography. Mixed companies like TIE, community groups and new writing companies, which may have policies towards women's writing and collaborative work, have not been listed below. Individual companies may be unchronicled and ephemeral, so the information will inevitably have omissions. Some information resources

formerly held by Women In Entertainment are available at the Fawcett
Library in London, whilst the New Playwrights Trust, the Lesbian Archive,
the Theatre Museum Study Room and the British Library are useful, as was
the British Theatre Association.[22] Reviews, listings and articles occur in
*Spare Rib, Time Out, City Limits, The Guardian, The Plot, Plays & Players,
Women's Review, Outwrite, Everywoman, Drama.*

Bemarro Sisters
Black Swan
Blood Group
Burnt Bridges
Beryl & the Perils
Beavers
Bloomers
Bag & Baggage
Box 3

Camouflage
Shirley Cameron
Changing Women
Charabanc
Character Ladies
Chuffinelles
Clapperclaw
Clean Break
Common Ground
Cunning Stunts

Rose English

Female Trouble

Gay Sweatshop
Annie Griffin

Hard Corps
Hesitate & Demonstrate
Hogwash
Hormone Imbalance

Ladies & Gentlemen
les oeufs malades
Lip Service
Little Women

Magdalena Project
Major Division
Manchester Women Live
The Millies
Monstrous Regiment
Mother Hen
Moving Parts
Mrs Worthington's Daughters

No Boundaries

Options Ltd

Parker & Klein
Pirate Jenny

Radical Actresses Guild
Raving Beauties
Red Ladder
Red Rag
ReSisters
Red Stockings
Rubber Jennies

Sadista Sisters
Second Wave Young Women's
    Project
Scarlet Harlets
Anne Seagrave
Sensible Footwear
Shameful Practice
Siren
Sola Energy
Spare Tyre
Sphinx

Tattycoram

Team Two   Women's Company
That's Not It   Women & Theatre (Birmingham)
Theatre of Black Women   Women's Comedy Workshop
Theatre Centre Women's   Women's Theatre Group
  Company   Women's Playhouse Trust
Three Women Mime   Women Under Glass
Trouble & Strife   Wayward Women

Visible Difference   Sylvia Ziranek

. . . Language, Loss, Love, Longing . . .

M is for Magdalena Project

Established in 1986, the Magdalena Project grew from discussions three years earlier between Jill Greenhalgh of Cardiff Laboratory Theatre, Geddy Aniksdal of Grenland Friteater and Julia Varley of Odin Teatret, about the way in which women's concerns were not addressed in male-dominated experimental theatre companies or their spheres of work. They wished to explore the possibilities of women's creativity and a female language in theatre, naming the Project after Mary Magdalen, the powerful and sexual figure relegated to the margins of Christianity as women's art work is marginalized. The first major event, in 1986, was an International Festival of Women in Experimental Theatre at Cardiff, involving thirty women from fifteen different countries who performed and ran participant workshops. Very successful, it generated new questions, areas for exploration and potential collaboration – since followed by stage projects, experimental voice workshops, women working with children, process and solo performances. While retaining their Cardiff base, Magdalena have also produced a collaborative show *Nominatae Filiae* with an international female cast under Zofia Kalinska, a Polish director, around the theme of demonic women. Despite relatively little exploration of the theatre-writer's role in developing a new female theatre language, the Magdalena will, with its indefatigable director Jill Greenhalgh, continue to confront contemporary feminist theory, mythology and theatrical practice with enormously fruitful results.[23]

. . . Mother, Men, Madness, Murder, Material, Meaning, Mime, Menstruation, Marginalization, Music . . .

N is for nineties

The future for women's theatre in the 1990s, as for writers working in the collaborative/experimental process, looks uncertain. The 1980s saw the demise of many women's companies; the survivors finding that scripting and devising processes with writers became a luxury that funding bodies were increasingly unwilling or unable to support. The Arts Council speaks the Thatcherite language of the 'pursuit of excellence' – as opposed to access – imaging excellence as the play springing like Athena fully armed from her father's head. This is the traditional mythology of authorship, which has always denied not only female creativity, but also collective creation and the interdependence of the individual writer and the world. Under Thatcherism, the emphasis lay on the marketable product, the management that hires staff for a particular production and value for money – small casts, compact sets and efficiency – rather than on process, experiment, collaboration and collectivity.[24] Further pressure on venues has meant that new writing, generally seen as a financial risk, was only worth taking on in a studio theatre, and subsequently many of these have closed, accounted as uneconomic and thus the first area for cuts when budget deficits began to bite.[25] Hence, women's writing, as with other experimental new work more volatile in process, is hard to anticipate and advance-sell as a distinct product. Inheritances of the collaborative process that remain include workshops exploring ideas towards a play or script-in-progress with a director, writer and actors; these have become common. Rarely are they part of an evolution towards eventual full production; the workshop often, for economic reasons, becoming an end in itself. Although money for this kind of developmental work, which is relatively cheap, may be available from trusts, foundations, Regional Arts Associations, even community-orientated business sponsors, a divorce of process from product is counterproductive. Meanwhile, mainstage presentations have become increasingly 'safe bets' or revivals, as rehearsal time has dwindled to two or even three weeks. With a number of theatres – regional, London and touring – on the brink of closing, the situation looks likely to get worse.[26]

Positive signs, though hard to identify, are the sheer persistence of groups and writers that continue to emerge; student, community and youth theatre initiatives – often collaborative – continue to provide a seed-bed from which new writers grow, despite the dearth of professional production. Many companies of the seventies and eighties, tenaciously defying economic difficulties, have adapted their work to changing circumstances, refining their processes and group dynamics, thus producing deepened work reflective both of changes in the Women's Movement and of complex debate within feminist literature. Meanwhile women playwrights and directors nurtured through the early collaborative process have, retaining their approaches, begun to move into larger theatres.

. . . Non-plays . . .

A critic once described my work as having a weak narrative. The critic came in looking for it and didn't find it. *Clam* was turned down by the

Arts Council when Bloodgroup applied for funds to put it on. They didn't know what it was. When it comes to definition they say 'Are you a poet or a playwright? Or are you a short storywriter?' They're very suspicious of people who diversify. They never asked Shakespeare if he was a poet or a playwright.

(Deborah Levy[27])

O is for Order, Orgasm, One-Woman Plays, Other . . .

. . . Open Texts

Much collaborative work is aimed to create spaces for the audience to identify with and implicitly add their own experiences to those being voiced by the actors. Thus such performance could be resonant with ritual communion, where the relationship between actor and audience was of participation in the shared experience of recounting and telling stories previously denied a public space:

> In Ireland still you have the Seannachies. They are storytellers. Because they told the story better than anybody else . . . the audience is there to actually add in to the storyteller. Now I have an interesting tape which is on this woman Biddy Early who is a nineteenth century clairvoyant and healer who challenged the clergy at a time when the Brits were trying to reform and centralise the structures of Ireland – because of early nineteenth century Land Reform . . . everyone around (the Seannachie) is adding things in. So if he says 'It was a narrow lonely road' they would add 'In the middle of the night.'
>
> (Margaretta D'Arcy[28])

P is for personal experience

> My name is Elzeta and I'm forty-seven years old. Me Madda and Farda were in England saving money fe send fe us, but meantime me and Manley was living with me Auntie . . . Uncle John, a tall brown skin man da lean him head against de door frame. Come ya, Elzeta, do! . . . He ask me how I was and I jump upon him big bed from England and start talk. Then him say – you know Elzeta, in dis world nobody get someting for nutting. You understan? Me say yes, but I didn't know what he was talkin about. Him start sweat on him nose so me decide to leave. As me try to get off de bed, he try and stop me. Me run for de door, but him reach it first and bolt it. Him say he woulda lick me if I didn't lie down pon de bed and take off me panty . . . Afterwards him get up and start to bawl, please Elzeta, no tell nobody, please.
>
> (ReSisters *Refuge Show*, 1984)

For an audience to hear the actor speaking so immediately of a powerful personal experience in an area usually surrounded by silence, brought a shock of recognition. Immensely moved and disturbed to hear their own seeming hidden experience validated, it could have felt like a betrayal to discover the experience was not the actor's own. Hence, especially around sensitive issues of 'coming out', Gay Sweatshop made the decision to employ only gay actors to play gay characters.

Q is for Questioning Orthodoxies, Quality

R is for redefining

> We know you are looking. Should we be? Shouldn't we be? After all they are performing. Or aren't they? . . . Bloodgroup constantly set up and knock down our notions of what is and what isn't performance in the theatrical sense, replacing it with the preparation and the after-taste, the leftout bits, the beyond the wings we never see. A ballerina accepts a bouquet of flowers and slowly pulls from it a series of items of silky underwear, she curtseys mechanically and then moves out of the spotlight. She scratches, shifts awkwardly, she's out of the lime-light but why won't she go away?[29]

. . . Race, Revolution, Roles, Relationships, Rationality, Rape . . .

S is for spare tyre

In 1979 Clair Chapman advertised in *Time Out*, hoping to contact women interested in creating a piece of theatre around Susie Orbach's *Fat is a Feminist Issue*. Eventually, through a workshopping period, the initial sixty replies emerged as a group of six. The first show, *Bearing the Weight* was a great success. Katina Noble recalls:

> Clair had read the book and it had changed her life totally. I had sorted out my compulsive eating problems but then heard Susie Orbach speak . . . We came together at a point in 1979, when . . . it was still fresh enough in our memories . . . so particularly in that first show, personal experience just poured out of us.

The company, now Chapman, Noble and Harriet Towell went on to create shows like *On the Shelf* about 'old maids', *Laugh Lines* about ageing, and others about health, family, sisters and the American dream. Working together for many years, they have evolved an effective creative formula, which minimizes the problems of working as a group:

> Everyone should be able to write exactly what they want, but I would like a final hand in the script. I think we need a style that pervades, a

consistency or we end up with a series of scenes without shape that add up to nothing so they've entrusted me with that which is wonderful.[30]

Siren

Known as the 'thinking women's theatre group', Siren was formed in Brighton in 1979, by Tasha Fairbanks, Jane Mostyn and Jude Winters. Originally a street theatre group active around abortion issues and the anti-Corrie Bill; inspired by radical feminism it saw itself as part of a political rather than theatrical continuum. Their theatre, apposite for street performance, stressed accessibility, mime, dance and clowning, with integral music, aiming for a weird and surreal effect. An early show, *Mama's Gone A Hunting*, was characteristic, and advocated a separatist solution to the institution of sexism. Initially created through a process of all three writing together line by line, Tasha Fairbanks's role merged more clearly in shaping and clarifying the script, until she identified herself as a writer. Literary and political elements struggle for precedence as Siren experiments with different processes: *Pulp*, 1986, was concerned with presenting a stylish show, elegant and affirming to a lesbian audience. Members have now specialized in various areas of theatre, intending to reform intermittently, and although – typically – none of Siren's work is published, they will send out scripts and videos.[31]

. . . Sexuality, Sexual Politics, Separatism, Stories, Seriousness . . .

T is for tyranny of structurelessness[32]

I don't think it's been solved how you organize collectively a large number of people within an ailing capitalist society, because you want your product – the theatre you have been doing – to get places fast and make some noise, you've got to circumvent a lot of collective ideals by the way and just say, 'We're going for this, and that's the deadline.' And in the contradictions of this situation, as I mentioned before – that was why I had to leave – there were no equal rights for women.

(Eileen Pollock, ex-member Belt & Braces[33])

How do you work collectively? If anyone's answered that question, please let me know. ReSisters are still deciding how to decide how to make decisions . . . after two years it still takes an hour to agree to how soon we should meet before a show starts! No hierarchy, equal responsibility doesn't seem to work – you can't force democracy. Actors, like most people who work, are used to having a boss . . . Suddenly they are put into a position where there's no director, no script, and sometimes no wages – panic! and there's no-one to blame, no-one to answer questions . . . So what happens? They focus on the most likely candidate in the collective – the one who always comes up with the bright ideas, the one who will answer questions, who doesn't mind more responsibility. They invest power into someone instead of sharing it collectively, and that power which was given out of lack of confidence, fear, feelings of inadequacy, inexperience, builds into a force of resentment against the person who has taken the power that was given. This is what happened in ReSisters. We are still searching for an answer.

(Angela Brinkworth 1985[34])

Throughout the 1970s and 1980s, the issue of group decision-making be-devilled groups, sparking heated debate at conferences, in journals and company meetings, where the record for length is held at eight hours by Joint Stock.[35] Emerging as a socialist theatre collective through working on David Hare's *Fanshen* about the process of revolution-making in a Chinese village, the group translated the play's continual self-questioning of individual and group into a major questioning of the company roles and structures. Further reinforced in feminist companies by the organizational practices of the Women's Movement where informal open discussions of consciousness-raising meetings were vital to empower individuals to speak their experiences, such methods, though creative and fruitful in theatre were in decision-making meetings not conducive to organizational efficiency. In the worsening economic climate of the 1980s, many companies disintegrated under the weight of disagreements, financial failure due to poor organization or were penalized by increasingly market-oriented funding bodies.

. . . *Text, Testimony, Training, TIE* . . .

U is for Urban, Urgency, Utopias . . .

V is for Violence, Voices, Victim, Visionary, Visual . . .

W is for writing

The relationship of the collaborative process and the individual writer is immensely fruitful, yet difficult. Encouraged by the devising process to begin to value their own experience and skills, women began to write independently of companies: Penny O'Connor and Adele Saleem of WTG, April de Angelis, Sheva Martin and Bonnie Greer of ReSisters, Yasmin Judd of Sphinx, for instance. Others, however, felt they had lost their own voice within the collective one, which sometimes homogeneously created a politically correct, accessible but rather shallow script.

Winsome Pinnock felt that her work with WTG on *Picture Palace* was perhaps most important for her development, showing her that collective process was not conducive to her own writing:

> I think it calls for being very technical, drawing the fullest technical possibilities out of what they want and not necessarily drawing on your own experience to such a large extent. I've always found it difficult . . . Sometimes in workshops you're writing what other people want. When WTG asked me to write a play about women and film, it was a subject I was interested in . . . but they had their ideas politically and in a way it was taken away from me and became theirs. And it was theirs, and that was right and in a way I should have accepted that I was writing a play for WTG and not for me.
> (Winsome Pinnock[36])

Within mixed contexts, a greater body of understanding about the collaborative process and ways of accommodating both individual and group needs, is developing in clarity and sophistication.[37]

> I wouldn't mind writing a first draft and then it being workshopped, but not before that. I can't really cope with all that input at the beginning. I think the workshop experience can really help in the process, if you do have very definite ideas about what you want to do. With the *Wind of Change* (with the Half Moon Young People's Theatre) there was a research period and then I was left to write, then there was another workshop period. There I felt I was speaking for myself and benefiting from the group input.
> (Winsome Pinnock[38])

Groups of women, and others, like Joint Stock, have, in developing the script-creating process, given a stronger voice within the work to actors. Despite the success of many writers since emerging as individuals, the approach is still viewed with suspicion by a critical establishment used to the canonical notion of the solitary, god-like, male authorial voice producing the fully-formed work of genius:

> For masterpieces are not single and solitary births; they are the outcome of many years of thinking in common, of thinking by the body of the people, so that the experience of the mass is behind the single voice.
> (Virginia Woolf[39])

. . . Wife, Women's Movement . . .

Y is for Youth Theatre, Young Women . . .

Z . . .

Notes

Introduction

1 Trevor R. Griffiths and Carole Woddis, *Theatre Guide*, Bloomsbury, 1988, p. 325.

2 For an overview of the 'semantic derogation of women' see Jane Mills, *Womanwords*, Longman, 1989, which has a comprehensive bibliography.

3 John Russell Taylor *Anger and After: A Guide to the New British Drama*, Methuen, 1962 (revised ed. 1969) and *The Second Wave*, Methuen, 1971; Katharine J. Worth, *Revolutions in Modern English Drama,* Bell, 1973; Oleg Kerensky, *The New British Drama*, Hamish Hamilton, 1977; Ronald Hayman, *British Theatre since 1955*, Oxford University Press, 1979.

4 John Russell Brown, *A Short Guide to Modern British Drama*, Heinemann, 1982; John Elsom, *Post-war British Theatre Criticism,* RKP, 1981; Gareth and Barbara Lloyd-Evans, *Plays in Review 1956–1980*, Batsford, 1985; David Ian Rabey, *British and Irish Political Drama in the Twentieth Century,* Macmillan, 1986; Richard Allen Cave, *New British Drama in Performance on the London Stage: 1970 to 1985*, Smythe, 1987; Colin Chambers and Mike Prior, *Playwrights' Progress: Patterns of Postwar British Drama*, Amber Lane, 1987.

5 See Michelene Wandor's *Look Back in Gender*, Methuen, 1987, for an interesting discussion of gender representation in post war drama.

6 See David Bradby and David Williams, *Directors' Theatre*, Macmillan, 1988, for a discussion of Littlewood's contribution to British theatre.

7 See Catherine Itzin, *Stages in the Revolution*, Methuen, 1980, pp. 32, 345.

8 For accounts of related issues see Roszika Parker and Griselda Pollock, *Old Mistresses: Women, Art and Ideology*, RKP, 1981; Dale Spender, *There's Always Been a Women's Movement This Century*, Pandora, 1983.

9 Some of the texts are: Robert Hewison, *In Anger: Culture in the Cold War*, Weiden-feld, 1981, *Too Much: Art and Society in the Sixties*, Methuen, 1986; Robert Hutch-ison, *The Politics of the Arts Council*, Sinclair Browne, 1982; Sheila Rowbotham, *Hidden from History*, Pluto, 1973, *Woman's Consciousness, Man's World*, Pelican, 1973; Alan Sinfield (ed.), *Society and Literature 1945–1970*, Methuen, 1983; Eliz-abeth Wilson, *Only Halfway to Paradise: Women in Postwar Britain: 1945–1968*, Tavistock, 1980; Janet Wolff, *The Social Production of Art*, Macmillan, 1981.

10 Helene Keyssar, *Feminist Theatre*, Macmillan, 1984; Sue-Ellen Case, *Feminism and Theatre*, Macmillan, 1988; Lesley Ferris, *Acting Women*, Macmillan, 1990; Michelene Wandor, *Understudies*, Methuen, 1981, *Carry on Understudies*, RKP, 1986, *Look Back in Gender*, Methuen, 1987; Karen Malpede, *Women in Theatre*, Drama Books, 1983.

11 Catherine Belsey, *Critical Practice*, Methuen, 1980, p. 91. The chapter 'The Interrogative Text' in which these two phrases occur provides the starting point of much of the discussion in this introductory section, and some terms used throughout.

12 Alison Higgins, a graduate of Sheffield University, founded the Hogwash Theatre Company, which has varied in number from four to ten female performers in October 1986. The group ran under the auspices of the Govern-ment Enterprise Scheme from 1 December 1986 to 1 December 1987, and has since managed to exist, touring to Midlands and Yorkshire mostly community venues, including some London fringe bookings. They have devised a variety of material including feminist cabaret and a work on Aphra Behn. An Inter-view with further details may be found in E. Aston and G. Griffin, *Stage Left: Women's Theatre Groups in Interview* (Berg, 1991).

13 Elaine Showalter, *A Literature of Their Own*, Virago, 1978, p. 13. Whereas Showalter defines these terms within the context of specific historical periods, this introduction extends her notions of content and form in a way that transcends chronology.

14 Patricia Erens, 'Towards a feminist aesthetic: Reflection–revolution–ritual', in P. Erens, ed., *Sexual Strategems: The World of Women in Film*, Horizon, New York, 1979, pp. 157 ff.

15 Erens, 'Towards a feminist aesthetic', p. 166.

16 Dale Spender, *Man-Made Language*, RKP, 1980. For extracts from and exposi-tion of the work of these French feminists see E. Marks and I. de Courtivron, eds, *New French Feminisms*, Harvester, 1981, and G Greene and C. Kahn, eds, *Making a Difference*, Methuen, 1985.

17 Jacques Lacan, *Ecrits*, RKP, 1977, especially Chapter One 'The mirror stage as formative of the function of the I'. See Kristeva's 'Signifying Practice and the Mode of Production', translated by G. Nowell-Smith in the *Edinburgh Film Festival Magazine*, 1976, and 'The Ruin of a Poetics', in S. Bann and J. Bowlt, eds, *Russian Formalism*, Scottish Academic Press, 1973, for an indication of Kristeva's extension of this idea of 'split' into language and its implications. A useful and clear exposition of the link between Kristeva and Lacan, can be found in an extract from T. Eagleton's 'Literary Theory: An Introduction', which is printed on pp. 213–216 of M. Eagleton, ed., *Feminist Literary Theory: A Reader*, Blackwell, 1986.

154   Notes

18 'The Ruin of a Poetics', p. 115.
19 As Chapter 1 indicates, some of Jellicoe's work, such as *The Sport of My Mad Mother*, is open to this kind of reading, due to its strong emphasis on interplaying visual discourses.
20 In her introductory note to the published text Churchill acknowledges her debt to Foucault's book: 'I . . . was so thrilled with it that I set the play not here and now but in nineteenth century France' (*Softcops*, Methuen, 1984, p. 6).
21 This as yet unpublished work by Goldman, a First Class Honours graduate who then became a Writer/Director in Residence at Essex University during the spring of 1990, and Tuck who is a PhD student, was consciously evolved through theories of women's language and performance strategies. It was presented on a shoe-string budget by Front Row Productions, a small company set up in 1989 by Edwyn Wilson and Nick Tobin, graduates of Bretton Hall, partly via the Government Enterprise Scheme – and thus typical of the limited financial backing available to new writers.
22 Susan Bassnett, *Magdalena International Women's Experimental Theatre*, Berg, 1990. Magdalena membership and further details can be obtained from: The Magdalena Project, Chapter, Market Road, Cardiff, CF5 1QE.
23 The essay on 'the Uncanny' (in Pelican Freud, vol. 14, *Art & Literature*, 1985) is a seminal one for psychoanalytic criticism, and especially for writing on the Gothic genre, such as R. Jackson, *Fantasy: the Literature of Subversion*, Methuen, 1981.
24 Antonin Artaud, *The Theatre and its Double*, Calder & Boyars, 1970, p. 44. There are many references in Kristeva's works to what she considers to be the polyphonic and semiotically charged elements in Artaud's work. For example J. Kristeva, *Desire in Language*, Blackwell, 1980, pp. 142 and 165, her 'Signifying Practice and the Mode of Production', and 'The Ruin of a Poetics', pp. 111–15.
25 J. Kristeva, *Desire in Language*, p. 136.
26 For further discussion of the question of gender in relation to the looking of the spectator, see Laura Mulvey, *Visual Pleasure & Narrative Cinema* reprinted in *Visual & Other Pleasures*, Macmillan, 1989, pp. 14–26.

1 Early stages: Women dramatists 1958–68

1 Raymond Williams, *Drama from Ibsen to Brecht*, (revised ed.), Pelican, 1973, p. 369.
2 R. Adam, *A Woman's Place 1910–1975*, Chatto & Windus, 1975, p. 175.
3 Jonathan Dollimore, 'The challenge of sexuality' in A. Sinfield, ed., *Society & Literature 1945–1970*, Methuen, 1983, p. 60.
4 V. Beechey, 'Women and Employment in Contemporary Britain' in V. Beechey and E. Whitelegg, eds, *Women in Britain Today*, Open University Press, 1986, p. 80.
5 John Osborne, *Look Back in Anger*, Faber, 1957, is an example of a play exhibiting misogynist attitudes while examining social issues.
6 Enid Bagnold, 'Foreword' in *The Chalk Garden*, Samuel French, 1956.

7 Enid Bagnold, Preface to *Call me Jacky*, in *Four Plays by Enid Bagnold*, Heinemann, 1970.
8 Toril Moi, *Sexual/Textual Politics*, Methuen, 1985, pp. 99–101.
9 G. Payne and S. Morley, eds, *The Noel Coward Diaries*, Weidenfeld & Nicolson, 1982, p. 449.
10 Bagnold, *The Chinese Prime Minister* in *Four Plays by Edith Bagnold*, p. 246.
11 Bagnold, *The Chinese Prime Minister*, p. 238.
12 Bagnold, *The Chinese Prime Minister*, p. 182.
13 Moi, pp. 99–101.
14 Bagnold, *Call Me Jacky*, p. 333.
15 Doris Lessing, 'Author's Note on Directing this Play' in *Play With a Tiger*, Pan, 1966, p. 295.
16 Lessing, 'Postscript', in *Play With a Tiger*, p. 296.
17 Lessing, 'Author's Note', in *Play With a Tiger*, p. 295.
18 Michael Billingon, 'Novel into Play – An interview with James Saunders', *Plays and Players*, March 1968.
19 E. Dipple, *Iris Murdoch: Work for the Spirit*, Methuen, 1982, p. 152.
20 R. Jackson, *Fantasy: the Literature of Subversion*, Methuen, 1985.
21 Joan Littlewood, 'Goodbye Note from Joan' in C. Marowitz, T. Milne, O. Hale, eds, *New Theatre Voices of the Fifties and Sixties*, Methuen, 1965, p. 133.
22 Stuart Hall, 'Beyond Naturalism Pure – the First Five Years', in *New Theatre Voices of the Fifties and Sixties*, Methuen, 1981, pp. 212–220.
23 Shelagh Delaney, 'Preface' to *The Lion in Love*, Methuen, 1967.
24 John Russell Taylor, *Anger and After*, Pelican, 1963, p. 112.
25 P. Roberts, 'Interview with Gaskill, Johnstone and Cuthbertson' *Plays and Players*, November, 1963.
26 Terry Browne, *Playwrights' Theatre*, Pitman, 1975. See Chapters 3, 5 and 9 for further references to writers with involvement with the Royal Court: particularly successful examples include Caryl Churchill and Timberlake Wertenbaker. During 1990–1, for instance, both have had new plays – *Mad Forest* and *Three Birds Alighting on a Field*, respectively – performed and revivals toured. Winsome Pinnock's *Talking in Tongues*, directed Upstairs by Hetty McDonald in 1991, is typical of the Court's current encouragement of black women writers.
27 'Ann Jellicoe talks to Sue Todd', in Ann Jellicoe, *'The Knack' and 'The Sport of My Mad Mother'*, Faber, 1985, p. 17.
28 Jellicoe, *The Sport of My Mad Mother*, p. 103.
29 Jellicoe, *The Sport of My Mad Mother*, p. 104.
30 Jellicoe, *The Sport of My Mad Mother*, p. 104.
31 Jellicoe, *The Sport of My Mad Mother*, p. 108.
32 Jellicoe, *The Sport of My Mad Mother*, p. 119.
33 Ann Jellicoe, 'The Rising Generation' in A. Durband, ed., *Playbill Two*, Hutchinson, 1969, p. 45.
34 Jellicoe, 'The Rising Generation', p. 54.
35 Jane Arden, *Vagina Rex & the Gas Oven*, Calder & Boyars, 1971, p. 32.
36 Jane Arden, *Vagina Rex & the Gas Oven*, Calder & Boyars, 1971, p. 63.

2 Claiming a space: 1969–78

1 Michelene Wandor, *Carry on Understudies*, RKP, 1981, pp. 32–5.
2 See Susan Todd, *Women & Theatre: Calling the Shots*, Faber, 1984, *Carry on Understudies*, Trevor R. Griffiths and Carole Woddis, *Bloomsbury Theatre Guide*, Bloomsbury, 1988, particularly entry 'Women in Theatre', pp. 325–6, for accounts of the struggle for women directors and performers.
3 See Catherine Itzin, *Stages in the Revolution*, Methuen, 1980, and Sandy Craig, ed., *Dreams and Deconstructions*, Amber Lane, 1980, for fuller accounts.
4 Michelene Wandor, ed., *Strike While the Iron is Hot*, Journeyman, 1980.
5 Quoted from correspondence with Sarah Richards, Administrator, 28 September 1989.
6 Taken from *Red Ladder Theatre Company: 1989–1992 – A Plan for the Next Three Years*.
7 Quoted from WTG's first press release, in *Carry on Understudies*, p. 51.
8 Comment derived from correspondence with Alison MacKinnon, 30 August 1989.
9 Luce Irigary, quoted in Mary Jacobus, *Reading Women*, Methuen, 1987, p. 65.
10 Catherine Belsey, *Critical Practice*, Methuen, 1980, pp. 70, 90–2.
11 Catherine Belsey, *Critical Practice*, pp. 90–2.
12 *Guardian* Women's Page, 21 February 1984; Angela Neustatter, *Guardian*, 16 February 1977; *Sunday Telegraph*, 19 June 1977; Pauline Peters, *Observer*, 3 February 1980.
13 Gems's 'Afterword' to *Dusa, Fish, Stas and Vi*, in Michelene Wandor, ed., *Plays by Women 1*, Methuen, 1982, p. 71.
14 Gems's 'Afterword' to *Dusa, Fish, Stas and Vi*, in Michelene Wandor, ed., *Plays by Women 1*.
15 Wymark's 'Afterword' to *Find Me*, in Michelene Wandor, ed., *Plays by Women 2*, Methuen, 1983, p. 127.
16 See Catherine Belsey, *Critical Practice*, pp. 85–92, for an exposition of Lacan's notion of the 'Split Subject', which is relevant to the staging of the split self.
17 The relationship of Self/Other can be related to the notion of the Uncanny factor of the double as explored in Freud's essay 'The Uncanny' (Pelican Freud, vol. 14, *Art and Literature*, 1985, pp. 339–76). The essay also explores the connection between repression and repetition compulsion – the return of the repressed.
18 Pelican Freud, vol. 7, *On Sexuality*, 1977, pp. 221–5; Pelican Freud, vol. 4, *The Interpretation of Dreams*, 1976, pp. 363–6; see also Marthe Robert, *The Origins of the Novel*, Harvester, 1980.

3 Waving not drowning: The mainstream, 1979–88

1 See Sandy Craig, ed., *Dreams and Deconstructions*, Amber Lane, 1980 and John McGrath, *A Good Night Out*, Methuen, 1981.
2 Michelene Wandor offers a broadly similar analysis in *Carry On Understudies*, 1981, but although I agree with her about the importance of the revelation of the

detailed texture of women's lives, and the difficulties of voyeurism, I think that the mind/body split that she doesn't consider reinforces her contention that there is both a radical feminist and a feminine dynamic in the play. The film of *Steaming* sidestepped some of the issues by allowing the women to win their fight and by making the council project a leisure centre rather than a library.

3 Reprinted in *London Theatre Record*, 1983.

4 For a full description of Joint Stock's work see Rob Ritchie, ed., *The Joint Stock Book*, Methuen, 1987.

5 Page numbers for *Cloud Nine* are cited from *Churchill: Plays One*, Methuen, 1985.

6 See Catherine Itzin, *Stages in the Revolution: Political Theatre in Britain since 1968*, Methuen, 1980, pp. 286–7.

7 Wandor, *Understudies*, p. 68. Wandor develops the argument in similar terms on pp. 171–2 of *Carry on Understudies*.

8 Churchill herself sanctioned changes for Tommy Tune's 1981 New York production, which brought Betty's monologue and a different song to the end of the play, but in all the British texts the original arrangement is maintained. Churchill has remarked that the effect of Tune's changes was to throw more emphasis on Betty as an individual and to make the ending more emotional and uplifting whereas the original was more ironic. See the interview with Churchill in Betsko and Koenig, *Interviews with Contemporary Women Playwrights*, Beech Tree Books, 1987.

9 Christopher Brown, *Brueghel,* Phaidon, 1975; John Willett, ed., *Brecht on Theatre*, Methuen, 1964, p. 158.

10 This passage from *Understudies*, p. 68 does not appear in *Carry on Understudies*.

11 Lisa Tuttle *Encyclopedia of Feminism*, Longman, 1986, entries for 'radical feminism' and 'separatism', pp. 268, 289.

12 The *Guardian* and *Evening Standard*, quoted from *London Theatre Record*, 1984.

13 Quoted from *London Theatre Record*, 1984.

14 Andrea Dunbar, *Rita, Sue and Bob Too*, with *The Abor* and *Shirley,* with an introduction by Rob Ritchie, Methuen, 1988, p. viii.

15 Quotations from Benedict Nightingale, *New Statesman* and Martin Walker, *The Guardian*, in *London Theatre Record*, 1982. For a taut and imaginative treatment of a similar theme, see also Eve Lewis's *Ficky Stingers* (1986), a powerful short play about a closed society in which the dynamics of a mixed gender crowd who go round together ensure that the fact that one of them has been raped by a member of the group is simply squeezed out of existence.

16 *First Run*, p. 98.

17 Similar elements are also present in some of her other work such as *All You Deserve* (1986), in which solidarity and friendship between students emerges in the face of a threat to close part of an FE college (cf *Steaming*) or the early *Away From It All* (1982), a satire on the package tour industry, in which themes that would be treated with greater assurance in the trilogy made an early and less controlled appearance.

18 She translated Ariane Mnouchkine's *Mephisto* for the RSC's 1986 production.

19 *New Anatomies* occupies pp. 297–339 of *Plays Introduction*, Faber, 1984. The note is on p. 298.

20 Max Stafford-Clark, *Letters to George*, Nick Hern, 1989, p. 189.

4 Sister George is dead: The making of modern lesbian theatre

1 See Bob Cant and Susan Hemmings, eds, *Radical Records: Thirty Years of Lesbian and Gay History*, Routledge, 1988; Catherine Itzin, *Stages in the Revolution*, Methuen, 1980; Philip Osment, *Gay Sweatshop: Four Plays and a Company*, Methuen, 1989 for accounts of these developments. Methuen's *Plays by Women* series; Jill Davis's two anthologies, *Lesbian Plays*, Methuen, 1987, and *Lesbian Plays: Two*, Methuen, 1989; and Philip Osment's Gay Sweatshop volume are important sources of primary material.
2 *Lesbian Plays*, p. 24.
3 *Lesbian Plays*, p. 24.
4 Trevor R. Griffiths and Carole Woddis, *Bloomsbury Theatre Guide*, Bloomsbury, 1988, p. 95.
5 *Gay News*, March, 1979.
6 For more on Fleming and Hard Corps see *Lesbian Plays*.
7 *Lesbian Plays*, p. 112.
8 *Lesbian Plays: Two*, pp. 33–4.
9 *Bloomsbury Theatre Guide*, p. 163.
10 Quoted from *Lesbian Plays: Two*, p. vi.

5 Black women playwrights in Britain

1 Women Talking from *A Dangerous Knowing*, Sheba, 1985.
2 As far as possible, I have indicated where scripts may be obtained if not published. I would be very interested to hear of or receive copies of plays not mentioned, and would encourage playwrights and companies to lodge copies of their work with both the British Library and the New Playwrights Trust, Interchange Studios, Dalby Street, Kentish Town, London, NW 3NG where they can be accessible for reading, to encourage further productions and study of work by black women. NPT, with Black Audio and Film Collective, have recently commissioned a Black Playwrights Directory, to list all published and produced black and Third World playwrights and screen writers. Page references given are to published versions listed in the bibliography. No page reference is given for unpublished scripts.
3 Naseem Khan, *The Arts Britain Ignores*, Commission for Racial Equality, 1979.
4 Sandy Craig, ed., *Dreams & Deconstructions*, Amber Lane, 1980, pp. 59–75.
5 Prabhu Gupta mentions in *Black British Literature*, p. 119 that Una Marston wrote the first play performed by a black company in Britain. She had other plays produced in the 1930s in Jamaica, published poetry, and presented 'Caribbean Voices' for the BBC.
6 Susan Croft, Interview with Theatre of Black Women, *The Plot*, 2, 1985.
7 See quotation about *Pyeyucca* in Alphabet of Apocrypha (p. 206, Chapter 9). Poems by Evaristo and Hilaire, including work from *Pyeyucca*, are included in Maud Sulter, ed., *Passion: Discourses on Black Women's Creativity*, Urban Fox Press, 1990. Sulter is herself a visual artist who also creates performance art, a field where black women and men are only recently beginning to emerge. See

Michael MacMillan, *Live Art and Cultural Diversity*, Art Council, 1991, for discussion of this area.

8 Croft, Interview with Theatre of Black Women, *The Plot*, 2, 1985.

9 See Alphabet of Apocrpypha (Chapter 9) for further discussion.

10 See Julie Holledge, *Innocent Flowers: Women in the Edwardian Theatre*, Virago, 1981.

11 Alice Walker, *In Search of Our Mothers Gardens*, Women's Press, 1984, p. xi.

12 References to *England is de Place for Me* are to the unpublished script, not the recently published revised Sheffield version.

13 From 'The Voices from Nowhere' by Pat Ashworth, in The *Guardian*, 11 October 1989.

14 From 'Moving On' by Sheryl Garratt in *City Limits*, July 1984.

15 LIFT, London International Festival of Theatre, has been responsible for bringing to Britain important black work, including *The Colored Museum*, Methuen, 1987, Reduta Deux Company, Sistren's *Fallen Angel & The Devil Concubine*.

16 Oyeleye's account of working as a director at the English National Opera is included in Sulter, ed., *Passion: Discourses on Black Women's Creativity*, Urban Fox Press, 1990. Oyeleye is also Chair of the Writers' Guild Women's Committee.

17 Kathie Perkins, ed., *Black Female Playwrights: An anthology before 1950*, Indiana University Press, 1989.

18 See article by Jyoti Patel and Jez Simons in 'Doing the Write Thing' *Bazaar Magazine*, issue 9, 1990.

19 Quotations and references to *Ishtaar Descends* are to an unpublished manuscript version, not the partly revised recently published Sheffield edition.

20 Quotation from publicity for *Chameleon*, by Yasmin Sidwha.

21 See Sulter, ed., *Passion*.

22 Review in *Spare Rib*, April 1990.

23 Jyoti Patel and Jez Simons, interviewed by Croft, Derby 1990.

24 Paulette Randall, interviewed by Croft, London 1989.

6 On the margins: Women dramatists in Wales

1 Elaine Morgan in correspondence with Margaret Llewellyn-Jones, January 1990.

2 D.I. Rabey and C.C. Savill, 'Welsh Theatre: Inventing New Myths', *Euromaske: European Theatre Quarterly*, 1, Fall 1990, pp. 73–5.

3 Carl Tighe, 'Theatre (or Not) in Wales' in Tony Curtis, ed., *Wales: the Imagined Nation*, Arrowsmith, 1986, p. 245.

4 See Susan Bassnett, *Magdalena: International Women's Experimental Theatre*, Berg, 1990.

5 The conference included workshop sessions on gender and performance, one led by Gillian Hanna, with a self-directed overspill group. Mine Kaylan, an academic, gave a paper on finding a language to describe women's performance, and Margaretta d'Arcy also spoke and set up a workshop. Despite the high percentage of women participants, the majority of speakers were men.

6 Tighe, pp. 248–50.
7 Write On Festival Leaflet, obtained from Made in Wales, Mount Stuart House, Mount Stuart Square, Cardiff, CF1 6DQ. Telephone (0222) 484016/7.
8 See the introduction and notes 13 and 15 below for the notion of women's theatre language, a possible Ecriture Feminine.
9 These plays were not dated in correspondence with the author.
10 Script report, The New Playwrights Trust.
11 According to Nicola Jorden Davies's agent, the working title of the resource project is *Topless Women*.
12 *Self Portrait*, Amber Lane, 1990; *Variations* in A. Castledine (ed.) *Plays by Women Vol. 9*, Methuen, 1991.
13 Three possible modes of women's drama (female/reflectionist, feminist/revolutionary, female/ritualistic) are defined in the Introduction. See the notes to the Introduction for bibliographical information on the notion of 'l'Ecriture Feminine'.
14 S. Yeger, *Self Portrait*, Amber Lane, 1990, p. 7.
15 This confusion of sensations coming from all areas of the theatre space could be seen to combine Artaudian notions of total theatre with the post-Freudian theory developed by Kristeva that the pre-speech polymorphously perverse pleasures of the individual are akin to the semiotic drives which she sees as subversive of the linguistic and patriarchal order – hence this production could be read as an example of a theatrical Ecriture Feminine.
16 Robin Thornber, of The *Guardian*, '*Self Portrait* is one of the most exciting, intriguing and satisfying new plays I've seen this season.' Quoted on the cover of the published text.
17 Yeger's stage work includes *Alice & Other Reflections, Watching Foxes, Geraniums, Dancing in the Dark, Variations on a Theme by Clara Schumann*, and the community plays *The Ballad of Tilly Hake* (commissioned by Ann Jellicoe) and *A Day by the Sea*.
18 Tighe, pp. 248, 259; Rabey and Savill, p. 75.
19 See Belsey, *Critical Practice*, pp. 70, 92 for the connection between classical realist closure and dominant ideology.
20 These unpublished scripts, which were generously made available for this research, have un-numbered pages.
21 See the discussion of Mike Leigh in Griffiths and Woddis, pp. 173–4.
22 The strong emphasis on visual rather than verbally-based methods of creative devising might seem to offer more opportunities for embodying the subversive semiotic drives as defined by Kristeva.
23 Tighe, pp. 247, 242, 255.
24 Rabey and Savill, p. 73.
25 Tighe, p. 259.
26 Reginald John Scourse, a Headteacher, wrote several Anglo-Welsh plays based on local community themes, such as *Bang in the Centre*, a comedy about a youth and community centre, and *All Our Tomorrows*, a nostalgic play that explored educational issues and frustrated creativity. These performances by local amateurs were typical of the opportunities for would-be playwrights in Wales before television became a major influence in the community.

27 The Grand Swansea had a ballet company, then *Shirley Valentine*, followed by Barbara Dixon, then Les Dawson in *Run for Your Wife*, a show for children, and *Grease*. Theatr Clwyd was showing films apart from one week devoted to a co-production with the Mercury Community Theatre of Hochhhuth's *Soldiers*. The Sherman was closed for much of August but had the Crucible TIE team, the *Adrian Mole* musical, another musical (*Perfectly Frank*) and a Welsh children's pantomime. The Torch was alternating a musical version of *Mr Polly* with, of course, *Under Milk Wood*.

7 Irish women playwrights since 1958

1 In 1898, Lady Gregory, W.B. Yeats and Edward Martyn founded the Irish Literary Theatre. This then merged with Fay's National Drama Society in 1903 to form the Irish National Theatre Society, which was presented with the Abbey Theatre by Annie Horniman the following year.

2 Mary O'Malley was one of the founders of the Lyric Theatre in Belfast in 1951. She should not be confused with the London born author of the same name who wrote *Once a Catholic*.

3 'Towards Post-Feminism?', *Theatre Ireland*, No 18, April–June 1989, p. 35. The women interviewed were Lynne Parker, co-founder and director with Rough Magic; Mary Elizabeth Burke-Kennedy, co-founder of Focus, founder of Story-teller's Company, actress, director and playwright; Marie Jones, co-founder of Charabanc, actress and playwright; Eleanor Methven and Carol Scanlon, actresses and co-founders of Charabanc; and Brenda Winter, co-founder of Charabanc, and, more recently, founder of the Theatre-in-Education company Replay.

4 The Theatre journal, *Theatre Ireland*, has done much to remedy this situation, and has given considerable space to women directors, designers, actresses and authors.

5 The focus of this study is mainly on texts that are available in published form, although other areas of women's involvement in theatre will be referred to. Because recent texts are not easily available, there may well be omissions. I would welcome any of these being brought to my attention. I should like to thank Victoria White, Claire Wilson, members of Charabanc, and especially Carolyn Swift and Margaretta D'Arcy for their assistance and suggestions.

6 Terminology relating to Ireland tends to be politically coloured. I have used the terms Northern Ireland and the Irish Republic when referring to established political or cultural institutions. In most other cases, I have referred to the six and the twenty six counties or to the north and the south of Ireland. The latter form does not correspond entirely to the political boundaries, as Donegal, which is part of the Republic, is the most northerly county of Ireland.

7 The recent appointment of Garry Hynes as Artistic Director of the Abbey is an exception which bodes well for the visibility of women in Irish theatre.

8 See *Only the Rivers Run Free: Northern Ireland, The Women's War*, Eileen Fairweather, Roisin McDonagh and Melanie McFadyean, eds, Pluto Books, London, 1989, p. 266.

9 See Jenny Beale, *Women in Ireland: Voices of Change*, Macmillan, London, 1986.
10 The complex and interrelated political, social and economic factors that have
    led to the current unrest in the six counties can only be sketched in the briefest
    terms here. For further information on the role of women in the Northern
    Irish struggle, see *Only the Rivers Run Free: Northern Ireland, The Women's War*.
11 Mary Daly, *Women and Poverty*, Dublin, Attic Press, 1989, p. 98.
12 The continuing dominance of Catholic dogma on issues of divorce, contracep-
    tion and abortion in the south of Ireland has led to deep rifts among Irish
    women. This was particularly evident in the conflicts between pro-
    contraception and abortion groups such as the Contraceptive Action Pro-
    gramme (CAP) or Women's Right to Choose and the right-wing fundamen-
    talist groups Society for the Protection of the Unborn Child (SPUC) and the
    Pro-Life Amendment Campaign (PLAC) in the early 1980s.
13 I am indebted for much of this material to Pat Murphy and Nell McCafferty's
    book of women photographers' views of contemporary Irish women's lives in
    Women in Focus, Dublin, Attic Press, 1987.
14 These measures did not, of course, eliminate inequality. There is still much
    cause for grievance: 'the majority of women workers, north and south of
    Ireland, are segregated into all-female, low-paid, unskilled jobs, such as cater-
    ing and service' *Women in Focus*, p. 81.
15 *To Present the Pretence*, Eyre Methuen, 1977.
16 'Theatre in an Age of Reform', *Awkward Corners*, London, Methuen, 1988, pp.
    177–78.
17 In *Contemporary Irish Dramatists*, Macmillan, 1989, Michael Etherton sees the-
    atre in the West of Ireland as a vital source of theatrical and ideological
    regeneration. While the arts in both Belfast and Dublin remain marked by
    British colonization, the West of Ireland 'effectively resisted English cultural
    imperialism' (p. 64).
18 See Michael Etherton, *Contemporary Irish Dramatists,* for further details.
19 See *The Guardian*, 19 April 1991.
20 *Bar and Ger* was published in 1980 by Samuel French who also published *A
    Galway Girl* in 1981.
21 The play was published in London by Faber and Faber in 1973.
22 Introduction to *Goodnight Sisters*, Attic Press, Dublin, 1988, p. 1.
23 *The Nightingale and not the Lark, The Porch*, and *Invisible Man*, Raven Arts Press,
    Dublin, 1988.
24 This also emerges in the third play in the trilogy, *Invisible Man,* which contrasts
    the emotional repression of Tony, who cannot express his love for his dying
    father, and his lover, Mack who freely offers his love.
25 See, for example, John B. Keane's *The Field*.
26 See the introduction.
27 In *The Crack in the Emerald*, Nick Hern Books, 1990.
28 Margaretta D'Arcy, *Awkward Corners*, Methuen, 1988, p. 137.
29 Philomena Muinzer, discussing a television play by Jennifer Johnson, broadcast
    by the BBC in March 1980, and set amongst a Catholic family in the Bogside
    area of Derry, comments that *'Shadows on our Skin* . . . appealed for humane
    relations between the two communities without examining the complexities

that prevent them, and in this was typical of the Ulster genre, The Answer Without A Question'. See Philomena Muinzer, 'Evacuating the Museum: the Crisis of Playwrighting in Ulster', *New Theatre Quarterly,* Vol III, No. 9, Feb 1987, p. 45.

30 *Ourselves Alone,* with *A Woman Calling* and *The Long March,* was published in London by Faber and Faber in 1986. Page references are given in brackets after the quotation.

31 Christina Reid, *Joyriders and Tea in a China Cup,* Methuen, 1987.

32 Recent plays include *The Belle of the Belfast City,* produced at the Lyric Players Theatre in Belfast in 1989 and *My Name Shall I Tell You My Name,* presented at the Young Vic, London, in March 1990.

33 Diderik Roll-Hansen, 'Dramatic Strategy in Christina Reid's *Tea in a China Cup',* *Modern Drama,* vol XXX, no. 3, Sept 1987, p. 393.

34 One of Marie Jones' plays – *The Hamster Wheel* – has been published in *The Crack in the Emerald: New Irish Plays,* Nick Hern Books, London, 1990. It explores the frequent dilemma in Irish life, of women who are faced with the responsibility of caring for invalid husbands and relatives.

35 Emilie Fitzgibbon, 'All Change: Contemporary Fashions in Irish Literature', in *Irish Writers and the Theatre,* Masaru Sekine, ed., Colin Smythe, 1986, p. 45.

8 Transformations and transgressions: Women's discourse on the Scottish stage

1 Liz Lochhead, *Mary Queen of Scots Got Her Head Chopped Off,* Penguin, 1989, p. 11.

2 Poem by Joan Ure in 'Scottish Writing and Culture', Scottish Theatre Archives, MSS 1513, no. 194, 1968.

3 Liz Lochhead in interview with Jenny Brown, *Off the Page,* STV, 1989.

4 David Hutchison, *The Modern Scottish Theatre,* Molendinar Press, 1977, p. 141.

5 In 'Women's Playwrights in Contemporary Scottish Theatre', *Chapman* 43–4, *Scottish Theatre,* Spring 1986, vol VIII, no. 6; vol IX, no. 1.

6 Scottish Theatre Archive, MSS 1513, no. 194, 1968.

7 'I am a feminist but . . .' in Susan Sellers, ed., *Delighting the Heart,* The Women's Press, 1989, p. 180.

8 Winged Horse was set up in 1979 to present new plays by Scottish-based authors, with more women than men in the casts, and to encourage women writers.

9 An alphabet of apocrypha: Collaborations and explorations in women's theatre

1 A number of places do hold collections of information of women's theatre. To locate scripts it is worth contacting (in London) the Fawcett Library, where the Women in Entertainment Archive was lodged after they folded; the New

Playwright's Trust for unpublished scripts; the British Library Manuscripts section, where any professionally produced play should be lodged and the Theatre Museum Study Room, Covent Garden. Bristol University Drama Department has recently established a permanent Women in Theatre Archive (contact Linda FitzSimmons).

2 April de Angelis, Interview of Angela Brinkworth, August, 1989.

3 Kathy Acker, *Lulu Unchained* in *Performing Arts Journal,* **30**.

4 Stella Hall in *Performance Magazine,* **22**.

5 Kathleen Betsko in discussion at International Women Playwrights Conference, Buffalo, New York, 1988. Kathleen Betsko and Rachel Koenig, eds, *Interviews with Contemporary Women Playwrights*, Beech Tree Books, 1987.

6 Virginia Woolf, *A Room of One's Own*, Penguin, 1945.

7 Catherine Itzin, *Stages in the Revolution*, Methuen, 1980.

8 See Susan Croft, Chapter 5.

9 Virginia Woolf, *A Room of One's Own*.

10 April de Angelis.

11 April de Angelis.

12 Interview with Clean Break, April de Angelis, Summer, 1989.

13 Interview with Theatre of Black Women, Susan Croft, *The Plot*, vol 1, no. 2, 1986.

14 See the Introduction of this book for further exposition of these terms.

15 See, for example, Changing Women: *Patterns* by Barbara Burford; Hard Corps: *John* and *Les Autres* by Adele Saleen; Monstrous Regiment: *Enslaved by Dreams* and *Point of Convergence* devised by Chris Bowler and *Alarms* by Susan Yankowitz.

16 Theodore Shank 'Paintings You Can See Into: Hesitate & Demonstrate (England)' in *The Drama Review*, Spring, 1983.

17 See for example: Eileen Phillips, ed., *The Left & the Erotic*, Lawrence & Wishart, 1983; Snitow, Sansell, Thompson, eds, *Desire, the Politics of Sexuality*, Virago, 1984; Rosalind Coward, *Female Desire: Women's Sexuality Today*, Paladin, 1984; Carolyn Vance, ed., *Pleasure & Danger: Exploring Female Sexuality*, Routledge, 1984.

18 See for example: Laura Mulvey, *Visual & Other Pleasures*, Macmillan, 1989; Teresa de Lauretis, *Alice Doesn't: Feminism, Semiotics & Cinema* London, Macmillan, 1984; Annette Kuhn, *The Power of the Image: Essays on Representation & Sexuality*, Routledge, 1985.

19 Betsy Wing (translator of Catherine Clement and Helen Cixous *The Newly Born Woman*, Manchester University Press, 1989) defines jouissance thus:

> Total sexual ecstasy in its most common connotation, but in contemporary French philosophical, psychoanalytic and political usage, it does not stop there, and to equate it with orgasm would be an over-simplification. It would also be inadequate to translate it as enjoyment. This word, however, does maintain some sense of access and participation in connection with rights and property; constitutions guarantee 'the enjoyment of rights'; courts rule on who is to enjoy what right and what property. It is, therefore, a word with simultaneously sexual, political and economic overtones. Total access, total participation, as well as total ecstasy are

implied at the simplest level of meaning – metaphorical – women's to capacity attain something more than total, something extra – abundance and waste (a cultural throwaway), real and unrepresentable.

20 Extract from Helene Cixous' *Incarnation*, translated by Susan Croft, published in *L'Indiade ou L'Inde de Leure Reves et quelques ecrits sur le theatre*, Theatre Du Soleil, 1989.

21 Interview with Siren, Susan Croft, Summer, 1989.

22 See note 1.

23 For further information see Susan Bassnett, *Magdalena: International Women's Experimental Theatre*, Berg, 1989.

24 This point is explored in more detail in Elaine Aston and Gabrielle Griffin, eds, *Stage Left: Women's Theatre Groups in Interview*, Berg, 1991, which contains lengthier interviews with Spare Tyre and Siren among others.

25 Both studios and Young People's Theatre attached to large buildings have been shown to be particularly vulnerable. Y.P.T.s are another site for new writing, collaborative and developmental work.

26 In London, in June 1990, the Half Moon Theatre had recently folded whilst The Albany Empire, home to Second Wave Young Women's Project and Playwrights Festival was on the verge of collapse.

27 Deborah Levy, interviewed in *The Plot*, vol. 1, no. 1, 1986.

28 Margaretta D'Arcy in *The Plot*, vol. 1, no. 1, 1986.

29 Stella Hall in *Performance Magazine*, **22**.

30 Interview with Spare Tyre, Susan Croft, Summer, 1989.

31 Interview with Siren, Susan Croft, Summer, 1989.

32 The concept was originally identified in Jo Freeman's 1974 essay *The Tyranny of Structurelessness* and was circulated by the Anarchist Workers Association, but was not immediately influential. It identifies many of the problems of hidden structure and leadership by default described by Brinkworth and others. For further discussions of collective problems see Charles Landry, David Morley, Russell Southwood and Patrick Wright *What a way to Run a Railroad: an Analysis of Radical Failure*, Comedia, 1985.

33 Eileen Pollock, interview with Susan Croft, in *The Plot*, vol. 1, no. 3, 1986. She and other company members later set up Bloomers.

34 Unpublished diary, Angela Brinkworth.

35 Rob Ritchie, ed., *The Joint Stock Book*, Methuen, 1987.

36 Interview with Winsome Pinnock, Susan Croft, Summer 1989.

37 See for example *The Joint Stock Book*; Richard Pinner, *Contract in Writing* NPT; *New Playwrights Trust Reports* NPT. Much relevant discussion took place at NPT/Theatre writers Union Contracts Conference, March 1989; particularly on problems of control and copyright of devised scripts, especially as significant for women. Transcripts are available from Lizbeth Goodman, Open University.

38 Interview with Winsome Pinnock, Susan Croft, Summer, 1987.

39 Virginia Woolf, *A Room of One's Own*.

Bibliography

Bibliography of published plays

★ indicates that works by these writers also appear in the list of unpublished work

Adshead, Kay. *Thatcher's Women* in Remnant, *Plays by Women 7.*
Arden, Jane. *Vagina Rex & the Gas Oven*, Calder & Boyars, 1971.
★Aron, Geraldine. *Bar & Ger*, French, 1980.
★Aron, Geraldine. *A Galway Girl*, French, 1981.
Bagnold, Enid. *The Chalk Garden*, French, 1956.
Bagnold, Enid. *The Chinese Prime Minister* in *Four Plays by Enid Bagnold*, Heinemann, 1970.
Bagnold, Enid. *Call Me Jacky*, in *Four Plays.*
Brewster, Yvonne, ed. *Black Plays 1*, Methuen, 1987.
Brewster, Yvonne, ed. *Black Plays 2*, Methuen, 1989.
Christie, Agatha. *The Mouse Trap,* French, 1956.
Christie, Agatha. *The Verdict*, French, 1958.
Christie, Agatha. *The Unexpected Guest*, French, 1958.
Christie, Agatha. *Go Back for Murder*, French, 1960.
Christie, Agatha. *An Afternoon at the Seaside, The Rats, The Patient (three 1-act plays)*, French, 1963.
Churchill, Caryl. *Light Shining in Buckinghamshire,* Pluto, 1978.
Churchill, Caryl. *Traps*, Pluto, 1978.
Churchill, Caryl. *Cloud Nine*, Pluto, 1979, revised ed. Methuen, 1984.
Churchill, Caryl. *Vinegar Tom,* in Wandor, *Plays by Women 1.*
Churchill, Caryl. *Top Girls*, Methuen, 1982, revised ed. 1984.
Churchill, Caryl. *Fen*, Methuen, 1983.

Churchill, Caryl. *Softcops*, Methuen, 1984.

Churchill, Caryl. *Plays One: Owners, Traps, Vinegar Tom, Light Shining in Buckinghamshire, Cloud Nine*, Methuen, 1985.

Churchill, Caryl. *Serious Money*, Methuen, 1987.

Churchill, Caryl. *Plays Two: Softcops, Serious Money & Fen*, Methuen, 1989.

Churchill, Caryl. *Icecream*, Royal Court/Nick Hern, 1989.

Churchill, Caryl. *Shorts (ten short plays)*, Nick Hern, 1990.

Churchill, Caryl and Lan, David. *A Mouthful of Birds*, Methuen, 1986.

Considine, Ann and Slovo, Robyn, eds. *Dead Proud: from Second Wave Young Women Playwrights*, Women's Press, 1987.

Cooke, Trish (a.k.a. Roselia Jean Baptiste), *Back Street Mammy* in Harwood *First Run*. (An extract from an earlier version of this, and her *No Place Like Home* also in Considine and Slovo, *Dead Proud*).

Daniels, Sarah. *Masterpieces*, Royal Court/Methuen, 1984.

Daniels, Sarah. *Masterpieces*, revised ed. Methuen, 1986.

Daniels, Sarah. *Ripen Our Darkness* and *The Devil's Gateway*, Methuen, 1986.

Daniels, Sarah. *Neaptide*, Methuen, 1986.

Daniels, Sarah. *Byrthrite*, Methuen, 1987.

Daniels, Sarah. *The Gut Girls*, Methuen, 1989.

Daniels, Sarah. *Beside Herself*, Methuen/Women's Playhouse Trust, 1990.

*D'Arcy, Margaretta (with Arden, John), *The Non-stop Connolly Show*, Pluto, 5 vols, 1977–8, Methuen, 1986; *Vandeleur's Folly*, Methuen, 1981; *The Ballygombeen Request* first version *Scripts 9* (New York); revised version as *The Little Gray Home in the West*, Pluto, 1982.

Davis, Jill, ed. *Lesbian Plays*, Methuen, 1987.

Davis, Jill, ed. *Lesbian Plays 2*, Methuen, 1989.

Dayley, Grace. *Rose's Story*, in Wandor, *Plays By Women 4*.

Deegan, Denise. *Daisy Pulls It Off*, French, 1985.

Delaney, Shelagh. *A Taste of Honey*, Methuen, 1982.

Delaney, Shelagh. *The Lion in Love*, Methuen, 1967.

*Devlin, Ann. *Ourselves Alone* with *A Woman Calling* and *The Long March*, Faber, 1986.

Dodgson, Elyse. *Motherland*, Heinemann, 1984.

Dodgson, Elyse, ed. *First lines: Young Writers at the Royal Court*, Hodder, 1990.

Dunbar, Andrea. *Rita, Sue and Bob Too* with *The Arbor* and *Shirley*, Methuen, London, 1988.

Dunn, Nell. *Steaming*, Amber Lane, 1981.

Evans, Lisa. *Stamping, Shouting & Singing Home* in Remnant *Plays by Women 7*.

Faku, Dorcas. (with Taylor, Diane). *Wenzani*, Polypton & West Six, 1984.

*Frumin, Sue. *The Housetrample*, in Davis, *Lesbian Plays 2*.

*Gannon, Lucy. *Raping the Gold*, Chappell, 1988.

Gems, Pam. *Dusa, Fish, Stas, & Vi*, in Wandor, *Plays by Women 1*.

Gems, Pam. *Three Plays: Piaf, Camille & Loving Women*, Penguin, 1985.

Gems, Pam. *Queen Christina*, in Remnant, *Plays by Women 5*.

*Ghose Nandita. *Ishtar Descends*, in Gray, *Second Wave Plays*.

Gideon, Killeon. *England is de Place for Me*, in Gray, *Second Wave Plays*.

Gray, Frances, ed., *Second Wave Plays: Women at the Albany Empire*, Sheffield, Academic Press, 1990.

Hansberry, Lorraine. *A Raisin in the Sun,* in Remnant, *Plays by Women 5.*

Harwood, Kate, ed., *First Run: New Plays by New Writers,* Nick Hern, 1989.

Harwood, Kate, ed., *First Run 2: New Plays by New Writers,* Nick Hern, 1990.

Hayes, Catherine. *Skirmishes,* Faber, 1982.

Hayes, Catherine. *Not Waving,* Faber 1984.

Horsfield, Debbie. *The Red Devils Trilogy,* Methuen, 1986.

Jacobs, Pauline (with the Bemarro Sisters). *A Slice of Life* (extract in Considine and Slovo, *Dead Proud*).

Jellicoe, Ann. *The Knack* and *The Sport of My Mad Mother,* Faber, 1985.

Jellicoe, Ann. *The Rising Generation* in Alan Durband, ed. *Playbill Two,* Hutchinson, 1969.

Jinton, Soraya. *Lalita's Way,* in Dodgson, *First Lines.*

*Johnson, Jennifer. *The Nightingale & not the Lark, The Porch* and *The Invisible Man,* Raven Arts Press, Dublin, 1988.

Kay, Jackie. *Chiaroscuro,* in Davis, *Lesbian Plays.*

*Kayla, Lisselle. *When Did I Last See You* (extract in Considine and Slovo).

Keatley, Charlotte. *My Mother Said I Never Should,* Methuen, 1988.

*Klein, Debbie. *Coming Soon,* in Davis, *Lesbian Plays 2.*

Lessing, Doris. *Play With a Tiger,* in *Plays of the Sixties,* Pan, 1973.

Lewis, Eve. *Ficky Stingers,* in Remnant, *Plays by Women 6.*

Littlewood, Joan. *Oh What a Lovely War,* Methuen, 1963.

*Lochhead, Liz. *Mary Queen of Scots Got Her Head Chopped Off,* Penguin, 1989.

*Lochhead, Liz. *Blood & Ice,* in Wandor, *Plays by Women 4.*

Luckham, Claire. *Trafford Tanzi,* in Wandor, *Plays by Women 2.*

MacDonald, Sharman. *When I Was a Girl, I Used to Scream and Shout . . .,* Faber, 1985.

*McIntyre, Clare. *Low Level Panic,* in Harwood, *First Run.*

*McIntyre, Clare. *My Heart's a Suitcase,* Nick Hern, 1990.

*Morgan, Elaine. *Waiting Room,* French, 1958.

*Morgan, Elaine. *The Soldier & the Woman,* French, 1961.

Mortimer, Jeremy, ed. *Young Playwrights Festival 1988,* BBC, 1988.

*Munro, Rona. *Piper's Cave,* in Remnant, *Plays by Women 5.*

Norman, Marsha. *'Night Mother,* Faber, 1983.

O'Brien, Edna. *A Pagan Place,* Faber, 1973.

O'Malley, Mary. *Once A Catholic,* Amber Lane, 1978.

O'Malley, Mary. *Look Out, Here Comes Trouble,* Amber Lane, 1979.

Ogidi, Ann. *Ragamuffin,* in Mortimer, *Young Playwrights Festival.*

*Oshodi, Marie. *Blood, Sweat & Fears,* in Brewster, *Black Plays 2.*

Osment, Phillip, ed. *Gay Sweatshop: Four Plays & a Company,* Methuen, 1989.

Page, Louise. *Tissue,* in Wandor, *Plays by Women 1.*

Page, Louise. *Salonika,* Methuen, 1983.

Page, Louise. *Real Estate,* Methuen, 1984.

Page, Louise. *Golden Girls,* Methuen, 1985.

Page, Louise. *Beauty & The Beast,* Methuen/Women's Playhouse Trust, 1986.

Page, Louise. *Diplomatic Wives,* Methuen, 1989.

*Pinnock, Winsome. *Leave Taking,* in Harwood, *First Run.*

*Pinnock, Winsome. *A Rock in Water,* in Brewster, *Black Plays 2.*

*Pinnock, Winsome. *A Hero's Welcome,* in *Plays International,* April 1989.

*Reid, Christina. *Joyriders & Tea in a China Cup*, Methuen, 1987.

Posener, Jill. *Any Woman Can* in Davis *Lesbian Plays*.

Remnant, Mary, ed. *Plays by Women*, vols 5–7, Methuen, 1986–8.

*Rudet, Jacqueline. *Money to Live*, in Remnant, *Plays by Women 5*.

*Rudet, Jacqueline. *Basin*, in Brewster, *Black Plays 1*.

Shange, Ntozake. *for coloured girls who have considered suicide when the rainbow is enuf* Methuen 1980.

Shange, Ntozake. *Spell no 7*, Methuen, 1986.

Sulkin, David, ed. *Festival Plays*, Longman, 1986.

Thomas, Heidi. *Indigo*, Amber Lane, 1988.

Thomas, Heidi. *Shamrocks and Crocodiles*, Amber Lane, 1988.

Townsend, Sue. *Bazaar and Rummage: Groping for Words* and *Womberang*, Methuen, 1984.

Townsend, Sue. *The Great Celestial Cow*, Methuen, 1984.

Townsend, Sue. *The Secret Diary of Adrian Mole Aged 13: the play*, Methuen, 1985.

Wandor, Michelene (scripted). *Care & Control*, in Wandor, ed. *Strike While the Iron is Hot,* Journeyman, 1980.

Wandor, Michelene, *Spilt Milk* in R. Rook, ed. *Play Nine*, Arnold, 1981.

Wandor, Michelene. *Aurora Leigh*, in Wandor, *Plays by Women 1*.

Wandor, Michelene. *Five Plays: To Die Among Friends, Old Wives' Tale Whores d'Oeuvres, Scissors* and *Aid Thy Neighbour*, Journeyman, 1984.

Wandor, Michelene, ed. *Plays by Women*, vols 1–4, Methuen, 1982–5.

Welburn, Vivienne. *Johnny So Long* and *The Drag*, Calder and Boyars, 1967.

Welburn, Vivienne. *Clearway*, Calder and Boyars, 1967.

Wertenbaker, Timberlake. *New Anatomies,* in *Plays Introduction*, Faber, 1984.

Wertenbaker, Timberlake. *The Grace of Mary Traverse*, Faber, 1985.

Wertenbaker, Timberlake. *Our Country's Good*, Methuen, 1988.

Wertenbaker, Timberlake. *The Love of the Nightingale* and *The Grace of Mary Traverse*, Faber, 1989.

Wymark, Olwen. *Three Plays: Lunchtime Concert, The Inhabitants* and *Coda*, Calder & Boyars, 1967.

Wymark, Olwen. *The Gymnasium & Other Plays*, Calder & Boyars, 1971.

Wymark, Olwen. *Loved*, French, 1980.

Wymark, Olwen. *Find Me*, in Wandor, *Plays by Women 2*.

Wymark, Olwen. *Best Friends, The Committee* and *the Twenty-second Day*, Calder, 1984.

*Yeger, Sheila. *Self Portrait*, Amber Lane, 1990. *Variations* in A. Castledine (ed.) *Plays by Women Vol. 9*, Methuen, 1991.

Secondary sources – reference

Acker, Kathy. *Lulu Unchained*, in *Performing Arts Journal,* **30**.

Adams, Ruth. *A Woman's Place 1910–1975*, Chatto & Windus, 1975.

Artaud, Antonin. *The Theatre & Its Double*, Calder & Boyers, 1970.

Aston, Elaine and Griffin, Gabrielle, eds, *Stage Left: Women's Theatre Groups in Interview*, Berg, 1991.

Banks, Morwenna and Swift, Amanda. *The Joke's on Us*, Pandora, 1987.

Bann, Stephen and Boult, S. eds. *Russian Formalism*, Scottish Academic Press, 1973.

Bassnett, Susan. *Magdalena: International Women's Experimental Theatre*, Berg, 1989.

Beechey, Veronica and Whitelegg, Elizabeth, eds. *Women in Britain Today*, Oxford University Press, 1986.

Belsey, Catherine. *Critical Practice*, Methuen, New Accents, 1980.

Betsko, Kathleen and Koenig, Rachel, eds. *Interviews with Contemporary Women Playwrights*, Beech Tree Books, 1987.

Bradby, David and Williams, David. *Directors' Theatre*, Macmillan, 1988.

Brown, Christopher. *Bruegel*, Phaidon, 1975.

Browne, Terry. *Playwrights' Theatre*, Pitman Publishing Ltd, 1975.

Bryan, Beverley, Dadzie, Stella and Scafe, Suzanne. *The Heart of the Race: Black Women's Lives in Britain*, Virago, 1985.

Cant, Bob and Hemmings, Susan, eds. *Radical Records: Thirty Years of Lesbian and Gay History*, Routledge, 1988.

Case, Sue Ellen. *Feminism & Theatre*, Macmillan, 1988.

Cave, Richard Allen. *New British Drama in Performance on the London Stage: 1970 to 1985*, Smythe, 1987.

Chambers, Colin and Prior, Mike. *Playwrights' Progress: Patterns of Postwar British Drama*, Amber Lane, 1987.

Clement, Catherine and Cixous, Helene. *The Newly Born Woman*. Trans. Betsy Wing. Manchester University Press, 1985.

Coward, Rosalind. *Female Desire: Women's Sexuality Today*, Paladin, 1984.

Craig, Sandy, ed. *Dreams & Deconstructions*, Amber Lane, 1980.

Curtis, Tony, ed. *Wales the Imagined Nation*, J.W. Arrowsmith, 1986.

Daly, Mary. *Women & Poverty*, Dublin Attic Press, 1989.

D'Arcy, Margaretta. *Awkward Corners*, Methuen, 1988.

De Lauretis, Teresa. *Alice Doesn't: Feminism, Semiotics & Cinema*, Macmillan, 1984.

Dipple, Elizabeth. *Iris Murdoch: work for the Spirit*, Methuen.

Eagleton, Mary. *Feminist Literary Theory: A Reader*, Blackwell, 1986.

Elsom, John. *Post-war British Theatre Criticism*, RKP, 1981.

Erens, Patricia, ed. *Sexual Strategems: The World of Women in Film*, Horizon, 1979.

Etherton, Michael. *Contemporary Irish Dramatists*, Macmillan, 1989.

Ferris, Lesley. *Acting Women: Images of Women in Theatre*, Macmillan 1990.

Fitzsimmons, Linda. *File on Churchill*, Methuen, 1989.

Fitzsimon, Christopher. *The Irish Theatre*, Thames & Hudson, 1983.

Ford-Smith, Honor, ed. *Lionheart Gal: Life Stories of Jamaican Women*, Women's Press, 1986.

Foucault, Michel. *Discipline & Punish*, Penguin, 1987.

Freud, Sigmund. *Pelican Freud, vol. 14: Art & Literature*, Pelican, 1985.

Gardiner, Caroline. *What Share of the Cake? The Employment of Women in the English Theatre*, Women's Playhouse Trust, 1987.

Greene, Gayle and Kahn, Coppelia. *Making a Difference: Feminist Literary Criticism*, Methuen, 1985.

Griffiths, Trevor R. and Woddis, Carole. *Theatre Guide*, Bloomsbury, 1988.

Guptara, Prahbu. *Black British Literature: An Annotated Bibliography*, Dangaroo Press, 1986.

Hayman, Ronald. *British Theatre since 1955*. Oxford University Press, 1979.

Hewison, Robert. *In Anger: Culture in the Cold War*, Weidenfeld, 1981.

Hewison, Robert. *Too Much: Art and Society in the Sixties*, Methuen, 1986.

Hutchinson, David. *The Modern Scottish Theatre*, Molendinar Press, 1977.

Hutchison, Robert. *The Politics of the Arts Council*, Sinclair Browne, 1982.

Itzin, Catherine. *Stages in the Revolution*, Methuen, 1980.

Jackson, Rosemary. *Fantasy: the Literature of Subversion*, Methuen, 1981.

Kerensky, Oleg. *The New British Drama*, Hamish Hamilton, 1977.

Keyssar, Helene. *Feminist Theatre*, Macmillan, 1984.

Khan, Naseem. *The Arts Britain Ignores*, Commission for Racial Equality, 1976.

Kelly, Ann. *Cultural Policy in Ireland*, Museum's Trust, 1989.

Kristeva, Julia. 'Signifying practice and the mode of production'. Trans. G. Nowell-Smith in the *Edinburgh Film Festival Magazine*, 1976.

Kristeva, Julia. 'The ruin of a poetics' In *Russian Formalism*. Ed. S. Bann and J. Bowlt.

Kristeva, Julia. *Desire in Language*, Blackwell, 1980.

Kristeva, Julia. *Revolution in Poetic Language*, Columbia, 1984.

Kirkpatrick, D.L., ed. *Contemporary Dramatists*, St James Press, 1988.

Kuhn, Annete. *The Power of the Image: Essays on Representation & Sexuality*, Routledge, 1985.

Lacan, Jaques. *Ecrits*, RKP, 1977.

Landry, Charles, Morley, David, Southwood, Russell and Wright, Patrick. *What a Way to Run a Railroad: an Analysis of Radical Failure*, Comedia, 1985.

Lloyd-Evans, Gareth and Lloyd-Evans, Barbara. *Plays in Review 1956–1980*, Batsford, 1985.

London Theatre Record, 1981, ed. and published by Ian Herbert, Twickenham.

McGrath, John. *A Good Night Out*, Methuen, 1981.

Malpede, Karen. *Women in Theatre*, Drama Books, 1983.

Marks, Elaine and de Courtivron, Isabelle, *New French Feminisms*, Harvester, 1981.

Marowitz, Charles, Milne, Tom and Hale, Owen, eds. *New Theatre Voices of the Fifties & Sixties*, Eyre Methuen, 1965.

Marwick, Arthur. *British Society Since 1945*, Penguin, 1982.

Mills, Jane, *Womanwords*, Longman, 1989.

Moi Toril, ed. *Kristeva Reader*, Blackwell, 1986.

Mulvey, Laura. *Visual & Other Pleasures*, Macmillan, 1989.

Murphy, Pat and McCafferty, Nell. *Women in Focus*, Attic Press, 1989.

Owesu, Kwesi. *The Struggle For Black Arts in Britain*, Comedia, 1986.

Owesu, Kwesi. *Storms of the Heart: an Anthology of Black Arts & Culture*, Camden Press, 1988.

Parker, Roszika and Pollock, Griselda, *Old Mistresses: Women, Art and Ideology*, RKP, 1981.
Phillips, Eileen, ed. *The Left & the Erotic*, Lawrence & Wishart, 1983.
Rabey, David Ian. *British and Irish Political Drama in the Twentieth Century*, Macmillan, 1986.
Ritchie, Rob, ed. *The Joint Stock Book*, Methuen, 1987.
Rowbotham, Sheila. *Hidden from History*, Pluto, 1973.
Rowbotham, Sheila. *Woman's Consciousness, Man's World*, Pelican, 1973.
Russell Brown, John. *A Short Guide to Modern British Drama*, Heinemann, 1982.
Russell Taylor, John. *Anger & After*, Methuen, 1962, (revised ed., 1969).
Russell Taylor, John. *The Second Wave*, Methuen, 1971.
Sekine, Masaru. *Irish Writers & the Theatre*, Smythe, 1986.
Showalter, Elaine. *A Literature of Their Own*, Virago, 1978.
Sinfield, Alan, ed. *Society & Literature 1945–1970*, Methuen, 1983.
Sked, Allan and Cook, Chris. *Post-War Britain*, Penguin, 1979.
Snitow, Ann, Sansell, Christine and Thompson, Sharon, eds. *Desire: The Politics of Sexuality*, Virago, 1984.
Spender, Dale. *Man Made Language*, RKP, 1980.
Spender, Dale. *There's Always Been a Women's Movement This Century*, Pandora, 1983.
Stafford-Clark, Max. *Letters to George*, Nick Hern, 1989.
Sulter, Maud (ed.). *Passion: Discourses on Blackwomen's Creativity*, Urban Fox Press, 1990.
Todd, Susan. *Women & Theatre: Calling the Shots*, Faber, 1984.
Tuttle, Lisa. *Encyclopedia of Feminism*, Longman, 1986.
Vance, Carolyn, ed. *Pleasure & Danger: Exploring Female Sexuality*, Routledge, 1984.
Wandor, Michelene. *Understudies*, Methuen, 1981.
Wandor, Michelene. *Carry on Understudies*, RKP, 1986.
Wandor, Michelene. *Look Back in Gender*, Methuen, 1987.
Willett, John, ed. *Brecht on Theatre*, Methuen, 1964.
Williams, Raymond. *Drama From Ibsen To Brecht* (revised ed.), Pelican, 1973.
Wilson, Armit. *Finding a Voice: Asian Women in Britain*, Virago, 1979.
Wilson, Elizabeth. *Only Halfway to Paradise: Women in Postwar Britain: 1945–1968*, Tavistock, 1980.
Wolff, Janet. *The Social Production of Art*, Macmillan, 1981.
Woolf, Virginia. *A Room of One's Own*, Grafton (Collins), 1977 (originally Hogarth Press Ltd, 1929).
Worth, Katharine, J. *Revolutions in Modern English Drama*, Bell & Sons, 1973.

Unpublished scripts/performance references

Listed below are the performances mentioned/discussed in this book, for which, as far as is presently known, published scripts are not available. The sign ★ indicates that contact with the writer, or the typescript, may be available from the New Playwright's Trust. The sign † indicates that contact may be made through Made in Wales. Production dates are given when available. A ‡ indicates scripts by this writer appear in the bibliography of published scripts.

Andoh, Adjoa. *Just My Luck*, Theatre Centre, 1989.

Agard, Sandra. *Women & Sisters*, With Isaacs, Cassandra and Smith, Marcia, Royal Court YPT, 1986.

Archer, Robyn. *A Star is Torn*, 1982.

‡Aron, Geraldine, *Same Old Moon*, 1984.

Artiste, Cindy. *Dreams With Teeth* Contact, Manchester, 1987; *Half Hearts & Quarter Measures*, Avon Touring; *Face Value*, Contact, 1988; *Meridian* (from Alice Walker's novel) Contact, 1990.

Ahmad, Rukhsana. *Song for a Sanctuary*, Reading Asian Women Writers Workshop, 1990.

Awan, Helen. *Workshop*. Tara Community Theatre Group.

Bains, Lynn. *Nae Problem; Great Lovers of the World* (with Strathclyde Theatre Group) 1985; *The Lady Shall Say Her Mind Freely*, 1986; *Getting Past It*, 1987.

Bartlett, Ruth Dunlap. *The Cocoa Party*, Black Theatre Co-op, 1987.

Belle, Christine. *Word of Mouth*. Strange Fruit, Nottingham, 1988.

Bemarro Sisters. *Gloria*. Second Wave, Albany Empire, 1988.

Bennette Hume, Peggy. Mainly children's plays for Roots Inc.

Bhuchar, Sudha and Langdon Smith, Kristine. *House of the Sun* (from Meira Chand's novel), Theatre Royal Stratford East.

Binchy, Maeve. *End of Term*, Peacock Theatre, Ireland, 1976; *The Half-Promised Land*, Peacock Theatre, 1979.

Bourcier, Yvonne, see Wertenbaker.

Reinburg, Petronella. Various plays for L'Ouverture Theatre Company.

Buckler, Jane. *Burd Mary*,† Write On Festival, 1988; *Steady State*, Write On Festival, 1989; *The Slow Approach of Night*, R.A.D.A., July 1990.

Bunyan, Carol. *To Come Home To This*, 1981; *Waving*, 1988.

Burford, Barbara. *Patterns*, Changing Women at Oval House, 1984.*

Burke-Kennedy, Mary Elizabeth. *Curigh the Shape Shifter*, 1980; *Women at Arms*, Dublin Theatre Festival, 1988.

Charabanc (Irish Company). *Lay Up Your Ends*, Tyrone Guthrie Centre, Annaghmakerrig, 1983. (with Jones, Marie) *Oul delf & False Teeth*, 1984; *Gold in the Streets*, 1986; *The Girls in the Big Picture*, 1987; *Somewhere over the Balcony*, 1988.

Cole, Shorelle. *Blind Faith*, Second Wave, Albany Empire, 1988.

Cooper, Mary. *Heartgame* (with women's drama group as part of Jawaani double bill with *Prem*), Asian Co-operative Theatre, 1988.

‡D'Arcy, Margaretta (with Arden, John). *A Pinprick of History*, 1977.

Davies, Nicola Jorden. *After Eeyore,* * Green Grows*.

Deb'Bora, *Where Do I Go from Here*. Akimbo Productions 1984.

Di Mambro, Ann Marie. *Hocus Pocus*, 1986; *Visible Differences*, 1986 (T.I.E.); *Joe* (monologue), 1987; *Sheila*, 1988; *The Letter Box* (monologue), 1989; *Tally's Blood*, 1990.

Downie, Ann. *The White Bird Passes*, 1986; *Watching Waiters*, 1986; *The Way to go Home*, 1987; *Waiting on One*, 1987; *The Yellow on the Broom*, 1989; *Biting the Hands*, 1989, BBC TV Play on One.

‡Dunn, Nell. *The Little Heroine*, 1988.

‡Dunn, Nell and Henri, Adrian. *I want*, written 1972, staged 1983.

Essa, Saira. *You Can't Stop the Revolution*, Temba, 1988.

Evaristi, Marcella. *Dorothy & the Bitch*, 1977; *Scotia's Darlings*, 1978; *Hard to Get*, 1980; *Wedding Belles & Green Grasses*, 1981; *Commedia*, 1982/3; *Checking Out*, 1986; *Terrestrial Extras,* 1986; *The Hat* (radio), 1989; *Visiting Company*, 1989.

Evaristo, Bernadine. *Tiger Teeth Clenched Not to Bite*, Theatre of Black Women, 1982 with Hilaire, Patricia; *Silhouette*, Theatre of Black Women, 1982; *Pyeyucca,* Theatre of Black Women, 1984/5.

Fairbanks, Tasha. *Mama's Gone a Hunting,* 1981; *Pulp*, 1985.

‡Frumin, Sue. *Bohemian Rhapsody,* 1980; *Rabbit in a Trap*, 1982; *Raising the Wreck,* 1985; *Home Sweet Home,* 1987.

Gallagher, Miriam. *Fancy Footwork*, Exit, 1983.

‡Gannon, Lucy. *Keeping Tom Nice*, 1986.

Gay Sweatshop, devised. *What the Hell is She Doing Here*, 1978.

George, Christine. *Family Bliss*, Albany Empire, 1989.

‡Ghose, Nandita. *Land*, Oval House, 1988; * *Bhangra Girls*, Red Ladder, 1989.

Glover, Sue. *The Seal Wife*, 1980; *An Island in Largo*, 1981; *The Straw Chair*, 1988.

Goldman, Lisa and Tuck, Sarah. *On the Bridge*, Oval House, January 1990.

Green, Maro and Griffin, Caroline. *More*, 1985.

Greer, Bonnie. *Zebra Days*, ReSisters, 1988.

Griffin, Annie. *Almost Persuaded, Blackbeard the Pirate*.

Griffin, Caroline. See Green, Maro.

Griffiths, Paula. *A Hanging in Hannika*, BBC Radio Wales, 1985; Write On Festival, 1986.†

Gwynn, Helen. *Echo Lady*, Write On Festival, 1989.†

Halpin, Mary. *Semi-Private*, Winner of the Irish Times Women's Playwriting Competition 1982, revived Tivoli, Dublin, 1989.

Hamilton, Gloria. *Pulse,* Umoja; *Mercy*, publication details unclear; *In Nobody's Backyard*, Umoja, 1985; *Success or Failure,* Umoja, 1988.

Hard, Corps, with Parker, Karen and Klein, Debbie. *For Ever*, 1985.

Harris, Ruth. *The Children*, Theatre of Black Women, 1988; *The Cripple*, Theatre of Black Women, 1986.

Hartigan, Anne. *Beds* (out of Annaghmakerrig workship), Dublin Theatre Festival, 1982; *La Corbiere,* Dublin Theatre Festival, 1989.

Hepburn, Judith. Various Plays with Carib Theatre.

Hilaire, Patricia. *Just Another Day*, Royal Court Young Writers Festival, 1982; *Hey Brown Girl*, Theatre of Black Women, 1982; see also work with Evaristo.

‡Horsfield, Debbie. *Away frim it All*, 1982; *All You Desire*, 1986.

Hynes, Garry. *Island Protected by a Bridge of Glass,* Edinburgh Fringe First, 1980.

Isaacs, Cassandra. See AGARD.

‡Johnson, Jennifer. *Shadows on Our Skin*, TV play.

Judd, Yazmine. Various Plays for Sphinx and others.*

K, Jacqui. *A Black Woman's Diary*, Roots Theatre, 1990.

Kay, Ada. *The Man from Thermopylae*, 1961.

Kay, Jackie. *Twice Over*, 1988.

‡Kayla, Liselle. *Don't Chat Me Business*, ReSisters, 1990;* *Don't Pay Dem No Mind*, Hi Time Theatre Co., Black Mental Health Conference Islington, 1988.

Kearsley, Charlotte. *Waiting,* 1982; *Under the Web,* 1987.

Kesson, Jessie. *Another Time, Another Place*, now TV film; *Go West, Wild Woman*, Castle Douglas Unity Players, 1974; radio work.

‡Klein, Debbie. See Parker and Hard Corps.

‡Lochhead, Liz. *Dracula*, 1985; *Shanghaied*, 1983; *Same Difference; Jock Tamson's Bairns*, 1990.

Lawson, Thelma. *Safe As Houses*, Theatre Centre, 1990.

Lewis, Pat. *Iron them Dry*,† rehearsed reading, Write On, 1988.

Looi, Sue-Lin, *All Sewn Up* (with Porter, Beth), Eastern Actors Studio, 1989.

Macheol, Zindika. (See Zindika).

Magee, Paula. *In Nomine Patris; Spacemen & Party Frocks*, Theatre about Glasgow, 1986; *Breast is Best*, TV play; *Daddy's Wedding*.

Martin, Cheryl. *Late Night Ice Cream*, Pit Prop Theatre Company, Manchester.

McCafferty, Nell. *Worm in the Bud*, Project Arts Centre, Dublin, 1985.

‡McIntyre, Clare. *I've Been Running*, 1986.

‡McIntyre, Clare and Nunn, Stephanie. *Better a Live Pompey*, 1981.

McLeod, Jenny. *Cricket at Camp David*, Bolton Octagon, 1989; *Island Life*, Monstrous Regiment & Nottingham Playhouse, 1987.

McNair, Sarah. *Les Autres (That Lot)*.

‡Morgan, Elaine. *Love for Liz*, Theatre Royal, Windsor; *Licence to Murder*, Guildford and Vaudeville, London; *What's got into You?* Welsh tour; *Happy Ever After*.

‡Munro, Rona. *Fugue*, 1983.

Murray, Melissa. *Hormone Imbalance*, 1979; *Ophelia*, 1979; *The Execution*, 1982; *Body Cell*, 1986.

Nassauer, Sharon and Stewart-Park, Angela. *I Like Me Like This*, 1979.

O'Connor, Penny. *Dig Volley Spike*, 1988.

‡Oshodi, Marie. *From Choices to Chocolate*, Workshop, Riverside Studios,★ 1987; *The S Bend*, Royal Court Young Writers Festival, 1984; *Here Comes a Candle*, Oval House, 1990.

O'Suilleabhain, Siobhan. A range of works in Gaelic.

Oyeleye, Olusola. *Many Voices One Chant*, Battersea Arts Centre Young Directors Festival, 1987.★ Also plays for Theatre Centre, Harmony and others.

Parker, Karen and Klein, Debbie. *Blood on the Lino*, 1990.

Patel, Jyoti (with Simons, Jez). *Awaaj*, Royal Court YPT, 1987; *Prem*, Battersea Arts Centre Young Directors Festival, 1987 and Asian Co-operative Theatre, 1988; *Kit, Sona & Ba*, Leicester Haymarket Studio, 1989.

Pearse, Gabriela (with Pearse, Jean). *Miss Quarshie & the Tiger's Tail*, Theatre of Black Women, 1986.

‡Pinnock, Winsome. *The Wind of Change*, Half Moon YPT, 1987; *Picture Palace*, Women's Theatre Group, 1988.

Pritchard, Marged. *Byd o Amser; Cylmau; Goriad yn y Drws*.

Raif, Ayshe. *Another Woman*, 1983; *A Party for Bonzo*, 1985; *Fail Safe*, 1986.

Randall, Paulette. *Fishing*, Royal Court Young Writers Festival, 1984★ and Black Theatre Season, 1985; *A Pudding like a Night on the Sea*, BBC Radio.

Randawa, Ravi. Tara in Education.

‡Reid, Christina. *The Belle of Belfast City*, Lyric Players Theatre, Belfast, 1989; *My Name Shall I Tell You My Name*, Young Vic London, 1990.

Reid, Netta Blair, *The Shepherd Beguiled*, 1957, Theatr Alba, 1982.

Richmond, Gilian. *The Last Waltz*, 1986.

Ritchie, Aileen. *Can ye Sew Cushions; Shang-a-lang*, 1986; *Asking for It*, 1989; *Walking My Baby Back Home*, 1989.

‡Rudet, Jacqueline. *God's Second in Command*, Royal Court Theatre, 1987; *Take Back What's Yours*, Croydon Warehouse, 1989.

Saleem, Adele. *John*, 1984.

Saville, Charmian. *The Consecrator,*† Write On Festival, 1988.

Schofield, Julia. *Love on the Plastic*, 1987.

Shapiro, Jacqui. *One of Us*, 1983; *Trade Secrets*, 1984; *Dead Romantic*, 1984; *Winter in the Morning*, 1988.

Shu-Fern, Lin. *The Sale of the Century*, Workshop, 1989.*

Sidhwa, Yasmin. *Chameleon*, Unlock the Chains Collective, Tara Arts Centre, 1990.

Smith, Kathleen J. *Buddha; Women Without Men; The Bronte Story*.

Smith, Marcia. *Women & Sisters* (see Agard and Isaacs).

Stajno, Yasa. *Salt River*, Pascal Theatre Co., 1988.

Stewart-Park. See Nassauer.

Swift, Caroline. One-woman play on *Lady Gregory*, Peacock Theatre, Ireland, 1987/8.

Syal (Meera) Feroza. *One of Us* (with Shapiro, Jacqui), National Student Drama Festival, 1983.

Walsh, Dolores. *In The Talkin Dark*, Winner of the Society of Irish Playwright's Award, 1987.

‡Wandor, Michelene. *Aid thy Neighbour*, 1978.

Watkins, Christine. *Adult Ways*†. Write On, 1986.

‡Wertenbaker, Timberlake and Bourcier, Yvonne. *Abel's Sister*, 1984.

Women's Theatre Group. *Double Vision*, 1982.

Yaw, Sandra. *Zerri's Choice*, Women's Theatre Group, 1989.*

‡Yeger, Sheila. *Alice & Other Reflections; Watching Foxes; Geraniums; Dancing in the Dark; Variations on a Theme by Clara Schumann; The Ballad of Tilly Hake; A Day by the Sea; Yellow Ochre*.

Zindika. *Paper & Stone*, Black Theatre Co-op, 1990.

Further information

Further plays by US, Caribbean and other international Black women writers produced in Britain.

Braithwaite, Diana. (US). *Mrs Jones Does Not Live Here Any More*, Porsche Club, Birmingham, Kajoyo Festival, 1989.

Brown, Hyacinth. (Jamaica). *BUPS*, Roots Theatre Co., St. Matthews Meeting Place, London, SW2, 1989.

Burrows, Vinie. (US). *Walk Together Children*, 1986.

Cumper, Pat. (Jamaica). *Fallen Angel & the Devil Concubine*. Graduate Theatre Co., London International Festival of Theatre, 1989.

Glouden, Barbara. (Jamaica). *Flash Trash*, Half Moon, 1986; *The Pirate Princess*, 1986.

Holland, Endesha Ida Mae. (US). *From The Mississippi Delta*, Young Vic, 1989.*

Owen, Rena. (New Zealand, Maori). *The River That Ran Away*, Clean Break, 1988.

Parker, Sheryn Hylton. (Jamaica). *Bring me Tomorrow,* Northampton Arts Centre & Tour, Kajoyo Festival, 1989.

Schwartz-Bart, Simone. (Guadeloupe). *Mon Beau Capitaine*, Institut Francais, 1989.

Theatre groups and group-devised work

See Alphabet of Apocrypha (Chapter 9), particularly the subsections 'Collaborative' and 'List', and Chapter 2, for discussion of groups, with reference to collectively devised and attributed work. Some of this work can be found in the Anthologies listed under Published Works, for example see under Brewster, Considine and Slovo, Davis, Dodgson, Gray, Harwood, Mortimer, Osment, Remnant, Sulkin, Wandor.

Index of dramatists

Index of plays

General index